S0-AAZ-885

CELEBRITY
Diss & Tell

CELEBRITY

Diss & Tell

Stars Talk About Each Other

Boze Hadleigh

**Andrews McMeel
Publishing**

Kansas City

05 06 07 08 09 10 SHD 10 9 8 7 6 5 4 3 2 1

ISBN-13: 978-0-7407-5473-9
ISBN-10: 0-7407-5473-4

Library of Congress Control Number: 2005924875

www.andrewsmcmeel.com

Attention: Schools and Businesses

Andrews McMeel books are available at quantity discounts with bulk purchase for educational, business, or sales promotional use. For information, please write to: Special Sales Department, Andrews McMeel Publishing, 4520 Main Street, Kansas City, Missouri 64111.

To Ronnie . . . thirty years

CELEBRITY
Diss & Tell

I love to kiss, and I love to tell.

−KATE HUDSON

To want the world is fire. To obtain it is smoke.

−Turkish saying

Half the people in Hollywood are dying to be discovered. The other half are afraid they will be.

−LIONEL BARRYMORE

CONTENTS

ZINGED!

Marilyn Monroe was fabulous, but in my opinion she was too fat.
—Model-turned-actress LIZ HURLEY

Russell Crowe is fat, and no one ever talks about that. And Jack Nicholson comes into a room fifteen minutes before his head does.
—Actress-writer NIA VARDALOS (*My Big Fat Greek Wedding*), on criticism that she has too many curves for a Hollywood star

It's a TV show? I thought *Table for Five* was slang for the behind on Jennifer Lopez.
—JOAN RIVERS

This awful director [Michael Bay] told me on the set of *Pearl Harbor* that he chose me for the role because I wasn't pretty. I was so depressed! I'd just lost seventy pounds after being pregnant, and I thought I was looking good. [Co-star] Ben Affleck sort of reassured me that I was.
—KATE BECKINSALE (*Van Helsing*)

I am doing a movie, and would you want a part that appears to be a charming, well-bred Englishman but turns out to be a shallow bastard? I thought you would be perfect.
—WOODY ALLEN, in a fax to *Hugh Grant*

You have to look behind the facade. People think that, because he was English, Alfred Hitchcock must have been very polite. . . . He directed me on TV as a kid, and he was a fat, sadistic bastard.

—BILLY MUMY (*Lost in Space*)

I would openly celebrate [Quentin] Tarantino's death.

—Producer DON MURPHY, after working with the director

A better window-dresser than film director.

—Producer JULIA PHILLIPS (*The Sting*), on former decorator *Joel Schumacher* (*Batman and Robin*)

He played my father in my first picture. His attentions were very unfatherly. When it was over I went up to him and said, "Thank goodness I don't have to act with you anymore." He simply said, "I didn't know you ever had, darling."

—KATHARINE HEPBURN on *John Barrymore*

How difficult can it be to fly a plane? I mean, John Travolta learned how.

—GRAHAM CHAPMAN of *Monty Python*

Andy Warhol is the only genius I've ever known with an IQ of 60.

—Author GORE VIDAL

Woman goes to a doctor. Says, "Make me like Bo Derek." He gives her a lobotomy.

—CONAN O'BRIEN

I wouldn't vote for her if she stood on her head and spit nickels out.

—LAUREN BACALL, on *Rosie Perez*'s Oscar nomination

He has a woman's name and wears makeup. How original.
> **—ALICE COOPER (who did it first), on fellow singer _Marilyn Manson_**

Michael Jackson's album was only called _Bad_ because there wasn't enough room on the sleeve for "Pathetic." **—PRINCE**

Madonna I find particularly revolting. If anyone talks like that in my living room, I would kill them. **—WHITNEY HOUSTON**

The Russians love Brooke Shields because her eyebrows remind them of [former leader] Leonid Brezhnev. **—ROBIN WILLIAMS**

I like Kate Hudson. She's cute and bubbly, a younger version of you-know-who [mom Goldie Hawn]. But she has a boy's front. That's where she resembles her dad.
> **—Comedian-host DICK MARTIN (_Rowan and Martin's Laugh-In_)**

What's with Brad Pitt and clothes? He'd rather dress like a street person, and he keeps his hair cut short enough to hide his manly blond beauty. Or doesn't he feel blond beauty is manly?
> **—ROSIE O'DONNELL**

I'd hate to be next door to her on her wedding night.
> **—PETER USTINOV, on tennis champ _Monica Seles_**

I've met Chelsea Clinton, at a gay [male] club in London called Heaven. I saw her dancing around, and actually we traded numbers. I was going to invite her to [a play], but she never answered my calls. So she's a b*@&#. **—BOY GEORGE**

It scares me to death, having two young girls, that Britney Spears is one of the world's role models!

—LISA RINNA (*Melrose Place*), married to Harry Hamlin (*L.A. Law*)

My mother [Sharon] is a role model. I'm not. And *she definitely* is not!

—KELLY OSBOURNE, who keeps a voodoo doll of singer *Christina Aguilera* in her dressing room

I remember when Britney Spears was oh-so virginal, and I made this comment about how women should take the sexual initiative and Britney should stop acting so coy. . . . I guess she found her image and maybe her voice wasn't selling enough, so she took the Madonna route, which is *so* rehashed now. **—CHRISTINA AGUILERA**

Diane's voice wasn't as good as mine—everyone said so—and I had the vocal training, she didn't. But she wound up heading the Supremes 'cause her voice was more *commercial,* whatever that means, plus she was sleeping with the boss.

—FLORENCE BALLARD, who was eased out of the group (*Diana Ross*, born Diane, eventually had a child by Motown honcho Berry Gordy.)

I'm a better actress than Halle Berry. She sold out and lowered her standards, went topless, got all the publicity and the Oscar, so now she gets the big roles.

—ANGELA BASSETT (*What's Love Got to Do With It?*)

Halle Berry's mother is a blonde Englishwoman. Yet in the States Ms. Berry is regarded as black. This helps give her a lock on the few roles for black actresses. Yet it's also sexist and racist, in that male black stars can be dark-skinned but the females, if they play beautiful

leading ladies, must be lighter-skinned and slim. Where are the darker, heavier actresses? My guess is, on the unemployment line.
—Half-Welsh, half-Nigerian British singer SHIRLEY BASSEY

I'll never put Tom Cruise down. He's already kinda short.
—Producer DON SIMPSON

I am not thrilled by comparisons to Jim Carrey.   **—JERRY LEWIS**

He is to acting what Liberace was to pumping iron.
—REX REED, on *Sylvester Stallone*

Crap floats too. It stays up there [until] decency or common sense sweeps it away. . . . Look at Rush Limbaugh. He rose without a trace.
—AL FRANKEN, author of *Rush Limbaugh Is a Big Fat Idiot*

There are no heroes today. Name *one*. Michael Jackson?
—BETTE DAVIS

David Letterman's attitude is often sour lemons. Sarcasm is his feel-good m.o. He himself once said he put the "suck" in "success."
—Former guest SHIRLEY MACLAINE

Shirley MacLaine—who does she think she isn't?
—YVES MONTAND (*On a Clear Day You Can See Forever*)

Keith Richards looks like death warmed over.   **—JOE PISCOPO**

Peter O'Toole looks like he's walking around just to save funeral expenses.   **—Director JOHN HUSTON**

His name's Fifty Cents 'cause he's half the total. **—JA RULE**

I admit my age, Joan Collins doesn't. But she'll never see seventy again. You know, last week she spent two hours at the beauty salon. And that was just for an estimate. **—JOAN RIVERS**

I'm not saying Barbara Walters is old, but the first time she covered a President Johnson's inauguration it was *Andrew* Johnson's.
—RODNEY DANGERFIELD (Andrew Johnson succeeded Abraham Lincoln.)

A toupee-wearing hack has-been.
—BOBCAT GOLDTHWAIT, on *Charlton Heston*

I like Whoopi Goldberg. It's her hair that scares me. **—DON RICKLES**

He looks like a dwarf that fell into a vat of pubic hair.
—BOY GEORGE, on *Prince*

Ever notice how John Goodman and other really fat actors have so much hair on their heads? Not to cast aspersions, but isn't that called the Eunuch Syndrome? **—SAM KINISON**

Sleeping with George Michael would be like having sex with a groundhog. **—BOY GEORGE, on his hirsute singing rival**

Elvis Presley not only dyed his blondish hair black, which he thought was more butch, but in some of his movies he wore more eyeliner than some of his leading ladies.
—Co-star ALEJANDRO REY (*Fun in Acapulco*)

I did a movie with Duke [John Wayne] and was very surprised to find out he had small feet and wore lifts and a corset. Hollywood is seldom what it seems.
—ROCK HUDSON

Fabio is the latest craze in America. He is an icon to the women who read romance novels there, but I think the only big bosoms he's interested in are his own!
—MARCELLO MASTROIANNI

It's a little sad when the mom is prettier and thinner than the daughter.
—HOWARD STERN, referring to *Naomi* and *Wynonna Judd*

Marlon Brando used to be a big talent, a big star. Now he's just big.
—Costar BRIAN KEITH

Drew Carey—a small-screen legend in his own lunchtime.
—BUDDY HACKETT

I was out walking the other day. Passed Ray Walston. From *My Favorite Martian*. Nice guy. He loves nature in spite of what it did to him.
—FORREST TUCKER (*F Troop*)

The least sexy actor in America? Let me think . . . John Malkovich. From head to toe and including the name, he is completely unappetizing and unbelievable.
—GILDA RADNER

David Bowie has one blue eye and one brown eye. Two colors, which makes sense—he has two faces.
—GRAHAM CHAPMAN, of *Monty Python*

[Michael Jackson] cut off his nose to spite his race. **—MARVIN GAYE**

Where else but in America can a poor black boy like Michael Jackson grow up to be a rich white woman? **—RED BUTTONS**

My father gets face-lifts. He's had so many, he looks Chinese—which is handy, 'cause he likes to go out with Asian women.
—CARRIE FISHER, on *Eddie Fisher* (who was made a widower by a wealthy Chinese-American)

Tom Arnold was a third-rate comedian. Then he married Roseanne. Great example of a guy who made something of himself, by the sweat of his frau. Or is it the sweat of his sow? **—PINKY LEE**

She has great breasts of granite and a mind like Gruyère cheese.
—Director BILLY WILDER, on *Marilyn Monroe*

You're too little and too fat, but I might give you a job.
—Director D. W. GRIFFITH, on meeting future superstar *Mary Pickford*

I've directed some pretty tough customers—John Wayne, Clint Eastwood, and Ronald Reagan among them. But the toughest star I ever directed, in a film called *Jinxed*, was Bette Midler.
—DON SIEGEL (*Dirty Harry*)

When I directed *Tom Jones*, Edith Evans asked me, "I don't look seventy, do I? Now be honest." I replied, "No, love, you don't. Not anymore." **—TONY RICHARDSON**

In my movie *Querelle*, Brad Davis plays a sailor. He wears pants so tight you know what religion he isn't.
—Director RAINER WERNER FASSBINDER

Among other things, I directed Tarzan movies. Give me an actor like Johnny Weissmuller anytime. If I saw Weissmuller scratching his groin, I knew either his loincloth was too tight or he was pulling at his foreskin. A very uncomplicated actor.

—RICHARD THORPE

They ask me, "Was [Barbra Streisand] tough to work with?" I tell them, "Don't ask me. Ask my predecessor—the director she fired."

—MARTIN RITT (*Nuts, Norma Rae*)

There, darling, that's what I wanted. I knew you could do it.

—D. W. GRIFFITH, after slapping *Mabel Normand* [in 1912] so she could do a crying scene in *The Mender of Nets*

I knew she could do it.   **—A relieved BEN AFFLECK, after ex-fiancée *Jennifer Lopez* married someone else**

J. Lo's latest serial husband is Marc Anthony, the singer. I wouldn't compare her to Cleopatra, but she may have the same result on men. So far, J. Lo's tarnished the careers of the men she gets involved with, while Cleopatra finished off *her* Mark Anthony *and* his career.   **—JIMMY KIMMEL**

Whatever happened to Kathie Lee whatshername? On the other hand, wherever she is, she should only stay there.

—SANDRA BERNHARD

What on earth is an Ashton Kutcher? It sounds like some useless item you see being sold on TV. In fact, it is.

—BILL MAHER (*Politically Incorrect*)

Bob Hope would attend the opening of a supermarket.

—**MARLON BRANDO**

Paris Hilton, the publicity-hungry heiress, has her own show. It's called *The Simple Life.* Very apt. Though she's not intelligent enough to realize how really simple she is. —**CONAN O'BRIEN**

David Schwimmer is the luckiest guy there is. Total dork. No talent. Barely any personality. But he lands on *Friends,* and now he makes a million a week. —**GENE ANTHONY RAY (*Fame*)**

Kirstie Alley is a better actress than you think. On *Cheers* and other shows she manages to seem likable—and she is a terminal grouch. So if she has any ambition left, I think she can manage to come down from the three hundred pounds she's reportedly zoomed up to.

—**GERALD ANTHONY (*One Life to Live*)**

I've seen *Roseanne.* John Goodman is fine, [but] she's a pig.

—**LARRY (*DALLAS*) HAGMAN**

Audrey Hepburn is the patron saint of anorexics. —**ORSON WELLES**

All my life I wanted to look like Elizabeth Taylor. Now I find that Liz Taylor is beginning to look like me.

—**DIVINE, who weighed about three hundred pounds**

If Elvis had to die young, it's too bad he didn't die before he put on all the weight. His image would still be intact, and all these overweight impersonators would be out of work.

—**KELLY OSBOURNE**

An overfat, flatulent, sixty-two-year-old windbag, a master of inconsequence now masquerading as a guru, passing off his vast limitations as pious virtues.

—**RICHARD HARRIS, on *Michael Caine*, who referred to their having been alcoholics**

I would rather drink latex paint than be in a movie with Steven Seagal. —**HENRY ROLLINS**

Wet, she's a star. Dry, she ain't. —**FANNY BRICE, on *Esther Williams***

A triumph of the embalmer's art. —**GORE VIDAL, on *Ronald Reagan***

Given the things that I said about Reagan—that he's a criminal who used the U.S. Constitution for toilet paper—it wouldn't surprise me if my phone was tapped. —**JOHN CUSACK**

Shirley MacLaine's the sort of liberal that if she found out who she was going to be in her next life, she'd make a will and leave all her money to herself. —**Director COLIN HIGGINS (*Foul Play*)**

I saw this empty taxicab drive up, and out stepped [producer] Sam Goldwyn. —**Theater-owner SID GRAUMAN**

Marilyn Monroe was smart for only ten minutes in her entire life. And that was the time it took her to sign with Twentieth Century–Fox. —**ANNE BAXTER (*All About Eve*)**

That broad's got a great future behind her.

—**Star CONSTANCE BENNETT, on newcomer *Marilyn Monroe***

That dyke! **—ELIZABETH TAYLOR,**

in *Marilyn Monroe*'s presence, as reported by Norman Mailer

Miss [Elizabeth] Taylor is a spoiled, indulgent child, a blemish on public decency. **—JOAN CRAWFORD, in 1962**

When did Britney Spears go from girl-next-door to bimbo-next-door? And why? Or is that a financially naïve question?
—Mystery author CAROLYN G. HEILBRUN

I met President Clinton, a southerner like me and a sexy man. But I urged him not to come too close. He had enough problems at the time. **—CYBILL SHEPHERD**

The first year we were together, I think he broke his record for having been faithful. **—*Elvis Presley*'s girlfriend LINDA THOMPSON**

He had never been able to make love to a woman who'd had a child. **—*Elvis*'s wife and mother of their child, PRISCILLA PRESLEY**

God, it was awful. He can sing, but he can't do much else.
—NATALIE WOOD, who had a brief affair with *Elvis*

Elvis liked them young. Very young. Underage would do nicely.
—Co-star GLENDA FARRELL

Elvis wanted to perform overseas but never did. The reason was his manager, the so-called Colonel, who took 50 percent of his earnings. The man was an illegal alien from Europe. Never became a U.S. citizen, had no passport. If he left the country, he wouldn't be allowed back in. And what the Colonel said, Elvis did. He obviously had some sort of hold over Elvis. **—Writer ANTHONY BURGESS**

Cat Stevens is disgusting. America made him a star, then after he becomes a born-again Muslim he thinks anti-American terrorism is okay because it's via his fellow religionists. **—ALISTAIR COOKE**

I always felt Stephen Baldwin was the least savvy and most dimwitted of the Baldwin brothers. Now he's become a religious nut—you might say a cross fanatic—making idiotic comments that would embarrass anyone with a reasonable, rational mind.
—TERRY LESTER (*The Young and the Restless*)

President Bush says he's afraid of religious fundamentalists taking over Iraq. Hey, if it's good enough for the Republican Party. . . .
—JAY LENO

Let me take over. I can teach Pilates far better!
—MADONNA, commandeering a class that pal *Gwyneth Paltrow* was teaching to nine other women in her London home

No gym, no sex!
—PENNY LANCASTER's dictum to older boyfriend *Rod Stewart*

Lose weight or lose me! **—Ultimatum of KIMBERLY STEWART (Rod's daughter) to on-again, off-again boyfriend *Jack Osbourne***

My wife doesn't want me to do that, so I turned it down
—DAVID ARQUETTE, on declining a film role that required nudity (His wife is actress *Courteney Cox*.)

I did it for my boyfriend [Jordan Brotman] but also for me, and so I don't have to spend so much time with security people in airports. **—CHRISTINA AGUILERA, on removing ten pieces of body jewelry, all except her right nipple ring**

I'd rather he do it in front of me if he's going to do it at all.

> —*Matt LeBlanc*'s wife **MELISSA, on consenting to let him autograph the breasts of two bold female fans in their late teens**

I'm on a New York street. Susan [Sarandon] comes looking for me, out of the coffee shop. I'm talking to two young ladies. I have to remind her that some girls really are interested in acting, and I have an acting company of my own, The Actor's Gang, and that's really what those two girls were so excited talking to me about.

> —**Oscar-winner TIM ROBBINS**

The hardest job in the world is being married to someone most females perceive as a sex symbol.

> —**MAGGIE EASTWOOD,** *Clint*'s **former wife**

I was drawn to him because he seemed like a complex guy. . . . Then he turns out to be a guy with lots of complexes.

> —**MELANIE GRIFFITH, on ex-husband** *Don Johnson*

We have designed odor-free shoes for Miss [Melanie] Griffith because her existing shoes at home were not doing the job.

> —**MANOLO BLAHNIK SPOKESPERSON (***Griffith*'s **husband Antonio Banderas complained that her two-hundred-plus pairs of shoes were smelling up the closet.)**

I wouldn't advise most women to marry an actor. Most of the actors you meet today think that when they hear the word "character" it's something to play rather than something to aspire to.

> —**JENNI LYNTON, former film production assistant and ex-wife of** *Anthony Hopkins* **(***Hannibal***)**

My initial response was to sue her for defamation of character, but then I realized I had no character.

—**CHARLES BARKLEY, after hearing *Tonya Harding* label herself the Charles Barkley of figure skating**

In a *USA Today* interview, Vanna White said that since her son has been born she wants to work less. Vanna, you turn tiles for a living. If you worked any less, you'd be the triangle player in K.C. and The Sunshine Band.

—**DENNIS MILLER**

John [Kennedy Jr.] isn't as much of a worker as his sister Caroline. He has a lot of help running [the magazine] *George.* John prefers to socialize and hang out. . . . His idea of work is doing two interviews in one day.

—**Cousin ANTHONY RADZIWILL**

When I married Fang, he promised to love and honor, for better or for worse, for richer or poorer, but he's so lazy, he didn't do any of those things.

—**PHYLLIS DILLER**

I heard the chemistry in their love scenes wasn't too good. The filmmakers aren't too happy, but Jennifer Aniston and I aren't *too* disappointed.

—**MICHAEL DOUGLAS, whose wife *Catherine Zeta-Jones* co-starred with *Brad Pitt* in *Ocean's Twelve***

Did you hear—no pun intended—that Pat Benatar is now a spokeswoman for hearing aids? What is the rock world coming to?

—**MICK JAGGER**

Katharine Hepburn sounds more and more like Donald Duck.

—**LIBERACE**

Have you seen Robert Redford lately? He looks like the proverbial sun worshiper who's changed into a lizard. That *skin!*

—German actor KLAUS KINSKI

I don't think it's wise or particularly virtuous for people like Robert Redford to go around saying they're too full of integrity to have plastic surgery. He's probably had his eyes done anyway; everyone has. After a certain age, the alternative to cosmetic surgery is sagging and wrinkling. Take your choice, but don't moralize about it.

—Film-noir actress MARIE WINDSOR

How dumb do people like Joan Collins and Zsa Zsa Gabor think we are? They say they've never had plastic surgery, never mind a face-lift. People don't *look* that way at their age without a surgeon's help.

—CLORIS LEACHMAN

I love it. Sophia Loren reveals that the reason she's still a beauty is she eats pasta regularly. Well, so does Shelley Winters. . . . I guess it's too prosaic to say that one can remain beautiful if one watches one's weight, avoids the sun and smoking, and occasionally visits the nip-and-tuck man.

—AMANDA DONOHOE (*L.A. Law*)

Those two plastic surgeons on *Nip/Tuck*—I know it's fiction, but that show makes you afraid to go see a plastic surgeon. Especially that weaselly handsome one who has no scruples whatsoever. He'd make a very believable politician.

—DREW BARRYMORE (In fact, *Julian McMahon*'s father was a prime minister of Australia.)

Richard Gere and Cindy Crawford—he's elastic and she's plastic.

—SANDRA BERNHARD, on the temporary couple

There's nothing between me and Richard Gere but air.

—**DEBRA WINGER on romantic rumors**
about her and her *Officer and a Gentleman* co-star

Tom Selleck was a male model. That's more his calling. When he walks and talks, he has problems. He's rather goofy for a macho sex symbol, and his voice is sort of high-pitched, and his laugh—never mind! —**Former macho sex symbol ALDO RAY**

The least sexy actress I ever saw was *that girl*—yeah, the star of *That Girl*, Marlo Thomas. Like a Kewpie doll with a bad hairdo, and not even cute. —**CORNEL WILDE**

Doing love scenes with Clark Gable in *Gone With the Wind* was not that romantic. His dentures smelled something awful.

—**VIVIEN LEIGH**

The bland leading-lady blonde.

—**SIR ROBERT MORLEY, on *Kim Basinger***

John Wayne had four-inch lifts in his shoes. He had the overheads on his boat accommodated to fit him. He had a special roof put in his station wagon. . . . They probably buried him in his goddamn lifts. —**Co-star ROBERT MITCHUM**

Mom wasn't short, and Dad was a Cuban with a Latin male's pride. . . . [And] he did occasionally wear what they used to call elevator shoes. —**DESI ARNAZ JR., son of *Lucille Ball* and *Desi Arnaz***

The Cuban heel.

—**What WILLIAM FRAWLEY (Fred Mertz on *I Love Lucy*)**
sometimes called *Desi Arnaz* behind his back

The maddest Dan Blocker ever got at me was the first day of a new season of shooting. He came back having gained noticeable weight, and he was already heavy. During a break, I joked, "When's it due?" looking at his stomach. He pulled his shoulders back and whispered as intensely and loudly as he could, "I am not fat. I am big-boned."

—MICHAEL LANDON, on his *Bonanza* co-star

I once asked Milton Berle how big he gets when it's fully erect, 'cause even at half-mast it's world-class. And he said, "I don't know—I always black out first." **—SAMMY DAVIS JR.**

[Singer-actress] Kathryn Grayson not only kept her lovely figure, she's added so much to it.

—Dancer BOB FOSSE, on his *Kiss Me, Kate* co-star

Lily Tomlin has gracefully aged, wouldn't you say? This is so often true of actresses who have nothing to lose. That's not being mean. In the long run, they're often luckier and less depressed than those who were beauties. **—PAUL WINFIELD**

Judi [Dench] is stouter than I am, so she isn't wrinkling as much. She says she doesn't mind aging, so long as she doesn't keep shrinking. **—Friend and co-star MAGGIE SMITH**

I have the opposite problem.

—GRETA GARBO, when friend *Cecil Beaton* informed her,
"As I grow older, I find my private parts are shrinking."

Pamela Anderson recently said dating makes her "feel a little dirty." Pam, I have news for you. You can feel the same way by looking down at your blouse or—and you don't even have to leave the house—at a mirror. **—JOAN RIVERS**

I found out Carole [Lombard] wasn't a natural blonde. We're in her dressing room, talking. She starts undressing. I didn't know what to do. . . . She's talking away and mixing peroxide and some other liquid in a bowl. With a piece of cotton she begins to apply the liquid to dye the hair around her honey pot. She glanced up and saw my alarmed look, and smiled. "Relax, Georgie, I'm just making my collar and cuffs match."

—GEORGE RAFT (Some Like It Hot)

Elvis Presley equated blonde hair with floozies. So when he married, he wanted his wife to dye her hair jet-black. Which would also match his hair, which was dyed.

—Studio hairdresser SYDNEY GUILAROFF

That singer Billy Idol has the sneeringest, meanest-looking lower lip I've ever seen. It's sexy but stupid. Is he just doing a bad Elvis pout or was he born that way? **—FREDDIE MERCURY**

Did you catch Nicole Kidman accepting the Best Actress Oscar for her supporting role [in *The Hours*]? Either she has a stiff upper lip, from her British-Australian background, or a fresh batch of Botox, from her Beverly Hills dermatologist.

—TV commentator FRANK DECARO

Talk about the decline and fall of the Roman Empire. It's almost as shocking as the decline and fall of Jack Nicholson's face.

—UGO TOGNAZZI (La Cage Aux Folles)

It's rather obscene, pairing these old prunes like Clint Eastwood, Tony Hopkins, and so on, with leading ladies young enough, nearly, to be their granddaughters. How much further can sexism go?

—MARGARET CHO

Brooke Shields—or as I call her, Dress Shields—she's too tall to be a leading lady and too short to act.　**—Oscar-winner GERALDINE PAGE**

Hollywood? Don't speak ill of the dead. Who have we got? Elliott Gould, Richard Benjamin, and Dustin Hoffman. If those guys had been my roommates in college, I couldn't have got them a date.
—MORT SAHL, in the late 1970s

Why is it that today's actors look like male hookers? Alec Baldwin, Richard Grieco, Kiefer Sutherland, they look like they haven't slept for days—except maybe for money. And the other actors—James Woods, Gary Oldman, Stallone—they look like they're pimps. How did Tinseltown get so ugly?　**—ANTHONY PERKINS**

Now Michael Jackson says his skin turned white by itself. What about his nose, his lips, and his hair? Did they also decide to turn Caucasian by themselves?　**—BOY GEORGE**

You know Bette Midler? Big talent but a face like a lemon. Have you seen her husband? He makes her look almost beautiful. These star broads don't marry for love; they marry for contrast.
—SAM KINISON

Orson Welles always carries with him a little suitcase with his makeup. He never appears in a film with his real nose. He's ashamed of his small nose. He has to stick something on his nose, some putty.　**—French actress JEANNE MOREAU**

Julianne Moore is certainly unashamed [of screen nudity]. Time and time again she's proved she's a natural redhead.
                    —*Far from Heaven* co-star **DENNIS QUAID**

Honey, I don't envy any white woman whose lips are bigger than mine.   —**ISABEL SANFORD (*The Jeffersons*), on *Angelina Jolie***

Harry Cohn [head of Columbia Pictures] once interviewed me with an eye toward hiring me. As you may know, I lost my right eye at three. . . . He tells me I'm off-center on my vision and it'll show on the screen. So I do a screen test to prove it doesn't, and he calls me back into his office and explains, "Thank you, Mr. Falk, but for the same money I can get an actor with two eyes."
                              —**PETER FALK (*Columbo*)**

It proves what they always say. Give the public what they want and they'll come out for it.
                    —**RED SKELTON, on *Harry Cohn*'s crowded funeral**

I've studied up on it. Lots of actors you don't think are Jewish are— Michael Landon, Peter Strauss, Peter Falk, Barbara Walters, Tina Louise on *Gilligan's Island*. But I'm not. Honestly. It's been printed that I am. I don't stress it, insofar as I don't wish to seem bigoted.
                    —**MICHAEL CAINE (born Maurice Micklewhite)**

If it's good enough for Paul Newman. . . .
                    —**HARRISON FORD, on listing Judaism as his religion**
                    (Both stars are half-Jewish by parentage.)

I've heard, and several times I've read, that he's not a good kisser on the screen. Probably he was saving it for real life. *I* have no complaints. **—CALISTA FLOCKHART, on beau *Harrison Ford***

Pretty actors or ones with gimmicky names usually don't last. You know, like a beautiful Guy Madison—remember him?—or the ones named Tab and Troy and Dash. A Dustin Hoffman, with talent, can outlast any of those. **—*Tonight Show* host JACK PAAR**

Is that short for two packs a day? What is that, *Tupac Shakur?* Certain names are not distinctive, they're ridiculous, including guys that change their names to something from a foreign culture that has nothing to do with them.

—SHIRLEY HEMPHILL (*What's Happenin'!*)

With Ryan O'Neal, what you see is all you get. That's why he won't be a star by 1985. **—Actor-turned-novelist TOM TRYON**

Mr. Warmth, he ain't. He's a loner. Whether that's on account of having been roommates with Al Gore in college, I don't know. They're both rather robotic, and they're both actors. Only, Gore plays heroes and Jones plays villains.

—Director JAMES BRIDGES, on *Tommy Lee Jones*

Mel Gibson is somewhere to the right of Attila the Hun. He's beautiful, but only on the outside. **—SUSAN SARANDON**

People's faces reflect what's inside, eventually. Mel Gibson the handsome, casual, seemingly likable hunk, is almost unrecognizable now. **—REX REED in 2003**

Thanks to Mel Gibson, Jewish kids in schoolyards across the nation are being baited for something that happened two thousand years ago, and under Roman rule. His movie doesn't clarify that Jesus was Jewish.

—RODNEY DANGERFIELD, born Jacob Cohen, in a 2004 online interview about *The Passion of the Christ*

What ever happened to John Travolta? I heard he either joined some cult [Scientology] and got fat. Or he married and had a child. Which amounts to the same thing.

—French star GÉRARD DEPARDIEU in 1993

It even got into *Time* magazine—how [John] Travolta was going to leave—but the sect had too much on him. He was pressured to stay and told to finally get married.   **—LANCE LOUD (*An American Family*)**

I'm not a Richard Gere–type actor. I won't, to bring in a certain audience, jump in the sack and display nudity. If you want to see that, you can go buy a pornographic movie.   **—CHUCK NORRIS**

Is that embarrassing or what? Practically everybody in [*Chicago*] was nominated for an Academy Award except Richard Gere. How does that happen? I mean, he's arrogant and not too talented, but when does *that* deter the Oscar people? There's a *mystery* there.

—AMPAS member JACK THOMSON

Andy Dick admits he's bisexual. This doesn't mean he's twice as busy on Saturday nights. The guy has a face made for radio, though he's still trying to be a TV star. . . . But it's brave of him to be honest. The handsomer ones almost never are, particularly if they work in movies.   **—Comic JASON STUART, who came out by kissing Geraldo Rivera in 1993**

Think what Warren Beatty could have achieved if he'd been celibate.
—Sister SHIRLEY MACLAINE

You can keep the pretty party-boys. They're just for show. I like a man who can make me laugh. Looks fade, but a sense of humor is for keeps. I'll take a Woody Allen over a Warren Beauty [*sic*] any day.
—BETTE MIDLER

Woody Allen . . . is evil.
—MAUREEN O'SULLIVAN, mother of Mia Farrow, *Allen*'s then-mate, with whose adopted daughter he had an affair

I worked with Gig Young. We were in the same film. You don't get to know a man, and you never know what he's going to do. . . . He had a bland personality, nice looks, somewhat sad smile, and years later, soon after marrying another young woman, he kills her, then kills himself. And I always thought the best of people!
—JOAN BLONDELL

Kevin Costner has personality-minus. **—MADONNA**

Actresses, more than actors, used to have personality. Now, blondeness and implants are sometimes enough to jump-start a career. Look at that Pamela [Anderson] chick who used to be on *Baywatch*.
—ROSE MARIE (*The Dick Van Dyke Show*)

I am not, honest to God, *happy* about that.
—PAMELA ANDERSON, on finding out that ex-husband *Tommy Lee* was releasing a book the same time she was. (These two can write?)

Everyone's writing a book now. It's an epidemic. Even people who can barely read. Paris Hilton goes on TV and says she thinks she has a book in her. I think it ought to remain there.
  —EMMA THOMPSON, winner of American Oscars for writing and acting

The worst is how celebrities are all writing children's books. We used to have kiddie experts like Dr. Seuss and Mister Rogers. Now the celebs are horning in. Like they need the money. It's an ego thing. Seinfeld, Jamie Lee Curtis, Madonna—do we really want to inflict these alleged authors on our kids? **—BILL MAHER**

Anne Heche wrote a book titled *Call Me Crazy*. I'll buy that—the title, not the book. The scary thing is, she's now a mother. Pity *that* poor kid. **—ROSIE O'DONNELL**

Anne Heche admits she's bisexual, doesn't say she's opportunistic. She did come from a dysfunctional family. Her father was a Baptist minister who died of AIDS. When she left Ellen [DeGeneres], Anne was looking for a spaceship to take her away. If she hadn't been a celebrity, she might have been *put* away.
  —SCOTT THOMPSON (*The Kids in the Hall*)

When it comes to her sexual orientation, Queen Latifah has said she won't tell, that she'd rather have people die of curiosity not knowing. Correct me if I'm wrong, but I think she answered the question without meaning to. **—Actress LYNNE THIGPEN**

High ratings is sometimes another word for "closet." Before *Will and Grace*, his name was Sean P. Hayes and he played a nonstereotypical gay character in the movie *Billy's Hollywood Screen Kiss*. The actor was openly gay, doing interviews. The movie did, like, ten dollars in business. Now Sean Hayes plays a stereotypical gay on *Will and Grace* and refuses to say if he's gay. Truth in advertising is discouraged in show business. **—MICHAEL JETER (*Evening Shade*)**

It works like this. You're a sitcom semi-regular, you *can* be out of the closet. Say, like Dan Butler, who plays the straight sportscaster on *Frasier*. The guy who plays the men's father, he's pretty out, but then he's a senior citizen. However, the gay co-star who's on every week—one of the brothers, hint, hint—is semi-closeted. Lives in the gay community of Silverlake [in L.A.] with his male partner but hasn't officially *said*. Though in Hollywood, living with another guy is *almost* like being out, and big stars don't do it.
—Screenwriter DAVID NEWMAN (*Bonnie and Clyde*)

I didn't know till Isabel [Sanford, a.k.a. Louise Jefferson, on *The Jeffersons*] told me. So when I finally get to meet Sherman Hemsley [George Jefferson], I come right out and ask, "Do you like boys or girls?" Teasin' him. He just gives me a dirty look and says, "Adults."
—GENE ANTHONY RAY (*Fame*, the movie and the TV series)

How brave of Richard Chamberlain to come out as gay in his very first book. At almost seventy. **—Openly gay actor ALEXIS ARQUETTE**

Nathan Lane did finally come out—after he saw he would not develop into a movie star, once he had some major flops under his belt. To his credit, he said he couldn't in good conscience stay in the closet after the torture-murder of Matthew Shepard.
—Actor-coach JEFF COREY

I hate folks saying "come out." The only black dude I know that came out was Johnny Mathis, and that didn't bring him down 'cause it's no surprise and he's halfway to white anyway. If a black comes out, then he gets hated by whites *and* his community.

—HOWARD ROLLINS (TV's *In the Heat of the Night*)

No amount of money on earth would be enough for Nicole Kidman to seriously consider going out with Michael Jackson. The disgraced King of Pop had his people put a call in to ask her if he could be her date for the MTV Music Awards. . . . There was a time when A-list stars were calling Michael, begging to be seen with him. Remember Brooke Shields?

—TV producer and columnist CATHY GRIFFIN in 2004

Pretty darn low-rent and pathetic.

—CHRISTINA AGUILERA, on *Britney Spears*'s second wedding

She doesn't exactly bring a family feeling to the set.

—BROOKE BURNS, trying to deny feud rumors with new *North Shore* cast member *Shannen Doherty*

Jennifer [Lopez] is behaving very well. She does not want the stigma of a diva reputation, and she's being especially nice and generous with Jane [Fonda, in her screen comeback]. She admires that she had a long, distinguished career, without a trace of diva temperament. **—*Monster-in-Law* director ROBERT LUKETIC**

Why is that, Madonna? Did they add a Kabbalah lane in the Lincoln Tunnel? **—JERRY SEINFELD, to *Madonna*, who overheard his wife in a Manhattan Starbucks apologizing for being late; the singer advised her that she wouldn't have been tardy if she'd had the power of Kabbalah in her life**

You don't want to eat *that*.

> **—DEMI MOORE, to younger beau *Ashton Kutcher*, who ordered a steak at Dolce restaurant (He then switched to pasta.)**

Ellen DeGeneres has a smile for everyone but is tight with a dollar. Like numerous stars, she's plain cheap and is known as a lousy tipper. . . . Rumor has it that she chose her girlfriend, Alexandra Hedison, partly so she wouldn't have to buy new monogrammed items for her after breaking up with Anne Heche.

> **—TV host SKIP E. LOWE**

Sean Connery has been earning big bucks since the early 1960s, when he became James Bond. Yet he is the stingiest actor since Fred MacMurray [*My Three Sons*]—another Scotsman. . . . Sean has a pad in Toronto, where waiters try to avoid him because they're so sure of what they won't, or will barely, get.

> **—Canadian actor BRUCE DILLINGHAM**

You know Lara Flynn Boyle, from *The Practice*? She's either annoyingly cheap or a fanatic for fashion. She goes to restaurants or The Comedy Store, she doesn't take a purse, and she'll ask a comic or a patron to buy her a drink or whatever. And since she's attractive, but so thin, they usually do. A friend of mine asked her why she goes out without cash or a credit card. Lara said that a purse or a wallet would spoil her ultra-slender silhouette.

> **—JIM J. BULLOCK (*Alf*)**

Somebody criticized me for calling [LaToya] La Toilet, but that [Jackson] family is weird! I swear, this is true: When *Janet* travels on tour and goes to a new hotel, she demands that they install a brand-new toilet for her! And they talk about Howard Hughes. . . .

> **—JUDY TENUTA**

[Francis Ford] Coppola couldn't piss in a pot. **—BOB HOSKINS**

He's not a dancer. What he did in those dance scenes was very attractive, but he is basically not a dancer. I was dancing like that years ago, you know. Disco is just jitterbug.

—FRED ASTAIRE, on *John Travolta* in *Saturday Night Fever*

That German magazine said Tom Cruise is supposed to have a zero sperm count, and he sued. But because he claims all sorts of things but adopted two kids, and had none with either wife, isn't it somewhat logical to at least wonder if Cruise is or is not sterile? I think he overreacts. To everything! **—Director SAMUEL FULLER**

[Carroll O'Connor's wife] came up to us and said, "Isn't this a wonderful party?" We all agreed. Then she said, "But you know, the one thing Carroll misses is his privacy." And Maureen [Stapleton] said, "Well, don't worry, he'll get it back." **—ROY SCHEIDER (*Jaws*)**

Maureen Stapleton and I get confused for each other all the time! When she won an Oscar, I got so many congratulations, and as long as she's working, I don't mind being mistaken for her. But one time, she said to me, "If another jerk asks me if we're sisters, I'm going to say yes—and add, 'And Jean's the one who drinks!'"

—JEAN STAPLETON (*All in the Family*)

One thing you can say for O.J. Simpson: He never shed a drop of blood except in anger. **—ROBERT MITCHUM**

I loathe and detest men who beat their wives or paramours. George C. Scott is one, on a long list. I knew firsthand, from Ava

[Gardner]. Many actresses required expert makeup to camouflage the results of their husbands' or boyfriends' brutality.

—**MGM hairdresser SYDNEY GUILAROFF**

George C. Scott. Fine actor. Big drinker. Wife beater. What else do you want to know? —**Ex-wife COLLEEN DEWHURST**

I'm frequently asked what I saw in Mickey Rooney. In retrospect, I think one reason that I married him was what he saw in me. Don't forget, he was one of the biggest movie stars at the time, and I was fresh from the cotton and tobacco fields of North Carolina.

—**AVA GARDNER**

All my women friends think [Laurence Fishburne] is suave and smoldering, but off camera he's a goof. —**ALFRE WOODARD**

He was in love with both of us, at the same time.

—**LAUREN HUTTON, on writer-director *Paul Schrader*,**
during *American Gigolo*, which co-starred *Richard Gere*

Uma Thurman has a horrifyingly great brain. —**JOHN MALKOVICH**

Ricardo Montalban is proof that, compared with me, quantity is not quality.

—**Dwarf actor HERVÉ VILLECHAIZE, on his *Fantasy Island* co-star**

The least couth actresses I've ever worked with? Bette Davis and Jodie Foster. —**HELEN HAYES**

I'm number 10 [at the box office]. Right under Barbra Streisand. Can you imagine being *under* Barbra Streisand. Get me a bag. I may throw up.

—Her second-billed *Hello, Dolly!* co-star **WALTER MATTHAU**

She is good with the singing, but she could not pass for a Latin American except in Hollywood.

—*Madonna's Evita* co-star **ANTONIO BANDERAS**

In my scenes with Bo Derek I had to imagine I was not there as her acting coach. —**RICHARD HARRIS**, who played her father in *Tarzan*

There's no getting around that William Hurt is a nut. You don't realize that it isn't appropriate to walk up to him and go, "Hi, Mr. Hurt, nice to meet you," until he snaps at you.

—**NEIL PATRICK HARRIS (***Doogie Howser, M.D.***)**

She's a sexy bombshell, and those are the kinds of roles she does. I do all kinds of different things. It makes me laugh when she says she got offered *Selena*, which was an outright lie. If that's what she does to get herself publicity, then that's her thing.

—**JENNIFER LOPEZ**, on fellow Latina *Salma Hayek*

I have to be honest. The first time I saw Cher I thought she was a hooker. —**RONNIE SPECTOR** of the Ronettes

I was invited to a screening of *Samson and Delilah*, starring Victor Mature and Hedy Lamarr. Afterward, one of the studio brass asked me how I liked it. I replied, "I never like a movie where the hero's tits are bigger than the heroine's." —**GROUCHO MARX**

Keira Knightley's cute—beautiful, even. A Botticelli face on a boyish bod. Hope she can resist the pressure to add implants.
                    —Columnist MARK SENDRAK, on the *Bend It Like Beckham* star

I always thought Jane Fonda had a stunning figure. Did you see *Barbarella*? Why did she need to go and have her breasts enlarged? Just 'cause [husband] Tom Hayden had an affair with a younger woman? What kind of role model seeks to solve her private problems by making her bust bigger?
                    —SANDY DENNIS (*Who's Afraid of Virginia Woolf?*)

Because of her lavish spending habits, Pamela Anderson Lee is said to be having financial problems. Which is strange, because her two largest assets are liquid.   **—CONAN O'BRIEN**

Like a virgin, indeed! She is a woman who pulled herself up by the bra straps, and who has been known to let them down occasionally.   **—BETTE MIDLER, on *Madonna***

Britney Spears wondered what was up at a recent party in Bel-Air, when all the boys kept going into the next room—then would return, stare at her, and start laughing. Britney marched into the room and [saw] a website called "Bare Britney" that featured a Britney look-alike—totally naked. "That's not me," she assured the guys, pointing out that her nose was different, not to mention several other body parts. One of the cattier gals present was heard to whisper, "Besides, *that* girl's breasts are real." Meow!
                    —*Beverly Hills* (213)

Sharon Stone. . . . It's a new low for actresses when you have to wonder what's between her ears instead of her legs.
                    —KATHARINE HEPBURN, on the *Basic Instinct* star

Robert De Niro is quite boring now.   **—VINCENT GALLO**

Tom Cruise is so much less in person than on the screen. Mousy and vaguely hostile. Some people bring more life into a room when they enter it. Tom Cruise seems to do that when he *leaves* a room.

—Hollywood wife PAMELA MASON

Charlton Heston has made acting in period pictures an art. A minor art.   **—AVA GARDNER**

Very, very lucky.   **—NEIL PATRICK HARRIS, on *Leonardo DiCaprio***

I saw Russell Crowe and Hugo Weaving in some Australian film, and I thought surely if Hollywood snaps one of them up it'll be Weaving, who's more talented, subtle, and—as I later saw—more versatile. Wrong! Hollywood prefers the petulant, sometimes violent side of beef.   **—London radio host DWIGHT POPOVICH**

(*Weaving* has since appeared in the made-in-Oz *Matrix* films and *The Lord of the Rings* trilogy.)

I said to Marilyn [Monroe], "Why can't you get here on time, for $#@%'s sake?" And she replied, "Oh, do you have that word in England too?"   **—SIR LAURENCE OLIVIER**

Marilyn Monroe was never on time, never knew her lines. I have an aunt in Vienna. She would be on the set every morning at six and would know her lines backward. But who would go to see her?

—Director BILLY WILDER

Working with Marilyn Monroe in *The Misfits* nearly gave me a heart attack. I have never been happier when a film ended.

—CLARK GABLE (It was his and *Marilyn*'s final movie.)

Marilyn was frightened, insecure. . . . During our scenes in *How to Marry a Millionaire*, she'd look at my forehead instead of my eyes. A scene often went to fifteen or more takes, which meant I had to be good in all of them, as no one knew which one would be used. Yet I couldn't dislike Marilyn. She had no meanness in her, no bitchery.

—LAUREN BACALL

Actresses are judged more severely than actors. Jane Fonda went to Hanoi to see for herself. Sean Penn goes to Baghdad to see for himself, to see Saddam Hussein's side—and he hardly gets criticized, and some commend him for his principles. If Susan Sarandon had gone, she'd be Baghdad Sue for the rest of her life.

—Columnist MICKEY BARNETT

Now, I've always thought Martha Stewart dull, her shows trivial, and the Martha Stewart Syndrome shallow and materialistic. But it's foolish and shortsighted to throw the book at her and let the fellas committing swindles, fraud, and big-time white-collar crime go free. . . . In our society, the few women who super-achieve have to watch every word, every step, because if not, there's more punishment and more hate reserved for them than for like males.

—In *L.A.* magazine

I hated working with that b*@&#. She was the biggest b*@&# in the business. Thank God I'll never have to work with her again!

—TOM BOSLEY (*Happy Days*), on *Lucille Ball*

I wouldn't pay twenty-five cents to spit on a Georgia O'Keeffe painting. And I think she's a horrible person too. I know her. So arrogant, so sure of herself. I'm sure she's carrying a dildo in her purse.

—Writer TRUMAN CAPOTE

She is a joke monster who ought to be beheaded in a public auditorium. . . . To me, she's the most loathsome creature in America. I've seen her, and to see her is to loathe her. To read her is to absolutely vomit.

—TRUMAN CAPOTE, on writer *Joyce Carol Oates*

Here's what my father said when I told him I was gay. "There's two kinds of people I don't deal with: criminals and queers. You're sick, thwarted, and perverted, and you're no daughter of mine." That was twelve years ago, and I haven't seen him since.

—Writer-director NICOLE CONN (*Claire of the Moon*), who is close to her mother and stepfather

When my husband and I left to go to England right before *The Adventures of Ford Fairlane* came out, we said, "If it's a hit, we're not coming back." We were joking, but we weren't, really. Because if America had accepted Andrew Dice Clay's attitude toward women and gays and minorities and embraced that horrendous, horrible character, I don't think I could have lived here.

—RITA RUDNER

Beverly Hills is wonderful. The worst thing about it is that Andrew Dice Clay lives here. **—*Laugh-In* producer GEORGE SCHLATTER**

Skeet Ulrich is a fool who will have to invent a persona.

—VINCENT GALLO

In his circle it's common knowledge that Yasser Arafat is gay. But after all these years he's been persuaded to marry his secretary . . . just so this self-proclaimed terrorist's image doesn't possibly get tarnished. **—Writer ANTHONY BURGESS**

Gary Coleman recently admitted, at age thirty-two, "I'm a virgin." Sorry, but at thirty-two that's only the first half of a sentence.

—**Talk-show host SKIP E. LOWE**

Is there no crime in Beverly Hills, that the cops there seem to mostly congregate in and around parks and johns, flirting with and trying to entice men into an entrapment? Four years ago, they got Robert Clary of *Hogan's Heroes.* Now singer George Michael. Their biggest concern at the station is probably who'll be their third celebrity.

—*Frontiers* **magazine**

Bruce Lee was an egomaniac. He thought it was terrible that he had to be just a movie star when what he really wanted to be was a dictator. I'm not kidding. He wanted to rule China or Taiwan or somewhere!

—**LEE MARVIN**

Michael Landon can be a spoiled brat when he wants to be, and he often wants to be.

—**Fellow TV star DAVID JANSSEN (***The Fugitive***)**

Excuse me. *Speed* was the movie Sandra Bullock did with me that made her a star. I was already a star, thank you very much.

—**KEANU REEVES**

I'd been a fan of [Burt Lancaster]. But when I had this small role in a movie with him [*The Swimmer*], his ego was so big he wasn't going to let this poor little newcomer to motion pictures have her two seconds of glory in the sun.

—**JOAN RIVERS**

I was not so eager to direct John Travolta, but the deal was an attractive one. . . . We did have a huge fight. There is no need for details. It began when I dared to criticize his religion, or cult.

—**Oscar-winner ROMAN POLANSKI**

I can't act, but 90 percent of the actors and actresses now acting can't act. I never said that I *can* act. Jean-Claude Van Damme sure as hell can't act, though I don't know what he's said about it.

—DENNIS RODMAN

I'd scare her, I'd bribe her. I screamed at her. I had to feed her her lines one at a time. I couldn't believe it when she won the Oscar.

—Director PETER BOGDANOVICH, on prepubescent *Tatum O'Neal*

I won't say she was dumb, but one time Jayne [Mansfield] squealed out loud on the set [that] she had a terrific idea. The director stared at her, then said, "Treat it gently, dear. It's in a strange place."

—Co-star TONY RANDALL

He owns or co-owns a restaurant. It's called Chi. But why should I eat there? All *his* taste is in his mouth.

—Rapper BOW WOW, on *Justin Timberlake*

People seem to love me. I hope what I'm doing to Regis isn't cruel.

—KATHIE LEE GIFFORD, on her departure from their show, which subsequently rose 17 percent in the ratings

Bruce [Willis] used to say that when he quit bartending, the world lost its most popular bartender. He was so nostalgic about it. He did say there was one problem with the work: figuring out who was drunk and who was just stupid. No comment.

—*Moonlighting* co-star CYBILL SHEPHERD

Martin Mull was great on my show. He once said I should take up jogging. So I says, "Well, you don't jog," and he says, "I used to. But the ice kept falling out of my glass." **—ROSEANNE**

You know how they say men like to have sex, and women like to make love. But with Roseanne, she was all over me, really demanding. Sometimes I felt personally attacked, like I was the lone plate of linguine at a dieters' convention.

—TOM ARNOLD, post-divorce

I'm not crazy being compared with other actresses, and 'specially not with Mabel [King]. Just 'cause we're both round, dark, and I was on [the TV sitcom] *What's Happenin'!* that don't mean we had one blessed solitary other thing in common.

—Comedian SHIRLEY HEMPHILL (ironically, both women died in 1999)

You can continue to s—k the big d—k of Hollywood if you want to, but you can count me out!

—SEAN PENN, upset over wife *Madonna*'s then-success in the movies

Tom Cruise is scary. Very threatening, very controlling. You don't dare do or say the wrong thing around him, because bad things might happen to you. He's very powerful.

—*Star* columnist JANET CHARLTON in *In* magazine

She's cruel, shrill, and common. . . . She's grammatically challenged. . . . She's whining all the way to the bank.

—Columnist MARILYN BECK, on *Laura Schlessinger*

There have always been mixed emotions about Howard Cosell. Some people hate him like poison, and some people just hate him regular. **—BUDDY HACKETT, on the controversial sportscaster**

Meryl Streep, I think, is the Creep. Ooh, God, she looks like a chicken and [has] a mouth like a chicken. She's totally untalented as far as I'm concerned. **—TRUMAN CAPOTE**

I could rip her throat out. I can sing better than she can, if that counts for anything.

—**MERYL STREEP, after a year of preparing for the musical film *Evita*, which went to *Madonna***

I think it's about feeling desperate. Some people don't exist unless someone [else] is looking.

—**Feminist comedian ELAYNE BOOSLER, on why *Madonna* shares so many intimacies with the public**

Saul Bellow is a nothing writer. He doesn't exist. He's a dull man and a dull writer. Hello, Saul, how are you?   —**TRUMAN CAPOTE**

It's a stretch for him to play someone not quite as boring as he tends to be.

—**TED KNIGHT, on *Mary Tyler Moore Show* co-star *Gavin MacLeod***

Melanie Griffith is a child actress. Still. She couldn't play smart to save her life. In addition, she makes movies with [then-husband] Don Johnson. Being a dumb blonde must run in that family.

—**Director DEREK JARMAN**

Yes, I have acted with Clint Eastwood [in *The Beguiled*]. Or rather, I have acted opposite Clint Eastwood.   —**GERALDINE PAGE**

Gerry Page is a superb Method actress. I once asked what method she used. She said, without batting an eyelash, "Talent."

—**HELEN HAYES**

Natalie Schafer is famous as the actress who never acts with her hands below her elbows.

—**JIM BACKUS, on his *Gilligan's Island* co-star and "wife"**

Patty Duke's behavior was most erratic. I didn't know what to make of it. I thought she was a Method actress. Afterward, someone informed me she was merely a manic-depressive.

—ELSA LANCHESTER

Brendan [Fraser] is underrated because he makes things look easy. And he's easygoing. He's sometimes zany, daffy, loves practical jokes. If you didn't see him working, observe the craft and discipline, you might assume he's a raving lunatic!

—RACHEL WEISZ (*The Mummy*)

Keith Richards will make his screen bow as Johnny Depp's father in a *Pirates of the Caribbean* sequel. It remains to be seen to what degree, if any, Richards brings his notorious boozing and mayhem onto the set.

—Columnist EUNICE THIXTON

I loved William Holden, but I could not have knowingly married an alcoholic.

—AUDREY HEPBURN, on her infatuated *Sabrina* co-star

I wasn't at *all* surprised. Of course, I wouldn't be surprised with half the actors I have known!

**—Director OTTO PREMINGER,
on the suicide of *Rachel Roberts* (*This Sporting Life*)**

The way I heard it, when Pearl Harbor was attacked, Joan Crawford was on the set, in her chair, knitting. Someone rushed over and yelled, "The Japanese have destroyed Pearl Harbor!" Joan looked up and said, "Oh, dear. Who was she?"

—MARY ASTOR

What does an actor know about politics?

**—RONALD REAGAN, dissing foreign policy dissenter *Ed Asner*
(*Lou Grant*) and forgetting that at the 1992 Republican convention,
Reagan attributed words to Abraham Lincoln that he never said**

President of what? **—LILLIAN CARTER, when informed her
son *Jimmy* planned to run for President of the United States**

The only politician in history to pick a fight with a fictional
character and lose.

**—Comedian STEVE BHAERMAN, on Vice President *Dan Quayle*, who
tangled with Candice Bergen's TV title character *Murphy Brown***

Will I have to be married to have kids? Maybe I won't—just to piss
off Dan Quayle. **—GEENA DAVIS**

He looks like a female llama who has just been startled in her bath.

**—British prime minister WINSTON CHURCHILL,
describing French head of state *Charles de Gaulle***

[Sean Connery] is a big Easter Island statue, he's so damned old! At
least make him pollinate with someone like Meryl Streep. She's still
young enough to be his daughter. But no! They have to have
someone who's his great-granddaughter! Big fat fossil fuel—you're
doing love scenes! Just let him pump gas!

—Comedian JUDY TENUTA

Have you ever noticed how all newspaper composite pictures of
wanted criminals resemble Jesse Jackson? **—Bigot RUSH LIMBAUGH**

As a taxpayer, if I am going to pay for needles, I'd like to see the drug users doing something for society. Come and clean the streets, wash the cars—you know, do something. Not that I'd want Robert Downey Jr. in my garage or anything like that. **—KENNY G**

You can never assume prosperity in this business. People who do are a**holes. Look at Hammer. **—CHRIS ROCK**

She has mentioned that I was important to her, and that's very satisfying. However, a check would be better!
—DEBORAH HARRY, on being a role model to *Madonna*

After the [Las Vegas] engagement [MacLaine's] tips to the stagehands were not the usual envelopes containing $50. Instead, she handed out tiny pocketknives inscribed "Love, Shirley." So with my envelopes I passed out stainless-steel knives from the coffee shop with "Love, Joan" printed in nail polish. **—JOAN RIVERS**

Mary-Kate Olsen is one of the wealthiest young gals in the world, but there she was the other day, shopping at a secondhand thrift store right in the heart of Beverly Hills. I guess, like the rest of us, she can't resist a bargain. **—Columnist CATHY GRIFFIN**

I was part of one of the biggest movies of the year, but all I've gotten from being in *The Flintstones* is a lot of five-year-olds running after me in Thrifty drugstores. **—HALLE BERRY**

Bud [Abbott] and Lou [Costello] were famous for stealing props and furniture from the sets of their movies. Very few directors ever called them on it. But one got fed up with it, and one day Lou went home and saw that his grand piano he was so proud of was missing. He asked his wife about it, and she said, "You sent for the piano on the set." Soon after, the phone rang, and the director said, "Lou, when you bring back every single thing you've stolen from my set, I'll return the piano." Next day they swapped.

—JOE BESSER, one of the later Three Stooges

It was at Disney where workers had to go on strike. As a host, an associate, or a public figure, Walt could charm you. As a boss, he was an ogre. **—HERMIONE BADDELEY**

He was no director. He didn't know what to tell us. I think the only man [Cecil B.] DeMille ever envied was Hitler.

—Silent star JOHN GILBERT

The trouble with Cecil is that he always bites off more than he can chew—and then he chews it. **—Older brother WILLIAM DEMILLE**

We were never really close. We were working so hard and so long, that's all we were ever doing. Ours was the sort of relationship I imagine soldiers develop during wartime. The situation forces them together, and they make the most of it.

—JOHN LENNON, on songwriting partner *Paul McCartney*

I once mentioned to Bing Crosby that Sinatra was a singer who comes along once in a lifetime. "Yeah," commented Bing, "but why does he have to come in my lifetime?" **—Columnist JAMES BACON**

Lisa Marie Presley was walking through the cosmetics department at Barney's in Beverly Hills when a makeup artist offered to give her a free makeover, told her she could make her look like she has cheekbones. Lisa Marie, who's packed on a few pounds in recent months, exploded. "Cheekbones!" she screamed. "How dare you insult me?" And she stormed out of the store.

—Beverly Hills (213)

Notice how Robert Blake has been looking more and more like a troll over the years since *Baretta*? Now, do you imagine he ever believed the woman he's accused of murdering married him for his looks or his morbid companionship? We know what *she* had in mind, but what was he thinking? A lot of Hollywood men fancy themselves prize catches despite their looks or personality.

—JACKIE COLLINS

My mom told me that [director] Robert Altman told her I have no personality. I have one, I must have one, but I don't quite know what it is. **—JENNIFER JASON LEIGH**

I have never been a fan of Woody Allen. Many people say he's the funniest in the world, but I've never been able to appreciate his humor. I find him neurotic. **—GEORGE C. SCOTT (*Patton*)**

I was in *Everything You Always Wanted to Know About Sex (But Were Afraid to Ask)*. Woody Allen was the director. When I met him, I wondered how he could possibly be qualified to direct this movie.

—JOHN CARRADINE

Steven Spielberg always wanted to be a little boy when he grew up.
—RAINER WERNER FASSBINDER, on his fellow director,
several of whose early movies were youth-oriented

I won't talk about you on the show if it's not okay with you. But then Mommy's going to have to find a new job, and you might not be able to go to Disneyland anymore.

—KATHIE LEE GIFFORD, to son Cody

Part of Tiger [Woods] tries to follow in his mother's footsteps as a good Buddhist, and part of him is a disciplined professional. Another part is a bad boy—and spoiled.

—New wife ELIN NORDEGREN

Forget Freddy. Forget Jason. When it comes to monsters, Marlo [Thomas] is unequaled. Her pretensions, demands, and tantrums are legendary within the business. **—Her longtime majordomo, DESMOND ATHOLL, who wrote the tell-all book That Girl and Phil**

She's as beautiful as death, as seductive as sin, and as cold as virtue.

—Director LUIS BUÑUEL, on his star Catherine Deneuve

On the set with Charlton Heston, they were setting up, and we'd been sitting, side by side, in silence, some twenty minutes. Finally I turn to Chuck and say, "You know, I just can't sit next to somebody for nearly a half an hour and not even say hello." He turns to me slowly, very condescending, and says, "Well, I can."

—EDWARD G. ROBINSON

I liked Richard Gere before we started [*An Officer and a Gentleman*], but that is the last time I can remember talking to him.

—DEBRA WINGER

She doesn't want to be a friend, she would rather fight. Her mother is Spanish, I am Spanish, we are filming in Mexico and France—you would think we could get along. But I tell you, in me she meets her match! **—PENÉLOPE CRUZ, on *Bandidas* co-star *Salma Hayek***

The true facts are that it was [Dennis] Hopper who pulled a knife on Plaintiff, and it was Plaintiff who disarmed Hopper using only one hand. **—RIP TORN, who in 1994 sued *Hopper* for stating on a talk show that Torn had pulled a knife on him on a movie set**

I think I slugged some respect into the guy.
—Director QUENTIN TARANTINO, who fought with producer *Don Murphy* in a Hollywood restaurant

We were filming a scene [the director of *Jinxed*] didn't want to do. We started to fight over it. It got pretty ugly. He started calling me names, and he jumped out of his trailer and I followed him. His wife—she's very large, about six feet tall—grabbed me because I was getting ready to haul off and hit him. She held me from behind, and instead of me hitting him, he hauled off and hit *me*. I was livid. It was terrible, just traumatic.
—BETTE MIDLER, on *Don Siegel (Dirty Harry)*

Danny Bonaduce, the obnoxious redhead on *The Partridge Family*, beat up a transvestite prostitute who refused to give him sex. He then hid in a closet, literally, where he was found by police. Then he got married and is now trying for a comeback. . . . One wonders how many showbiz marriages are part of the publicity mix.
—Columnist RICHARD GULLY

When it came out in the *Enquirer* that Eddie Murphy befriends male hookers in drag, he said he was a married man and sued for

$5 million. Soon after, he dropped the suit and paid the paper's court costs for defending itself against him. Could this *possibly* mean they were telling the *truth*?

—Palm Springs columnist HAROLD FAIRBANKS

I have to 'fess up. One of the highlights of my early career was when they came to shoot *Hawaii* in Hawaii, where I lived. I got an extra's role as a missionary's wife on board the ship, and I threw up right on Julie Andrews, the star. Not to belittle her—and I did try to do it as tastefully as possible—but it was a shining moment in an otherwise dreary career. **—BETTE MIDLER**

Brittany Murphy apologized for revealing that her ex-boyfriend Ashton Kutcher has a small manhood . . . on a talk show while dishing about his relationship with Demi Moore. She said, "I suppose that to him age doesn't matter and to her size doesn't matter."

—Hollywood columnist ARLENE WALSH

As a director he was ten times more wonderful than he was as a lover.

—NASTASSJA KINSKI (*Tess*), on *Roman Polanski*

Short guys can be so touchy. I once told Sonny Bono that one nice thing about being short is that it rains on you later. The little putz got mad about it! **—JESSE WHITE (TV's Maytag repairman)**

I did my first movie with Bette Davis. And you know what she said to me? Oh, it just haunts me. I wonder if it's true, maybe she's right. She said, "You can't have a relationship and a career. You can't have both." **—ROSANNA ARQUETTE**

I saw Bette Davis in a hotel in Madrid once and went up to her and said, "Miss Davis, I'm Ava Gardner and I'm a great fan of yours."

And she behaved exactly as I wanted her to behave. "Of course you are, my dear," she said, "of course you are." And then she swept on.

—AVA GARDNER

Claire Trevor once went back to see Judith Anderson after a performance of *Medea*. She had been truly bowled over, and she said, "I simply can't find the words to tell you how superb you were." Judith Anderson just said, "Try."

—ROCK HUDSON, friend of the Oscar-winning *Trevor* **(*Key Largo*)**

Diane [*sic*] Ross does not have the gift of friendship. I give Diane credit for going a very long way on relatively little. She's exciting for audiences, but not for the people who thought they were her friends.

—MICHAEL PETERS, choreographer of the "Thriller" video

Say It With Music: Hilary Duff has taken a page out of the same book as Justin Timberlake and Eminem. She has written a song, "Haters," slagging Lindsay Lohan. . . . Hell hath no fury like a woman who's caught her boy cheating.   **—*Beverly Hills (213)***

Penélope Cruz is having a for-real affair, conducted *out* of the media glare, with Matthew McConaughey, . . . whose hits are nearly all with his leading ladies rather than his movies.

—Columnist SUSAN STANLEY

Hugh Grant is more ambivalent about girls than about wealth, first, or fame, second. He really likes it when people worship the ground he walks on—but they do it because it's prime property.

—London columnist GEORGE BYINGTON

If Hugh is grumpy, he's going to let you know. And he has absolutely no worries about how that's going to make anybody else feel.
—RENÉE ZELLWEGER, filming the sequel to *Bridget Jones's Diary*

Mel Gibson has got to be the center of attention, otherwise he gets very unhappy and leaves. And it seems he hates it if a woman is getting any attention when he's there. **—JANEANE GAROFALO**

I have had the displeasure of knowing Eddie Murphy. I won't spill any professional secrets. But I will say there's a reason you almost never see him doing interviews. He has nothing to say, couldn't say it well anyway, and his ego wouldn't want anyone else to be interviewed in his presence. **—LYNNE THIGPEN (*The District*)**

Well, Jackie [Kennedy Onassis] better not go on a talk show. She wouldn't know what to say. . . . I hate her. I used to be great friends with her. I hate her. I absolutely despise her. She's a very opportunistic, insincere, vain, rather mean person.

—TRUMAN CAPOTE

Jackie's younger sister Lee—Well, the way I feel about Jackie, that goes *triple* for Lee. And then some! **—TRUMAN CAPOTE**

ALL IN THE FAMILY

I don't discuss my mother in mixed company.

—MEG RYAN, at a press conference

My mother can drive me up a wall better than anyone I know. . . . After she'd been married eight times and was still giving me marriage advice, I said, "Mom, lay off!" **—Twice-married CHER**

I don't talk to Julia. It's kind of a dysfunctional family since Dad died. I don't talk to my mom either.

—Actor ERIC ROBERTS, *Julia*'s elder brother

I get such a kick out of being rude to fans and then saying I'm Alec.

—BALDWIN brother BILLY

My brother is a textbook example of sour grapes.

—JODIE FOSTER, upon *Buddy Foster*'s writing a tell-all book

I co-starred on *Mayberry R.F.D.* Then my kid sister was on the show, thanks to me and to her talent. Later I gave up acting, while she and our mom made Jodie's career more important than any relationship or any truth, and I was sort of squeezed out.

—BUDDY FOSTER, author of *Foster Child*

My brother has made an art of keeping his life a secret, and his public life is a lot different from his private life.

—Jazz musician RANDY FOWLER in 2004,
announcing a planned book on *Kevin Spacey*

My father left us when I was very young. I met him as a teenager. We spoke. No, *he* spoke, I listened. I knew he was successful. I didn't know all he would talk about would be his career. So I said to myself, one meeting is enough.

—MARIA SCHNEIDER (*Last Tango in Paris*), on French actor *Daniel Gélin*

He makes his living as an ultra-right-wing TV host in Orange County, California. He's gotten carried away with it.

—REBECCA DE MORNAY (*Risky Business*), on father *Wally George*

Well, she met Jane Fonda and got in with that crowd, so now we don't speak anymore.

—WALLY GEORGE

In everyday life, being pretty and having a big bust are assets. But when you're Natalie Wood's little sister, pretty is not enough, and a smaller bust is more admired.

—Then-actress LANA WOOD (*Diamonds Are Forever*)

I don't compete with my sister [Dolly Parton]. How could I? Most families only have one "star," and I do just my very best and am just satisfied with that. **—Actress STELLA PARTON (TV's *Nine to Five*)**

Natasha's better known. She's more ambitious, and she married a celebrity [actor Liam Neeson, *Schindler's List*].
—JOELY RICHARDSON (*Nip/Tuck*), Vanessa Redgrave's other daughter

Vanessa puts a lot of people on the defensive, especially in the U.S. She's tall, English, the last name begins with Red-, and her politics, especially the pro-Arab stance—well, we *don't* talk politics when we're together. **—American-based LYNN REDGRAVE**

On a good day, my mother can come on strong. Other times, she is, or can be, kind of scary. **—SYLVESTER, on *Jacqueline Stallone***

As a woman with backbone and a talented actress, my mother made enemies without opening her mouth. On the other hand, my dad on screen was mild and likable. He didn't start making enemies until he stopped saying the screenwriters' lines.
—MAUREEN REAGAN, on father *Ronald* and mother *Jane Wyman*

My dad's more three-dimensional than Opie Taylor [*The Andy Griffith Show*] or Richie Cunningham [*Happy Days*]. He even has a temper! He's a real person. But some people are disappointed by that.
—BRYCE DALLAS HOWARD, on actor-turned-director *Ron Howard*

Sometimes somebody might feel freer to get mad at a relative than at a total stranger. **—LINDSAY LOHAN (*Mean Girls*), on her father being jailed for allegedly hitting her uncle during a family fight**

Everyone is going on about how great Julia was in *Erin Brockovich*, but what did she actually do? Wear push-up bras. It wasn't great acting. **—ERIC ROBERTS, on his sister's Oscar-winning role**

I always wanted to act. Zsa Zsa didn't. But the American newspapers and television made her famous [first], all because of her love life.
—EVA GABOR (*Green Acres*)

My sister is more talented than me. But she can take no for an answer.
—JENNIFER LOPEZ

I hope Ashlee's reality-TV series on MTV is a hit. Only not *too* big a hit!
—Sister JESSICA SIMPSON

I'm the virgin in the family when it comes to Oscars. My father [Henry Fonda] has one, and my sister Jane has two. **—PETER FONDA**

People keep trying to give me a big compliment by saying, "Your voice is almost as beautiful as Barbra's."
—*Streisand*'s half-sister, singer ROSLYN KIND

My older sister [Shirley MacLaine]—you have to hand it to her. She's definitely outspoken. I don't know by whom. . . .
—WARREN BEATTY

Years go by, and he doesn't call or write. But that's fine with me. I don't have any complexes.
—SHIRLEY MACLAINE, during a past estrangement from *Warren Beatty*

My mom can't stand the [plain] shoes I wear, but I'm not crazy about her clothes. I once looked inside her closet and said, "When did the circus clowns move in?" Fortunately, I said it to a friend.
—*Cher*'s daughter, CHASTITY BONO

At some point, my daughter Jamie Lee [Curtis] became convinced she's the mother in our relationship. She means well—heart of gold and all that—but occasionally I have to pause and say, "Stop telling me what to do and how to live my life, dammit."

—JANET LEIGH (Psycho)

The one person on earth I'm scared of is my mother, Geraldine.

—DIANA ROSS

My mom is so cute. She's like this overgrown baby chick with big eyes, and I feel so protective of her. Like I should give her advice or something, which I know is ridiculous. And she makes me laugh more than anybody; she can be hilarious without even knowing it. She's a doll. . . . **—Goldie Hawn's daughter, KATE HUDSON**

Grown men were afraid of my mother. She was bigger than life, and her bite was as bad as her bark.

—Joan's adopted daughter, CHRISTINA CRAWFORD

I have a little dog. A bitch. That means female, darling. Her name is Zsa Zsa. Like my sister, who is also . . . a female. **—EVA GABOR**

Dad was a pushover, a real sweetheart. It was Mum I was intimidated by—you know, a writer [Mary Bell] and *terribly* serious.

—HAYLEY MILLS (Parent Trap)

Ryan's Daughter is not my best film, but it is the best thing that happened to me, professionally. It brought me the Academy Award, and that meant I could finally be known again as somebody other than Hayley Mills's father. **—SIR JOHN MILLS**

If any of my daughters becomes a world-famous actress, I'll have to cope with it. Henry Fonda would be my model. I only hope I'd be able to carry it off, hide the embarrassment as gracefully as he did.

—BRUCE WILLIS

My mother won't see some of my movies, because of sex or violence. And sometimes she'll criticize them, or a role I took, though in my first major movie offer I said no, because she'd worked too hard and sacrificed too much for me to appear nude on the screen.

—*Naomi*'s daughter, ASHLEY JUDD

My father was a prude. Never saw any of my stage shows, wouldn't go near 'em.

—BETTE MIDLER

I think in any family where someone's a big star, the rest of the family's real proud of them. And a little bit jealous. And a tiny bit resentful.

—*Loretta Lynn*'s sister, singer CRYSTAL GAYLE

My relatives don't know how to handle my fame. "I need a new roof for my house." They assume I'm rich. They'll say things like that because they don't know what else to say. I don't even go to family reunions anymore.

—JAMES EARL JONES

My father said, "Hey, Drew, you want to give me an autograph too? How 'bout putting it on a check?"

—DREW BARRYMORE

In *Miracle on 34th Street*, my little-girl character doesn't believe in Santa Claus. But I hardly did either, because when my mother took me to a store and I sat on his lap, he got out a piece of paper and requested my autograph.

—Former child star NATALIE WOOD

The worst thing is being a big child star. People know you're rich, and 'cause you're a kid, they think you're dumb. Or naïve. So they always want something. Like even a whole house.

—MACAULAY *"Home Alone"* CULKIN

When a child abruptly quadruples her family's income, some changes may be expected.

—Former number-one box-office star SHIRLEY TEMPLE

I used to have to go down to Palm Beach to coach [Shirley Temple], and she'd get involved in a badminton game with me, and her father would call her and she'd say, "I'm not ready, and *I'll* tell you when I'm ready. *I* earn all the money in this household." Of course, she's a different type of person now.

—Composer JULE STYNE (*Gypsy, Funny Girl*)

The main thing you learn about living in a big family is that the first one up in the morning is the best dressed.

—Biographer KITTY KELLEY

The mature thing to do when a relative keeps hurting you or withholding love is to finally drop them. Let go. But people are least mature when it comes to their parents. However, I did eventually, finally, let go of my mother.　**—Author TRUMAN CAPOTE**

I loved my mother so much—I was so attached to her—that I told my son that when she died, I was sorry but I'd have to go with her.

—SANDRA DEE

No, no question about it. My mother was my biggest influence and inspiration. Her real name was Désirée, which is French for "desired." She was the person I most desired at my side, and she attended virtually every [*I Love Lucy*] taping—you can hear her on the soundtrack [laughing and saying "uh-oh"]. I don't know that I'd have entered movies or gone into television without her enthusiasm and encouragement.   **—LUCILLE BALL**

My mother was more beautiful than me. She looked like Greta Garbo—she won a contest for it. But it was too soon for her, for women to have their dreams come true more easily. My mother pushed me into what became my career. She gave me my career.   **—SOPHIA LOREN**

Behind most successful men, they say, is a woman. Behind many successful women is a mother. A very encouraging, boosting mother. Or sometimes a very negative mother.   **—Psychologist DR. EVELYN HOOKER**

My mother thought I was nuts to want to be an actress. She never backed me up, kept saying I should become a secretary, preferably a government job, for the pension, the security. She had no belief in my talent.   **—BARBRA STREISAND**

If I'd had a mother, I might not have this driving ambition. But I don't know. Maybe my career is an attempt to replace her. I don't know.   **—MADONNA**

My mother said to me, "You're revolting. And on top of that, you're not even very feminine." Well, that led me to the stage, which is an accepting and comfortable place. So in a way I have my mother to thank.   **—Broadway star CAROL CHANNING**

I wanted to be an actor when I was a little kid. I begged, pleaded, cajoled, threatened my parents. Finally, I said if they didn't send me out on auditions, I'd never be happy. And I got my wish.

—BARRY WILLIAMS, a.k.a. Greg on *The Brady Bunch*

I felt so left out because I wasn't a BeeGee and my older brothers were. I don't know how I got the nerve to go into singing, except that it seemed to be the family business, and I had the nerve to think I might be good. You can't imagine the sheer relief, once I became a star myself. **—ANDY GIBB**

My mother got a lot of publicity out of me when I became an actress. She was proud I followed in her footsteps. She did not, though, want me to be a star. *That* was something else, and glamour and success were *her* monopoly.

—*Marlene Dietrich*'s daughter and biographer, MARIA RIVA

My father would be horrified if he knew I was making it in the pictures and that I'm not billed as [given name] Creighton Chaney.

—Silent star *Lon "Phantom of the Opera" Chaney*'s son
LON CHANEY JR. (*The Wolfman*)

My father said that if I became an actress it would be like being a prostitute. He would have nothing more to do with me. But when money arrives in a big quantity, it can change anyone's mind.

—BRIGITTE BARDOT, former French sex symbol

My father said no son of his could be an actor and be his son. So in my teens I left home forever and I never saw him again. And no one will ever know what I went through in the years until success finally came. **—PETER LORRE (*The Maltese Falcon*)**

If my daughter wants to act, I say good luck to her. But I'd really rather my son not do it. It's not a fit profession for a man.

—Ventriloquist EDGAR BERGEN, father of *Candice Bergen*

It was my mother who helped push me into the business, having recognized my budding genius at an early age. She took me to a children's audition at a theater where I did my little act and got hired immediately. The stage manager then took me back to my mother and said to her, "Shall we say three pounds a week?" and my mother replied, "I'm sorry, but we couldn't possibly afford to pay that much." **—SIR NOEL COWARD**

After I made it [in movies] and started, let's say, acting up a bit, my father, who was my manager, said to me, "You know, you're not the only talent or potential star in this family. Thank goodness you're not an only child." **—MACAULAY CULKIN**

My younger brother has my last name, put it that way. I don't know how much talent or charisma he has. Jim's just my brother, so I don't see any of that. **—JOHN BELUSHI**

My [oldest] son David had charisma as a kid, but it cleared up as an adult. **—Actor JACK CASSIDY, also father of Shaun and Patrick**

My father was quite competitive. He'd been very ambitious. He was competitive with his wife, Shirley Jones, and then when she and I had *The Partridge Family* and this incredible fame and fortune, he got a bit depressed about it.

—DAVID CASSIDY, *Shirley Jones*'s stepson

When you're colorful or a little hyper, or you take the initiative, friends and relatives sometimes call you obnoxious. Let's face it, I was the most colorful member of my fabulous family, so I sort of became the star and got the most publicity when we became *An American Family*. **—LANCE LOUD, of the 1970s PBS reality TV series**

I'm proud of my son. I always wanted Ben to become a big star. Naturally. Now I get good parts in his movies.

—Comic actor JERRY STILLER

My mother was jealous before I was a star. She resented my beautiful face, couldn't stand having a son that good-looking. She used to beat me. I think part of her motivation, at least subconsciously, was to disfigure my face. Not that my face made a career for me by itself, but it certainly helped. **—TONY CURTIS**

My mom [Janet Leigh] raised us. Dad was usually busy someplace else, being a movie star. **—JAMIE LEE CURTIS, daughter of *Tony Curtis*, one of whose sons committed suicide**

I'll never know exactly what drove my son to suicide, or to what degree I might have been to blame. **—GREGORY PECK**

The haunting question still is, would my only son have [killed himself] if I hadn't been an actor, with everything that accompanies being an actor, and a successful one? Other people's kids kill themselves, yet I can't keep from asking myself that question.

—Frequent Betty Grable co-star, DAN DAILEY

People don't care about the truth. If they liked a movie star and his image, they don't care what he did to his kids. Now, our dad and mother had four sons, then Mom died prematurely—and of four of us, two have taken their own lives. That's not a very good record.

—GARY CROSBY, son and biographer of *Bing Crosby*

Of course I'm sad. But I am not surprised. I'd been expecting it.
— **MICHAEL DOUGLAS, on the 2004 suicide of**
Kirk Douglas's youngest [of four] son *Eric*

I cannot begin to speak rationally about that. No comment.
— **MARLON BRANDO, on the suicide of his daughter** *Cheyenne* **after her**
lover had been fatally shot by her brother *Christian*

By the nature of show business and its higher incidence of divorce,
it makes for more dramatic lives. And if you don't think stardom
changes people's personalities, you haven't seen it close up. People
prefer the fantasy. My mother was certainly no monster, but she
certainly wasn't Lucy Ricardo either. Being her child was far from
easy, and it was not a barrel of monkeys. But a lot of people feel
betrayed if you start to tell the truth, so I don't talk about it much
now. — **LUCIE ARNAZ, daughter of** *Lucille Ball* **and Desi Arnaz**

If you call someone a child molester, someone who hits his wife,
like that, they'll give you a medal for your honesty. Unless you're
talking about someone in your family. Then they think *you're* the
villain. — **LATOYA JACKSON, who wrote a book about,**
then later reconciled with, her father and family

The elementary reason Michael Jackson launched into his project
of remaking his face was that he didn't want to look like his father,
Joe.
— **MABEL KING, who co-starred with** *Michael* **in the musical** *The Wiz*

When my daughters Natasha and Joely are informed by fans that
they resemble and perhaps even sound like their mother [Vanessa
Redgrave], there's frequently a pause afterward. Rather as if the

unspoken conclusion is "But of course you're only a fraction as talented." It is indeed very tough.
> **—Director TONY RICHARDSON (*Tom Jones, The Loved One*)**

The thing with being sisters is other people trying to decide who's prettier. *They* make it difficult.
> **—NICKY HILTON, sister of *Paris***

Don't you loathe those not-so-well-meaning individuals who try to pin a parent down and ask her, or him, "Now, which child do you love the most?"
> **—LYNN REDGRAVE, daughter of *Sir Michael***

If someone asks which is my favorite [son], I always say "Both." But I'm happier with the one who gives me more money or a bigger present. I mean, I'm only human.
> **—JACQUELINE STALLONE, mother of *Frank* and *Sly***

This is not to sound sexist, but with us it doesn't matter if writers want to say X is handsomest or Y is the hunk. Whatever. All the Baldwin brothers are a handsome bunch.
> **—ALEC BALDWIN**

The youngest is often the one who moves farthest away, usually to establish an independent identity. Lynn is wonderful, and wonderfully talented, and she lost the weight and became a spokeswoman for an American reducing firm. But she had the happenstance of being the younger sister of Vanessa, who was taller, slimmer, more beautiful, and exceptionally talented. So she moved to the States.
> **—*Lynn* and *Vanessa*'s actor-brother**
> **CORIN REDGRAVE (*Four Weddings and a Funeral*)**

My sister and me never complained about who's prettier. It was more like who's smarter? That lasts longer anyway.
> **—CYNDI LAUPER**

My brother's better-looking than me. One reason I'm so cool with that is he's gay. **—TOM ARNOLD**

Dennis and I were spared that situation of competing for the same roles like I'm sure's happened with the Bridges boys or the Baldwins. It was no contest. Dennis was the looker, and I wasn't. He was never in the running to play President Johnson.

—RANDY QUAID, who played L.B.J. on TV

Randy's at least as talented as I am. Still, in this business your face can determine whether you're going to be a character actor or a potential star. It's out of your hands—no pun intended.

—DENNIS QUAID

Sean's thinner than me. I *guess* he's more talented. But more people like me better. *I think.* **—CHRIS PENN (*To Wong Foo Thanks for Everything, Julie Newmar*), Sean's actor brother**

My father was a successful stage actor. I went into stage acting and then on to Hollywood. But if I'd had an older brother who'd become an actor first, I'd have chosen another field. I'm grateful I'm an only child. An older, bossy brother would have been my worst nightmare. **—ANTHONY PERKINS**

Twins don't have the problem of being dominated by the older one. It's great, because you're peers, and the other one can't be cuter or older. Or younger. **—MARY-KATE OLSEN, sister of *Ashley***

An older sister is naturally expected to set a good example, or even act as mother in the mother's absence. **—OLIVIA DE HAVILLAND (*Gone With the Wind*), elder sister of *Joan Fontaine*, whom she insisted not take their father's name when she too became an actress**

Everyone wants to know about the feud between my sister and myself. And why shouldn't I admit that I haven't been able to forgive her for not inviting me to our mother's funeral service—and for other cruelties? I married first, won the Oscar before Olivia did, and if I die first she'll undoubtedly be livid because I beat her to it.

—JOAN FONTAINE (*Rebecca*)

Pop wasn't dead yet, and here was Natalie already planning his funeral. Film friends were to be present. She looked on this as a performance. I realized she was indulging her private feelings rather than attempting to express what Pop was all about.

—LANA WOOD, shortly before the death of their father in 1980

(*Natalie Wood* died a year later, drowned.)

It's an interesting fact that in showbiz people will help their kids but not very often their siblings. Just one example was Shirley MacLaine. When her kid brother Warren Beatty came to Hollywood, she was a star. He grew rather bitter about having to do the rounds and go for auditions, with a star already in the family. And notice, he's never asked her to appear in any of his films since.

—*MacLaine*'s ex-husband, Japan-based producer STEVE PARKER

I told Jane if her son wanted to become an actor, I wasn't going to pull any strings for him.

—TED TURNER, ex-husband of *Jane Fonda*, mother of actor *Troy Garity*

I'm making my way on my own, and I'm doing it in a different way than Britney. I'm going to keep my standards higher and a little purer.

—Younger sister ASHLEE SPEARS

Show business is just in our blood, I suppose. But it doesn't hurt to have connections. **—JASON SCHWARTZMAN, son of *Talia Shire* (*Rocky*), sister of director *Francis Ford Coppola*, who's the father of writer-director *Sofia Coppola* and uncle of *Nicolas Cage***

Reflected expectations and fame can be rough on you. I never had it anywhere as rough as Lisa Marie does.
—NICOLAS CAGE, former husband of Elvis Presley's daughter

In my family, you can't compete. Why try? You have to compete with yourself. Be your best self and look straight ahead.
—JANET JACKSON

My father was gigantic, in more ways than one—and sort of a genius. I hate it when I read comparisons. There aren't any comparisons. The only thing in common was I'm his son.
—JOSH MOSTEL, son of *Zero*

Acting's always been a big, big interest of mine. The kids, they all got talent, they want to act big, professional. Ellen, John, Joey. At least one of them's going to make a name.
—Sometime acting coach HELEN TRAVOLTA

If a kid has a passion to act, why does a parent try and stifle that? I do actors' workshops to encourage kids, so I'd be hypocritical to turn around and stifle my kids' enthusiasm.
—WALTER ROBERTS, whose children *Eric*, *Julia* (born Juliet), and *Lisa* all became actors

No one in my family was theatrically inclined, and my mother is so down-to-earth that when she's in the audience . . . well, I'd rather not know, because it makes me so self-conscious and kills my sense of make-believe. Other than that, she's a jolly first-rate mum.

—GLENDA JACKSON, two-time Oscar winner
turned member of Parliament

My mom's very supportive. She made me feel comfortable when we worked together. Even though she's so talented and beautiful.

—EVA AMURRI, daughter of *Susan Sarandon*

My daughter has *nothing* to do with me or my life, and don't you dare ask me any questions about her!

—Comedic actress MARTHA RAYE

My mother was a mother! **—Stripper GYPSY ROSE LEE,**
whose memoirs, *Gypsy*, focused on *Mama Rose*

I did not write my book to get even.

—B.D. HYMAN, who wrote two books about her mother, *Bette Davis*

She lived off me, and I lent her husband money to start his own business, and they have both conspired against me—I, who was not the best mother in the world, but in *no* way abusive, and I always tried my best! **—BETTE DAVIS, on the *Hymans***

When I was very young, without my consent, my ears were pinned back [via plastic surgery] so that I wouldn't share that famous physical trait with my real father.

—JUDY LEWIS, the supposedly adopted daughter of *Loretta Young*
and *Clark Gable* (The unmarried—to each other—stars had
an affair while on location.)

It seems that if you don't want a book written about you, don't have a child! . . . I would have made a terrible parent. The first time my child didn't do what I wanted, I'd kill him!

—KATHARINE HEPBURN

I'm not child-less, dahling. I am child-free.

—Stage diva TALLULAH BANKHEAD

What if you have a daughter and she is prettier than you? Or she is ugly? **—GINA LOLLOBRIGIDA, who had a son**

My children come first. I never feel competitive with Mia, who is a fine actress. Except when I see her on screen. That's when I think, that should be *me*. And in a way, it is.

—MAUREEN O'SULLIVAN ("Jane" in the Tarzan movies), mother of actresses *Mia* and *Tisa Farrow*

My mother was constitutionally incapable of being the loving, kind, devoted mother you see so often in the movies.

—JOAN CRAWFORD

My mother was the *real* Wicked Witch of the West.

—JUDY GARLAND

She was a friend of mine—a trying friend, but a friend. . . . She never denied herself anything for me. . . . She did what she wanted to do. And I have no right to change her fulfillment into my misery. **—LIZA MINNELLI, daughter of *Judy Garland***

They say every woman eventually turns into her own mother. Debatable, but I can certainly think of worse fates.

—Actress **JESSICA CAPSHAW**, daughter of actress *Kate Capshaw*, wife of Steven Spielberg

If I thought I'd have to have the same life my mother did, I'd kill myself! —**ELSA LANCHESTER (*Bride of Frankenstein*)**

Ideally, no one's supposed to know I'm on the outs with my mother. But in this crazy business, everyone seems to know everything, and this type of thing makes news. —**AARON CARTER**

My mom was very manipulative. Devouring, even. Even romantically threatening, and then it was just my luck to work opposite several romantically inclined older actresses. —**TONY PERKINS**

I don't think most girls get along worse with their mothers than boys do, or guys with their fathers. It's just that we're more open about it. Somehow it's not such a taboo to bitch about your mother.

—**EMMA THOMPSON**

My dad was easygoing. Sometimes he seemed more of an older brother, though he did believe in discipline.

—Actor **JASON RITTER**, son of *John*

My father was very flawed as a father. I find it shows up in my own paternal shortcomings. —Playwright **EUGENE O'NEILL**

They say if you're abused as a child by your parent, you'll probably pass it on to your own offspring. It's an awful thought. Unfortunately, statistics bear it out.
—**CHRISTINA CRAWFORD, who didn't have children**

I'm convinced mothers are harsher toward their daughters than toward their sons. Our mother once said, while drinking heavily, that she wished she'd had a son. She saw my sister [actress June Havoc] and me as being or having what she couldn't. There was very deep-rooted jealousy. In a similar way, I think fathers are harder on their sons. I'm quite satisfied that I had [just] a son.   —**GYPSY ROSE LEE**

He once told me that his lifelong goal was that William DeMille should always be identified as Cecil B. DeMille's brother.
—**Actor and *C.B.* assistant HENRY WILCOXON**
(*William DeMille* was a successful silent-movie director first.)

Time is a great leveler. I remember when it felt unusual not to see myself described as Lloyd Bridges's son. Now they sometimes write about Dad as the father of Beau and Jeff Bridges.   —**JEFF BRIDGES**

[My daughter] has a good gay father, and I have one that's straight and pretty bad.
—**Writer-actor CARRIE FISHER, daughter of singer *Eddie***

Our mom's just like any other mom, except she's gay.
—**The BARBI TWINS**

My mother [literary agent Charlotte Sheedy] is gay, and she's been living with a woman for a long, long time. So when somebody says "lesbian chic" to me, it's like when did it become chic? I was growing up with it all the time.   —**ALLY SHEEDY**

My uncle's gay, and he inspired me with his personal qualities of kindness, generosity, and wisdom. But he says I inspired him when I came out. Most gays and lesbians of his generation never came out and have to look up to us younger people for that.

—MELISSA ETHERIDGE

I looked up to my brother Garry because he was older and he was successful and got me jobs on TV. Who else would hire me as an actress? We're both movie directors now, but it's never, ever about who's got the bigger hit movie.

—PENNY MARSHALL (*The Odd Couple, Laverne and Shirley*)

It was only on account of my thinking to go into politics that my big sister let me know, so I shouldn't someday read it in the papers, that she was really my mother. And the lady I *thought* was my mother was really *her* mother. That took a lot of adjusting to, on my part.

—Singer-actor BOBBY DARIN

I don't hold anything against them. They were really good people, and they did what they had to do.

—JACK NICHOLSON,
who grew up in a situation similar to Bobby Darin's

My mother loved that people often mistook us for sisters. It was the delight of her life.

—SANDRA DEE, whose stepfather sexually abused her for years

The most shocking thing in my life was when my sister was killed in a car crash. She was an actress before me, and so special and beautiful, full of life. I couldn't believe it. Sometimes I still can't.

—CATHERINE DENEUVE, originally known as the
younger sister of *Françoise Dorléac*

I tried acting, [but] I preferred to write, to create my own characters. Besides, Joan was already at it.

—Novelist JACKIE COLLINS

Maria's older sister Jackie, many believed, had a superior voice. Both trained, both loved music and opera. In the end, though, Jackie spent more time on the man in her life than on pursuing a career. Maria used her jealousy of Jackie to become a prima donna. When [Greek tycoon] Aristotle Onassis married Jackie Kennedy instead of her, Maria saw red twice. She detested the name "Jackie."

—STEVEN LINAKIS, cousin of *Maria Callas*

My mother is demented. Don't listen to anything she says.

—MARIA CALLAS, when her mother informed the press she was living in poverty despite her rich daughter

Father was a stockbroker, and Mother had a lot of time on her hands too. **—HERMIONE GINGOLD (*Gigi, The Music Man*)**

My daughter-in-law seems to get a lot of her bossy streak from her mother, and my son gets stuck in the middle, which isn't at all fair!

—SANDRA BECKHAM, mother of soccer star *David,* after the mother of *Victoria Beckham,* former Spice Girl "Posh," called a U.K. radio talk show to air her views on the turbulent marriage

Whoever I date comes under *very* close scrutiny by my dad. He's a nice guy but a ferocious watchdog where I'm concerned.

—NICOLE RICHIE, daughter of singer *Lionel*

My mom's a wonderful grandmother. . . . Her mother died [a suicide] when my mom was still young, so I also get to mother *her*. . . . I don't regret not having chosen acting.

—VANESSA VADIM, daughter of *Jane Fonda*

I said to my daughter Marlo, "If you had my nose, I'd advise [a career in] comedy. But you got your mama's nose, so go be a leading lady." **—DANNY THOMAS, father of *That Girl Marlo*, who in fact had a nose job**

Laughter is very important. Entertainers are underrated—we perform a service that's very significant. We do it no matter what. The show must go on. **—FRED GWYNNE [a.k.a. Herman Munster], whose daughter drowned while he was performing on Broadway (He didn't miss any performances.)**

When you've lost your only child, a large part of you that is invisible to others dies with him.

—MARY TYLER MOORE, whose son accidentally shot himself

People write that I only blame the drug dealer for my son's death. That's untrue. Tragically, my son did choose drugs. But I also blame a society that's gone soft on drugs and sees them glamorized now, and doesn't know how to handle drug dealers. In Malaysia, they're automatically executed.

—CARROLL O'CONNOR (*All in the Family, In the Heat of the Night*)

My father and mother don't see eye to eye on anything. They're out of my life now.

—ROSEANNE, also estranged from her sister and brother

My father was a proctologist, my mother an abstract artist. That's how I see the world. . . . My family wasn't the Brady Bunch. They were the Broody Bunch. **—SANDRA BERNHARD**

I don't discuss my private life or my past marriage or [my daughter]. All that's out of bounds. **—Secretly gay actor ROBERT REED, father to *The Brady Bunch*, who complained that the show wasn't realistic enough and had stereotyped him**

I was a little bit fearful that in a marriage I would be controlling. And I had my mother to take care of. **—JACQUELINE BISSET, on why she never married (Her father walked out on her mother, who had multiple sclerosis, when Jackie was twenty-four. Her French-born mother lived to eighty-six and died in 1999.)**

You can't really shock Hollywood. But Hollywood reacts to what shocks America, and when I married my ex-husband's son, people who were either my enemies or very, very stupid tried to depict it as incest. And it did hurt my career, Oscar or no Oscar. **—GLORIA GRAHAME (*Oklahoma! The Bad and the Beautiful*)**

A woman can trust her father. She can't necessarily trust her husband. Not even her only husband. **—LYNN REDGRAVE, who after many years of marriage found out that hers had gotten their son's girlfriend pregnant**

I trust my sister anywhere, 'cept on a tennis court. **—VENUS WILLIAMS, sister of *Serena***

I think there's a kind of ESP between sisters at times, and it makes that a very special bond. And maybe a little scary too. **—JESSICA SIMPSON, sister of *Ashlee***

Our mother wanted all three sisters to be successful, so she encouraged us to outdo each other. So if Eva said, "I got an excellent new role," Mother would say, "But wait till you hear what Magda or Zsa Zsa has done." And we're *still* competing!

—ZSA ZSA GABOR

I say get over yourself! I say it to those actors who moan and whine over how their famous relatives make it so tough on them in this business. I had a great-uncle who was Vice President of the United States, long before [Dan] Quayle, back when that meant something besides a possible job promotion. But his being famous and important has never hurt my career as an actor. Or helped it either. So big deal.   **—MCLEAN STEVENSON (*M*A*S*H*)**

It's embarrassing that wherever I go I am asked "How is your nephew?" and I can't answer them because I have never seen him.

**—JANET JACKSON, who sent word to *Michael*
that she wanted to visit, but got no reply**

Judy [Garland] did have a gay father, some gay husbands, and a few other assorted gay relatives and in-laws.

—Openly gay singer-composer PETER ALLEN, *Garland*'s ex-son-in-law

I believe Miss Raquel Welch got her good looks from her father. He is a plastic surgeon, isn't he?   **—GROUCHO MARX**

Fathers are depressing.   **—GERTRUDE STEIN**

My father was a typically macho [Bolivian] male, and sometimes he treated my mother terribly. Eventually, I stood up to him on her behalf, and he backed down. It was a wonderful and empowering moment, for me at least.   **—RAQUEL WELCH**

Father now found his [visiting] daughter growing attractive to him, especially in her bathing suit. . . . I was on guard. One evening he announced that [his new wife] was ill, possibly pregnant, that he would have his bed moved into my room. I rejected his proposal with some degree of coolness. His masculine pride was wounded. Soon we were enemies. **—JOAN FONTAINE (*Jane Eyre*)**

It was my father who told me I should develop my body, seeing as how I wasn't born with much of a brain an' it was the only thing I had to fall back on. **—SYLVESTER STALLONE**

I played my father's daughter [in *Tightrope*]—no big stretch. But this time [in *Midnight in the Garden of Good and Evil*] everyone's going to have their own opinions, like, "Oh, well, she probably got the role because she's Clint's daughter," or, "Blah, blah, blah." But I really don't care, because I worked hard for it. I auditioned and read.
—ALISON EASTWOOD

[My stepfather] bathed us little girls in the tub each night. The washcloth would tarry too long in intimate places. Olivia [de Havilland] and I, never given to confidences, did agree that something was odd. We were to have the same discussion eight years later, this time joined by Mother, with more serious consequences. Fathers and daughters, stepfathers and stepdaughters. The story is not new. **—JOAN FONTAINE**

It's sad enough when you have an anti-gay man like [Vice President] Dick Cheney who has an openly gay daughter. But when he's a national figure and actively works against the rights of gay and lesbian citizens, it's a national disgrace as well as hypocrisy.
—CHER, mother of openly gay *Chastity Bono*

My dad supported me, now I'm supporting him. Not just because we're related or both Democrats, but because it takes good people to make good politicians. **—GEORGE CLOONEY, at a fund-raiser for *Nick Clooney*'s bid for congressman from Kentucky**

I was at a social gathering one time, and somewhere behind me I heard a voice say, "I can't *stand* James Mason." I absolutely froze. For a moment, I felt furious and scared at the same time. Then another voice said, "I know. He acts the same in every movie." And I laughed with relief. My father's name is James Mason. No relation. **—MARSHA MASON (*The Goodbye Girl*)**

He is being exhumed to prove what is already strongly indicated by my facial resemblance and the word of several witnesses.

—AURORE DROSSET, "illegitimate" daughter of French star *Yves Montand*, who in 1997, six years after his death, received legal permission to have the body DNA-tested for paternity

I used to tell my kids about cigarettes, "If I see you smoking. I'm going to drown you and get it over with. Because I will not watch you kill yourself like that." Their father died of cancer due to smoking. **—NANCY SINATRA**

My parents are remarkable. My mother was a model, then she became a psychotherapist. My father is a professor and was the first American to be ordained as a Buddhist monk.

—UMA THURMAN, whose first name means "bestower of blessings"

I come from a family of health-care professionals, but I was too old for med school, so I thought about enrolling in the MacAlister School of Embalming.

—MICHAEL JETER, who became an actor instead

Dad [Peter Fonda] invented something called the Magic Key, which was a truth-definer. He'd say to me and my younger brother, "Which one of you broke the vase?" and we'd both deny it. Then he'd say, "I guess I'll just have to use the Magic Key." He'd then walk slowly to this drawer where there was a load of keys. He would pull out some common household key and one of us would get scared and break down and say, "I did it, I did it!"

—BRIDGET FONDA

My father's ninety-one now, but next to being a vegetable. He's in a convalescent home in Sacramento, and my brother and his wife look after him. The last time I went to see him he didn't recognize me, and that hurt me. He told my brother George, "That's not him. I know my boy, and that's not him." George said, "Did you look at his rings? Who else would wear all of that?" But my father said, "It's not him." I made my brother promise not to ever force me to go again. I don't want to remember him that way. **—LIBERACE**

I was born with a cyst on my shoulder. My mother told me this story, said it had little arms and legs and hair and everything. Now, this sounded completely medically untrue, but she told me it was a twin that never developed. My mother said it was quite large, the size of a softball. They just snipped it off. **—ANDY GARCIA**

Being a member of our family, Enzo gets only the best.

**—BRAD PITT, stepfather to *Jennifer Aniston's dog*,
for whom he bought a $1,000 Gucci leather bed**

Dogs can definitely get jealous, so after our son Roman was born, when we'd go out, my husband, Daniel, and I would take turns on who walked our dog and who'd push the baby carriage. It makes

the dog feel more secure, better about us, and better about
the new arrival. **—DEBRA MESSING (*Will and Grace*)**

The one thing I haven't done is publicize my family to enhance me. I
haven't taken a picture with the kids. . . . I don't have any rights as
a celebrity. They can write whatever they want about me—and they
do. But if somebody slanders, misrepresents, or writes something
untrue about my child, I have recourse to defend them. If I have
publicized them in pictures, they don't have any protections.

—MERYL STREEP

I feel cheated, never being able to know what it's like to get
pregnant, carry a child, or breast-feed. **—DUSTIN HOFFMAN**

Nepotism has reached a new low where Pamela [Anderson] Lee's
concerned. Her baby was chosen to enact an abandoned baby on a
beach in her series [*Baywatch*] and earned $60,000 for the
assignment. True, he may be more talented than [she], but that is
bald nepotism. It's also sexism: a male infant earning more than
the average adult actress. **—WILLIAM HICKEY (*Prizzi's Honor*)**

One day I could just step right over her—her lying on the floor—
and not feel a thing, not give a damn.
—MARLON BRANDO, on coming to terms with his mother's alcoholism

If the school bully or wiseass said to my daughter, or for that
matter my son, that she throws or plays like a girl, I would hope
she'd have the presence of mind to answer back, "Yeah—Martina
Navratilova!" **—CYBILL SHEPHERD**

My father, who's Cuban, was reluctant, but my parents did allow me to become a model and start traveling the world, starting in Japan, when I was sixteen. I had a sort of chaperone.

—CAMERON DIAZ (The "chaperone" was a fifteen-year-old model.)

She had a marvelous talent for mishandling money—mine. When I was put under stock contract at Metro and had a steady income for the first time, we lived in a four-unit apartment building. I suggested to Mother that we buy it as an investment and rent the other three apartments. She hit me in the mouth and invested the money in a nickel mine in Needles, California, that has never been found. We never got a nickel back. **—JUDY GARLAND**

My twin brother and I were discovered by Loretta Young—in church. She said we looked like "double angels." So she put us in her series. Years later, when word got around to her that we were bisexual, which a lot of twins are, she dropped us from her Christmas list like a hot potato. I wonder if she'd been nicer if I'd said I was a gay priest? **—DACK RAMBO (*Dallas*)**

When I was eighteen, my mother took me out for tea and said, "Alex, I just want you to know I'm a lesbian and I'm in a relationship with so-and-so." The thought going through my head was, "How do I give her this moment, which I'm sure she's been preparing for?" I didn't want to take it away from her, but I'd known this for nine years or something. It's just like, "Duh."

—ALLY SHEEDY

If there were a reason I'd rather my Alexandra not be gay, it would be the bigotry and discrimination she has to face on a regular basis.

—DAVID HEDISON (*The Fly*), whose daughter

is the girlfriend of Ellen DeGeneres

I think my family's less dismayed about my being lesbian than about my being less—or more, depending on your opinion—than feminine. One relative even said, "Look at Mary Martin. . . ."

—CANDACE GINGRICH, half sister of Newt (Broadway star *Mary Martin* married a gay man and had offspring, but also had longtime female partners)

I think relatives of gay people are sometimes the worst.

—DACK RAMBO (*Dallas*), referring to co-star *Larry Hagman* vetoing a lesbian story line for the show (L.H. is Mary Martin's son by her first, briefer marriage to a heterosexual.)

More-liberal stars publicly support their gay kids, like Cher, while others keep quieter, like Streisand. What floors me is conservatives who know they have a gay son or daughter and still oppose equal rights—people like Colin Powell, Phyllis Schlafly, Sonny Bono. . . . Such people make money off their anti-gay stands, but how far does love for money or power *go* with such people?

—KEITH CHRISTOPHER (*Another World, Guiding Light*)

First, Michael Jackson dangling his latest production out a Berlin hotel window. And now our own "crocodile hunter" Steve Irwin dangling his one-month-old son while feeding an eighteen-foot croc with the other hand. Makes one think some people don't *deserve* to have children.   **—Australian radio host DEXTER JEFFERS**

The people who manufacture my clothing line work in better conditions than most people in Third World countries.

—KATHIE LEE GIFFORD, about her presumably adult employees

If you adopt a child, what happens when the marriage goes sour? When Burt Reynolds and Loni Anderson fought, they could always leave Quinton with Dom DeLuise. But what about the kids who aren't that lucky?
—BILL MAHER

My father, George Hamilton, was a boxer in college. Which college? Uh . . . the College of the Performing Tan.   **—ASHLEY HAMILTON**

She ain't skinny, she's my sister.   **—Attributed to**
RICHARD CARPENTER, whose sister *Karen* died of anorexia nervosa

After a certain age, I moved back in with my mother—thought I'd look after her the rest of her years.   **—Golden-era character actor**
EDWARD EVERETT HORTON, whose mother reportedly lived to 106

Never let an interviewer get in the way of a good story. If you have one prepared about your mother and he begins by asking, "How's your father doing?" just proceed with, "Father is worn out coping with *Mother,* who. . . ." Say what you came to say, regardless.
—Author QUENTIN CRISP

Merle Oberon was half-Indian. Although Caucasian, many Indians are dark-skinned, and, as an Asian country, it was considered by the British, who then ruled it, as what we'd now call the Third World. Merle was determined to succeed in movies. When she arrived in London, she had a new biography for herself and passed off her Indian mother as her maid.
—Film historian DOUG MCCLELLAND

To my knowledge, there were no Russian ancestors on either side of the family.   **—SARA KARLOFF, daughter of *Boris*, who explained away his exotic (part Indian) looks by stating he was part Russian**

It makes no less sense to take your mother's name than to take your father's. It makes *more*, since you always know who the mother is but don't always know who the father is, and most kids after divorce are reared by the mother. However, in my case, as an actress, it would have been inconvenient to have my mother's last name, which is von Schlebrugge. **—UMA THURMAN**

Madonna's latest role is matchmaker. She's hoping for a lasting pairing of her openly gay brother Christopher Ciccone with Rupert Everett, Julia Roberts's co-star in *My Best Friend's Wedding*. Madge thinks they'd be a gorgeous couple. **—Columnist SUE CAMERON**

Norma [Shearer] got *her* brother a job in [MGM's] sound department. Despite his hearing problem, he finally became head of the department and made good. But my brother Al—I got him a job there [and] he'd fall asleep—he drank—they had to fire him. He was a bum—a *bother*, not a brother.
—JOAN CRAWFORD, on her only sibling

I think it [Rick's stardom] made him withdraw further into himself. It sort of came between us. He wasn't jealous of me, but he was of my career. He tried movies for a while—he became a successful executive—but he saw that my singing was like an ongoing moneymaker. **—RICK NELSON, on older brother *David***

Acting can be shallow. The roles. . . . After [graduating from] Harvard, I'm thinking about becoming a doctor, like my father.
—NATALIE PORTMAN, star of various *Star Wars* films

Stress from kids! **—ALANA HAMILTON STEWART, attending a fashion show with Farrah Fawcett, answering a question about how they kept their slim figures**

I know the pressure was on Jackie. Our father was an agent, very successful. . . . I had big success as an actress, and then Hollywood wanted me—this was all long before *Dynasty*, darling. When Jackie found her niche and became a big success, nobody was more thrilled than I.

—JOAN COLLINS, on her younger novelist sister *Jackie*

Simon [Cowell, her *X-Factor* co-judge] is a pompous little b*@&# who walks like he has a stick stuck up his a**.

—SHARON OSBOURNE, quoted in *Beverly Hills (213)*

(*Cowell* had publicly dissed daughter Kelly Osbourne's looks and alleged that Ozzy's accident was staged for publicity.)

I tried to leave home twice, but I missed my parents, so . . . now I *had* to leave, 'cause we're making [the reality series] *Life As We Know It* in Canada. I've even gotten my own little place and decorated it, so maybe this time I'll really stay away. **—KELLY OSBOURNE**

I don't regret it for an instant. It's brought Kelly and Jack fortune and a kind of fame, but that's not all it's brought them.

—AIMEE OSBOURNE, who didn't join her siblings and parents in their MTV reality show

I don't look like Jessica, and I avoid crossing career paths. Some people say it's tough competing with a popular older sister. Others say it has to be easier, because of her ditzy image. But I'm not competing! People always want to put us in the same boat just because we're sisters! **—ASHLEE SIMPSON**

Ashlee's a real blonde, like me, but now she's dyed her hair black—it's so Goth. And she's wearing smudge-black eyeliner. I guess she's experimenting.

—JESSICA SIMPSON (The sisters' careers are managed by their father.)

I never felt that much love for any woman. It's the most love I've ever felt—like a tidal wave, is a good comparison. Even changing his diapers! I'm even doing that! I don't mind it.

—COLIN FARRELL, on ten-month-old son *James*
(whose mother he did not marry)

My husband's love for my father's wine was a big reason we put aside all our differences. We're one big happy family again.

—MADONNA, who was estranged from father *Tony Ciccone*,
then invested some of her wealth to save his failing wine business

I'm trying to go sort of a middle road. My mother [actress Blythe Danner] turned down so many good parts in top movies so she could be with her family. She deserved a much bigger career.

—GWYNETH PALTROW

You have to stay in shape. My grandmother, she started walking five miles a day when she was sixty. She's ninety-seven today, and we don't know where the hell she is. **—ELLEN DEGENERES**

My mom said she learned how to swim. Someone took her out in the lake and threw her off the boat. That's how she learned to swim. I said, "Mom, they weren't trying to teach you how to swim."

—PAULA POUNDSTONE

I tell my friends and relatives, "If you ever see me getting beaten by the police, put down the video camera and come help me!"

—BOBCAT GOLDTHWAIT

Seems like Jerry Hall's kids are all going the fashionista route. Of course, Jade Jagger is a rising jewelry designer, and Elizabeth has trod the runways, but now James, Jerry's youngest, has left behind his stab at acting and will focus on the runway, having already modeled for Burberry and Tommy Hilfiger—and soon to bow for U.K. designer Kim Jones in Paris.   **—Columnist AVIVA MEYERSON**

Other than music, I didn't have very much in common with my brothers and sisters. Janet and I used to like the same movies.

—MICHAEL JACKSON

I feel very fortunate in that I grew up in a family with three out of four children being gay.   **—K. D. LANG**

I've got five, and she thinks I'll regret it when I'm older if I have any more.   **—JUSTIN TIMBERLAKE, whose mother persuaded him to cease adding to his tattoo collection**

Actually, you know, anywhere they speak Spanish that's not my mom's house would be cool.   **—WILSON CRUZ**
(*My So-Called Life*), when asked where he'd like to travel

Maybe I was born weighing more than thirteen pounds because I was supposed to be twins. The other was stillborn.

—LIBERACE, whose mother, Frances, when angry, would remind him of his "inherent insatiability and selfishness," blaming him for stifling his twin in the womb

Some family members held that Elvis was so obsessively and guiltily devoted to his mother because he felt responsible for the death of his twin, and so believed that he owed her twice the amount of love. **—Music historian RAO M. BERMAN**

I can't imagine Cher didn't know! I've known Chastity since she was young, and this girl was a total tomboy. I just assumed she was gay from when she was five. I can't imagine Cher could be in that kind of denial. But I guess she should talk to my dad.
—JASON GOULD, son of Elliott Gould and Barbra Streisand

How that got started, I have no idea. But I was not the Gerber baby. Trust me. **—HUMPHREY BOGART, whose mother was an illustrator (Besides, Bogart was born in 1899 and Gerber in 1927.)**

It's a gorgeous, romantic, perfectly beautiful wedding. What a perfect start for a marriage. **—JOAN COLLINS, who spoke too soon about daughter Tara's relationship (She separated from her French composer husband two and a half years after the wedding and fifteen months after the birth of their child.)**

My mother would tell [the governess] to go see to the luggage when we'd return from a trip, so she would be out of sight while the reporters, and more particularly the photographers, came around.
—IRVING THALBERG JR., on mother *Norma Shearer*, a superstar who preferred to give the impression that she reared her children herself

I am looking into it, just to have some help. **—GWYNETH PALTROW, on deciding to possibly hire a nanny for baby Apple**

How come nannies weren't invented when I was bringing up my tribe? I'd have killed to have one. Now that I can afford it, I don't need her. **—PHYLLIS DILLER, mother of five**

Jane and I support zero population growth. **—TED TURNER in 1998**
(But to support such a goal, a couple must have no more than two children; *Jane Fonda* had two, and Turner had five.)

Secure men are always flattered when their sons follow in their professional footsteps—unless the profession is acting, the most insecure profession of all.
—JAMES BRODERICK (*Family*), father of *Matthew Broderick*

Ashton Kutcher buys his lemonade here. Where do you buy yours?
—Sign on lemonade stand operated by twelve-year-old SCOUT WILLIS, daughter of Bruce and Demi Moore, whose younger beau is *Kutcher*

By her example, my mom [Patty Duke, former child star] taught me a lot of what to do in achieving and coping with fame and celebrity—and a lot of what not to do.
—SEAN ASTIN (*The Lord of the Rings*)

He is such a ladies' man, and he has suffered so much from it. I think this has been an influence. **—ENRIQUE IGLESIAS, son of *Julio*, confessing he was still a virgin at twenty-four**

I know I'll never amount to a fraction of what my father was, in the public's mind, anyway. **—*Errol*'s son SEAN FLYNN, a photographer who died in Southeast Asia during the Vietnam War**

I can tell you that my daughters do not treat me anywhere as reverently as my TV children did in *Father Knows Best,* and thank goodness!
—**ROBERT YOUNG**

My son Barry is my best friend. We enjoy working together, and do so often.
—**DICK VAN DYKE**

I remember interviewing Freddie Prinze Jr. when he was entering the business. . . . He was so grateful that I, unlike nearly everyone who spoke to him, didn't dwell on his famous father or the question of whether he really killed himself.
—Columnist **RICHARD GULLY**

My dad killed himself when I was young, and like all survivors of suicide, I've been suffering ever since. I love my father, but a good parent has got to resolve that death is not an option, that he has to stick around for the duration. Suicide is not just something you do to *yourself.*
—**MARIETTE HARTLEY**

Sometimes when I'm getting a little cranky or feeling ornery, one of my kids will remind me, "Dad, you're a role model. Stop it." And that usually does the trick.
—**BILL COSBY**

I'm proud of my relatives, [but] sometimes this is a very hard family to be part of.
—**JOHN F. KENNEDY JR.**

I never wanted it to be easy for my son to try and live up to my legacy. Why should it be easy? If it's too easy, it can't be worth very much.
—**KIRK DOUGLAS,** father of *Michael*

I dig my father. I wish he could open his eyes and dig me.

—PETER FONDA, son of *Henry*

I don't know why, but sons seem to have more to live up to. A daughter can dabble in the business or not, become famous in her own right or just marry and have kids. Anything she does is okay. I know my brother [Desi Arnaz Jr.] had it much rougher than me, growing up.   **—LUCIE ARNAZ, whose mother was Lucille Ball**

My brother [Chris] tells me that people are often surprised that he has a kind of sunny disposition. I take it they're surprised because he's my brother.   **—SEAN PENN**

What's not so cool is when people will say to my face, "How come you didn't stay thin like your brother Jeff?" I've been getting that for years. You'd think by now I'd have some clever comeback or line.

—Older brother BEAU BRIDGES

I remember at a party when someone was about to tell an off-color joke about nuns in front of Bob [Newhart], and I had to step in and tell the guy that Bob's sister really was a sister—a nun.

—PETER BONERZ (Jerry the dentist on *The Bob Newhart Show*)

My sister was the smart one. I looked up to her. The public doesn't always see the smartest or the prettiest or even the most talented one in the family. They see the pushiest one, the one who hung in there—and maybe the one who had the most to prove.

—JOAN RIVERS

I'm close to my sister. We're such friends. Because when you're famous, you never know who's a real friend and who wants something or is just a platonic groupie. Everyone *says* they're your friend. But if you still get along with your sister, you *know* she's your friend.   **—NICOLE KIDMAN**

It's a little depressing how even a member of your family will be somewhat suspicious of your motives. If you're in the industry, they imagine you want a job. If you're not, they imagine you want a handout, and they retreat behind their high walls, in their Caribbean mansion. Family or not, the rich and famous are more comfortable socializing with others who are rich and famous.

—ERIC DOUGLAS, younger half-brother of *Michael*,
and aspiring actor and comedian

My sister Maggie did me the biggest favor. She set me up with Kirsten Dunst [her co-star in *Mona Lisa Smile*]. We've been together two years. And we have a puppy named Atticus. And we'd all like to work together, capture us all on film happy and young.

—JAKE GYLLENHAAL

I'd like to do a movie with Peter, perhaps do for him what I was able to do for my father.   **—JANE FONDA, who produced**
***On Golden Pond*, which earned *Henry* an Academy Award**

I admire my sister [Joan]. She is talented, funny, and *up*. I can't imagine anyone not liking her. She always has a positive word for me.   **—JOHN CUSACK**

If I didn't have a happy marriage [to Oscar-winner Hilary Swank], I'd envy my brother more than I do.

—CHAD LOWE, *Rob*'s younger brother

I tell them, "Matt's the moody one, I'm the happy one."

—Younger brother KEVIN DILLON

It's crazy. Think about it. Someone finds out I'm John's brother and says, "You must be loaded." *He's* rich, I'm not. They think it works differently for celebrities than for a regular family? *Think* about it.

—JOEY TRAVOLTA, actor

I ain't rich, but I like to get my relatives their hearts' desires for their birthdays. I asked my fourteen-year-old nephew what he wanted for his birthday. He said he wanted a watch. So I let him.

—Comedian JACKIE "MOMS" MABLEY

In some quarters, my mother is regarded as a joke. They didn't know her at all, just the image. She was a good mother, but who I am today is far removed from her reality. She died a long time ago, and our careers are poles apart.

—MARISKA HARGITAY, daughter of *Jayne Mansfield*

We don't pick our families, and for better or worse, we shouldn't be judged by them. We should be judged, or measured, by the things and traits we choose and by what we achieve ourselves.

—ANGELINA JOLIE, daughter of *Jon Voight*

There's a tendency to think of actors as career-dominated or obsessed. It's true of some, not all. And not of me. I'd swap my whole career to bring my only son back to life.

—RUSSELL JOHNSON, a.k.a. The Professor on *Gilligan's Island*

OUT OF LOVE

They say the last straw was when Jennifer Lopez asked Ben Affleck to tell her honestly, "Why do people always take an instant dislike to me?" and he said, "It saves time." **—RODNEY DANGERFIELD**

Mattel has made it official: Barbie and Ken have split up. Apparently she found him too plastic.

—Talk-show host CAROLINE RHEA

He's cured me of ever wanting to get married again.

—HALLE BERRY, divorcing *Eric Benét*

Princess Diana believed in the Prince Charming myth and was shocked to receive only crumbs of affection from Charles. Of course, that meant she wound up with a crummy relationship.

—Screenwriter CALLIE KHOURI (*Thelma and Louise*)

Men cheat. Particularly husbands. They're hypnotized by the word *younger.* **—UMA THURMAN (*Kill Bill*), formerly married to actor *Ethan Hawke***

Latin men respect motherhood. So when a man's wife becomes a mother, he starts to, you know, look aroun'.

—DESI ARNAZ, ex-husband of *Lucille Ball*

Alcoholism is frightening in any man, but his cheating is what hits you where you live.

—LUCILLE BALL, recalling her first marriage to *Desi Arnaz*

I was man enough to admit I cheated on Vanessa. But she's still the most beautiful woman I've ever known.

—Basketball star KOBE BRYANT

Tolerating bad behavior from a husband won't make a man out of him. It only makes him more of a bad boy and a spoiled brat.

—BIANCA JAGGER, *Mick*'s ex

My husband said he needed more space. So I locked him outside.

—ROSEANNE, on *Tom Arnold*

I gave my new boyfriend the gate because I'm a vegetarian and I love animals. It was our first date, and at the restaurant I wondered what his favorite animal was. "Steak," he says.

—ALICIA SILVERSTONE

I learned the hard way what a husband really wants. He wants to get extremely close to somebody who'll leave him alone most of the time. **—KIM CATTRALL (*Sex and the City*)**

Honey, the word *men* starts with *m-e*. . . . I wanted to tell you about my lousy ex-husband, but he just died. And they say you should speak only good of the dead. All right, then: My ex-husband's dead. Good! **—Comedian JACKIE "MOMS" MABLEY**

For a while we pondered whether to take a vacation or get a divorce. We decided that a trip to Bermuda is over in two weeks but a divorce is something you can have forever.

—WOODY ALLEN, on *Louise Lasser* (*Mary Hartman, Mary Hartman*)

I've reached the point where I can say that I am indeed bisexual, always have been, and that I am also a good husband.

—Writer WILLIAM GOYEN, then married to Doris Roberts (*Everybody Loves Raymond*)

Only time can heal a broken heart, just as only time can heal his broken arms and legs.

—MISS PIGGY, on a (temporary) breakup with *Kermit the Frog*

To be happy for a year or so, get married. If you want to be happy for fifteen years, get a dog. And for a lifetime, get a garden.

—Divorcée MARTHA STEWART

I've seen it happen: how marriage and fatherhood can turn an energetic, sexy guy into a couch potato. I don't want mine to become a man who exercises only his caution.

—Singer KYLIE MINOGUE, who reportedly declined to wed actor beau *Olivier Martinez* (*Unfaithful*)

Sean [Connery] is the proverbial cheap Scotsman. He wouldn't tip a scale.
—First wife DIANE CILENTO

Dennis [Rodman] never apologizes about anything. I once told him he should learn remorse code.

—Ex-wife CARMEN ELECTRA (*Baywatch*)

I have heard it said that the fastest way to a man's heart is through his chest. **—LAUREN BACALL, referring to ex-boyfriend** *Frank Sinatra,* **who dropped her suddenly**

That—I think it was for sixteen months—circus was less of a marriage than a desperate grab for publicity, like this mutual greed for some limelight. Of course, the media were so happy to go along with it, regardless. The media are sad now. They prefer shenanigans to all but the hardest news.

—GEORGE MICHAEL, on the *Liza Minnelli / David Gest* **merger**

I do take Valentine's Day seriously. So a few years ago I tied up my boyfriend in the bedroom—and then in the living room for two whole hours I watched what *I* wanted on TV. **—PARIS HILTON**

Bill [Murray] forgot my birthday, but he once bragged that he's never forgotten a single Valentine's Day. As if corporate America would let you forget it. **—GILDA RADNER (***Saturday Night Live***)**

My husband, [director] Louis Malle, told me there is no Valentine's Day in France. But he promised to try and make every day romantic—a Valentine's Day. **—CANDICE BERGEN**

He wasn't romantic, but he was passionate, in a rough way.

—MEG RYAN, on co-star and temporary fling *Russell Crowe*

I was introduced to Kirk Douglas at a party. As soon as he heard I was an Australian actress, he smiled and said, "Yes, the Australians. A friendly and manly race. And I hear the men are nice too."

—DIANE CILENTO

When I worked with Jim Brolin [they played the Reagans], his wife Barbra [Streisand] visited on the set. They actually flirted with each other. So there's hope. Love can be better the second, third, or whichever time around. **—Australian actress JUDY DAVIS**

One item that can be broken, and broken more than once, yet keep on functioning is the human heart.
—SUZANNE PLESHETTE, soon after divorcing heartthrob *Troy Donahue*

Yes, we were really married, but it only lasted a few months, so it's not really worth answering in detail.
—TROY DONAHUE, on his 1964 marriage to *Suzanne Pleshette*

We talked about it ahead of time. We wanted it to last. We talked a *lot*. Our acquaintances thought we might have problems from my being Mexican. How silly. I thought if there were problems it would be from us being actors. So we agreed to put our marriage first, our work second. **—MARGO (*Lost Horizon*), who was married to *Eddie Albert* until her death**

Before tying the knot, I think it's a good idea to practice more conversation and less fornication.
—CANDICE BERGEN, who was married to *Louis Malle* until his death

With a baby, you don't and probably shouldn't know what you're getting. Imagine being the mother of Hitler, or of Stalin or Mao. But a man's already what he is, you're *not* going to change him. So you better find out all you can, for your own sake and that of any child you might have.

—JOAN PLOWRIGHT, widow of *Laurence Olivier*

I didn't marry Michael [Douglas]. His first wife got a humongous settlement once he left her for a younger woman [Catherine Zeta-Jones]. Michael behaved very badly toward me. Very. And I've hardly disclosed any of it, except to friends. I'm sure he's hoping I never write a book.

—Actress **BRENDA VACCARO** (*Midnight Cowboy*)

Burt [Reynolds] was a batterer. A violent man. I was the bigger star at the time. For whatever reason, he waited over twenty years before marrying anyone else [Loni Anderson]. And I think it [the second marriage] had a lot to do with publicity. By then his superstar status was turning from gold to green.

—**JUDY CARNE** (*Rowan and Martin's Laugh-In*)

If Clark had one inch less, he'd be the "Queen of Hollywood" instead of "The King." —**CAROLE LOMBARD**, *Gable*'s third wife, and the first not much older than him

Alec [Baldwin] has a big heart. We shared the same social conscience. But he has, as he will admit, a big, big temper.

—Ex-wife **KIM BASINGER**

No one's gonna know what it was, or how strong, between Kim [Basinger] and me. I don't kiss and tell. 'Cept sometimes in a song.

—**PRINCE**

Cary Grant didn't kiss, but he did tell.

—Co-star **INGRID BERGMAN**, who had a crush on him

When you marry a Latin, you have to expect more demonstrativeness than you're used to. At first you're a little uptight about it, but it's surprising how quickly you get used to it, grow fond of it.
—**EDDIE ALBERT (*Green Acres*), recalling *Margo***

When you're going with a star, a front-and-center star, you become aware how there'll always be a third party along, every time you go out. It becomes more of a circus than a relationship.
—**KIEFER SUTHERLAND, who was engaged to *Julia Roberts***

Her career was too central a part of her for it to have worked out.
—**BENJAMIN BRATT, another *Julia Roberts* fiancé**

My toughest job was being married to Barbra Streisand.
—**Ex-husband ELLIOTT GOULD**

Joan Crawford thought about marrying Clark Gable and even considered me for a while. But I don't think either Clark or I would have relished playing a supporting part in Miss Crawford's private life.
—**Co-star HENRY FONDA**

Poor Kiefer [Sutherland] and what he had to go through [after Julia Roberts canceled their wedding]. I worked with him on *Article 99*, and I think that's why I've stayed away from going out with actresses.
—**RAY LIOTTA**

Most actors keep a certain emotional distance from acting. It's a cultural thing. But actresses really get into it and always look forward to the next role. And each new husband is a new role too—a private and a public role.
—**BURT REYNOLDS, after the divorce from *Loni Anderson***

Even though she's beautiful and a totally convincing actress, I married [Meryl Streep] because it's for keeps, and she never wanted to live in Hollywood. **—Sculptor DONALD GUMMER**

Do Ida and I quarrel? Do we quarrel! But our disagreements are always less important than our daughters.
—Comedian-star EDDIE CANTOR (who founded the March of Dimes)

We have terrible fights but wonderful reconciliations.
—BARBRA STREISAND, on then-companion *Jon Peters*

We'd been friends for years. Merv Griffin introduced us. Robert [Clary] was my escort, and then my best man friend. He was cast in *Hogan's Heroes*, and he'd never been married, so everyone thought he should marry me. I went along, since he was fond of my son, and it's worked out very well.
—NATALIE CANTOR, one of Eddie's daughters

No, I got in trouble saying Tom [Cruise] had seriously considered the priesthood and could be more comfortable with a celibate lifestyle. I won't say any more. It's too easy for them to twist things. **—First wife MIMI ROGERS**

When Ellen [DeGeneres] and I met President Clinton and we were all talking, I had my arm around Ellen without realizing it. That's how we are. But we were *not* kissing; we save that for when we're alone. But a lot of the news stories said we were kissing, and I think that stems partially from homophobia and wanting to exaggerate our natural affection, making it seem outrageous or improper—journalistic exaggeration. **—ANNE HECHE**

In 1951 [singer] Johnnie Ray was entrapped by a plainclothes policeman. Back then, that could ruin you. In 1952 he therefore took a wife, for image's sake. And the truth is, as long as same-sexuality is stigmatized, it will push a lot of gay men into the arms, temporarily, of the bigots' daughters.

—Columnist and *Ray* friend LEE GRAHAM

If James Dean had lived longer than he did, he would have been urged or ordered by Jack Warner to get married. He was nowhere as discreet as, for instance, Rock Hudson, so it was just a matter of time. **—Stage co-star GERALDINE PAGE**

They were building up Jimmy Dean and Pier Angeli as a new dream couple. To draw more teenagers to the cinemas and away from the television sets, and also to heterosexualize the perception of Dean. Pier was terribly ambitious, and so was her mother. She was neurotically needy, and Jimmy tired of her clinging. She was determined to marry a celebrity, and got [singer] Vic Damone. In the end, she killed herself. **—GLORIA GRAHAME, ex-wife of Nick Ray, who directed *Dean* in *Rebel Without a Cause***

Merv [Griffin] and I are just very good friends, darling.

—EVA GABOR (However, after a lawsuit by an alleged lover of *Griffin*, she switched to saying they were engaged.)

Frances Bergen [Candice's mother] and I are very good *friends*. We are *not* romantically involved. **—Actor CRAIG STEVENS (Alexis Smith's widower), refuting a 1996 newspaper claim that he and *Bergen* were a "couple"**

Seems the longest-lasting marriages of all are the sex-free ones, specifically gay husband and lesbian wife—at least in showbiz: the likes of Lunt and Fontanne, Charles Laughton and Elsa Lanchester, Alexis Smith and Craig Stevens, Cole Porter and Linda Lee, and on and on. **—Sexologist BOB BERKOWITZ on CNBC's *Real Personal***

The unfortunate truth is that in this town men and women do compete. The happiest marriage I've seen in Hollywood is Billy Haines and Jimmy Shields. **—JOAN CRAWFORD, pal of former silent star *Haines*, who was with *Shields* almost fifty years**

I'm the only actor who ever married a congressman. **—Two-time Oscar-winner MELVYN DOUGLAS, on actress-turned-congresswoman *Helen Gahagan Douglas***

Hollywood still prefers fiction. In 2004 they make a musical about Cole Porter, a love story about a gay man and his wife, leaving out that she was either asexual, bisexual, or lesbian. And by casting Kevin Kline and Ashley Judd, reversing the fact that Linda was fifteen years older than her husband. **—REX REED**

Life's never *slow* for us! Part of my year I give to my work, part is just my husband's. I shut down and we travel around [in a motor home] to where he needs to be. **—ASHLEY JUDD, married to a race-car driver**

Yeah, it's only right. I'm dropping it right away. **—REBECCA ROMIJN STAMOS, on dropping husband *John Stamos*'s name after their split, reportedly caused by her career upswing and his wanting to have kids**

You'd sort of think she'd just discovered it. She uses it a lot.
—**JULIAN MCMAHON** (*Nip/Tuck*), on then-girlfriend
and co-star *Shannen Doherty*'s temper

He tended toward anger and depression. But he was more inclined toward hurling chairs than visiting a psychiatrist or a marriage counselor. —**LONI ANDERSON**, on ex *Burt Reynolds*

Ike just thought that once you signed that marriage contract you became his possession, though it wasn't a two-way street.
—**TINA TURNER**, who escaped the abusive marriage

If the shoe fits. —**FRANCES FISHER**, comparing ex-boyfriend
and father of her child *Clint Eastwood* to *O.J. Simpson*

Gregg [Allman] was my second and last husband. I like romance, I like relationships—no, wrong! I like *good* relationships. A lasting marriage, these days it's like gambling. The odds are against you. A couple of mistakes, and you should wise up, not go back to the roulette table. Besides, Gregg was into drugs. He wouldn't give that up, so I gave him up. —**CHER**

I'd been very sheltered. That alcoholism existed was news and a great shock to me. The marriage couldn't survive it.
—**SHIRLEY TEMPLE**, whose first husband was actor *John Agar*

It got kind of boring—the gambling and all those poker tournaments, and just watching.
—**JENNIFER LOPEZ**, on ex-fiancé *Ben Affleck*'s passion

Antonio [Banderas] cannot throw away a pair of pants, doesn't matter how old. He thinks of them as old friends. You should see his closet.
                                                    —MELANIE GRIFFITH

After [Alexis Smith] died I got rid of [her] 680 cookbooks.
                                        —CRAIG STEVENS (*Peter Gunn*)

Since George [Hamilton], I haven't had a single conversation that revolves around suntanning.   **—Ex-wife ALANA HAMILTON STEWART**

We were together seven months, but I must've witnessed, like, seven years or more of shopping.   **—Backstreet Boys singer**
                             NICK CARTER, on ex-girlfriend *Paris Hilton*

For some reason, Randy likes to buy me things. It's really his idea.
                               —PARIS HILTON, on beau *Randy Spelling*,
                                    son of media mogul Aaron Spelling

My idea was not to get this publicity. It was to confess my life [in a book]. My lovers are part of my life. Brigitte Bardot and Catherine Deneuve think I told too much of my life. Jane [Fonda] does not think so.   **—French director ROGER VADIM,**
                               who was sued by *Bardot* and *Deneuve*

When I was with Terence [McNally], the more homophobic critics were unfair to him, insinuating that I was writing his plays for him, or helping him. It was quite stupid of them, because it's eminently clear that our subject matter and writing styles are distinct.
                        —EDWARD ALBEE (*Who's Afraid of Virginia Woolf?*)

My wife Henny doesn't mind my being stopped for autographs. But she has grown weary of fans asking, "Where's your wife, where's *Lovey?*" They think—and you have no idea how *many* think this!—that I'm married to Natalie Schafer in reality, because I was married to her on *Gilligan's Island*. And *that's* back when I was still youngish!
—JIM BACKUS

A fan once came up to me, really sweet, really naïve, and asked me if I'd married Bruce Willis. After I regained my composure, I smiled and said, "Bite your tongue." **—CYBILL SHEPHERD**

I'm not even considering saying "I do" until I have his full-fledged commitment. I wouldn't want to be someone whose marital record overshadows her career.
—Singer KYLIE MINOGUE, on actor *Olivier Martinez* (*Unfaithful*)

With or without [a contract], sooner or later a man is going to cheat. You can bank on it. **—FARRAH FAWCETT, whose seventeen-year relationship with *Ryan O'Neal* was allegedly broken up by his affair with actress Leslie Stefanson (Years later they reunited, but reportedly split again when he left Farrah for Leslie.)**

It's not a political relationship. It's a relationship that happened and that happens to be partly political. **—JOHN CUSACK in 2004, on dating *Alexandra Kerry*, daughter of Senator John Kerry**

It's just a nice getting together. Can't someone have privacy anymore? We went out a few years ago, and now we're going out again. That's all. But the hacks go and lie and say we're getting married! That really pisses me off.
—GEORGE CLOONEY (The nonfiancée is British actress *Lisa Snowden*.)

I got filmed going out of a restaurant by *Hard Copy*. They said, "Here Antonio is, getting into this car with his new girlfriend." It was my sister! I went out with my sister to dinner.

—ANTONIO SABATO JR.

It was a date, but it was a platonic date. A segment of the press wanted to make it salacious or incestuous or something.

—BARRY WILLIAMS, who dated his *Brady Bunch* mother
Florence Henderson once

Sarah [Jessica Parker, his wife] understands. You can have pet names for someone and it's perfectly innocent. Nicole Kidman and I bonded, making *The Stepford Wives*. When we talk on the phone, she calls me Babyface and I call her Goddess. If it weren't innocent, nobody would know about this. I wouldn't tell it.

—MATTHEW BRODERICK

I could have a business lunch with someone who's heterosexual, like Charlize Theron, or bisexual, like Drew Barrymore, or gay, like Ellen DeGeneres, but as long as she's female, the tabloid press will misrepresent it as a romance. Worse, if my boyfriend's seated right next to me, he'll either be cropped out of the photo or not mentioned at all. The media sells what it *wants* to sell, not facts or reality. **—RUPERT EVERETT (*My Best Friend's Wedding*)**

I hope my marriage lasts longer than hers, of course, but I am a truly great fan of hers. **—RENÉE ZELLWEGER, who at auction**
bought the wedding dress of *Katharine Hepburn*,
who lived with her husband only a few weeks

Larry's [Olivier] first wife, Jill Esmond, was a bigger star than he was when they married. When she went to Hollywood with a contract, he tagged along, hoping to get into pictures. The papers kept it hushed up when she left him for another woman. I think they settled in Wimbledon. **—SIR JOHN GIELGUD**

Jane [Fonda] left Tom Hayden after he began an affair with a younger woman. One who wasn't half as attractive as Jane. In my opinion, he used her fame and money for his political ends.
—Brother PETER FONDA

I look at other women, but I do nothing. But Melanie [Griffith], who is beautiful, is insecure. She returns to the surgeon for an injection or a little tuck, to fight the wrinkles. I tell her that in Europe we don't *hate* wrinkles. She says we're not in Europe, so back to the surgeon. **—ANTONIO BANDERAS**

If I ever have a face-lift, and I doubt I ever will, it won't be for Jim [Brolin]. It'll be for *me*. **—BARBRA STREISAND**

The [very heated] custody fight is history. We're trying to make a go of it again—from scratch, except for our son Eliot.
—Former flight attendant GRACE HIGHTOWER, who broke up with *Robert De Niro* after she allegedly caught him cheating and broke one of his ribs

It was a whirlwind time—fun and wild—[but] I'm not even sure why we broke up.

—WINONA RYDER, on her relationship with *Johnny Depp*

I like her, I can understand—sort of—how she feels. But it's really just between us two. **—CAMERON DIAZ, on *Justin Timberlake*'s mother, who opposes the idea of her son marrying an older woman and bigger star**

One time [longtime companion Fannie Flagg] decided she was spending too much money at the beauty parlor. She'd wax herself. Well, that was tedious and boring, so she thought she'd singe the hair off her legs. However, she dropped the match, and I was treated to the spectacle of Fannie, her crotch in flames. **—Fellow author RITA MAE BROWN (*Rubyfruit Jungle*)**

Maybe people are more sophisticated today. When I found out [actor] Jeff Chandler was a cross-dresser, I was beside myself. I had a hundred questions—too embarrassed to ask any of them. My passion certainly cooled, and all the more so when I saw how many garments he had in polka dots. I could never stand polka dots. **—ESTHER WILLIAMS**

My brother-in-law [Alexis Arquette] cross-dresses often, but I told David he makes a lousy-looking female. Besides, he might scare the baby. **—COURTENEY COX**

Oh, Mr. Thalberg, I've just met that extraordinary wife of yours with the teensy-weensy little eyes! **—British stage star MRS. PATRICK CAMPBELL, on *Norma Shearer,* to MGM honcho *Irving Thalberg***

Merv Griffin does claim to have invented *Jeopardy!* In truth, his wife invented it, but he got the credit and the rewards. But do not ask me about the marriage. My lips are sealed. **—Sidekick ARTHUR TREACHER**

I figure if I don't talk about it much, it has a better chance of making it.
—TIGER WOODS, on his new marriage to Nordic model *Elin Nordegren*

It sounds romantic, being married to a poet. There's not too much poetry in bills, taking out the garbage, and crises to do with your offspring. **—Poet STAN RICE, husband of novelist *Anne Rice***

We're still friends, but not while his new girlfriend's around—and not in front of the children.
—JERRY HALL, ex-wife of *Mick Jagger*, who has homes in France, New York, and Mustique but not in London (Rather than stay in a London hotel, he stays at Hall's home, but only when unaccompanied.)

I do have some pleasant memories, even though he was unfaithful and cheap. By all accounts, Mick has not changed.
—Ex-wife BIANCA JAGGER, now a social activist

It was, like, "Are you kidding me?" He's old enough to be my dad. It's disgusting. *Please.* **—MILLA JOVOVICH, on being propositioned by sexagenarian *Mick Jagger***

The ones who come on to young actresses and models are typically more secure than the vast numbers of men in Hollywood who prefer to deal with prostitutes. The powerful Don Simpson was one—so renowned for using and abusing them that when he did come onto an actual actress she'd be insulted to be zeroed in on by him. **—Veteran press agent BEEBE KLINE (*Simpson* produced *Top Gun, Flashdance, Beverly Hills Cop*, and so on.)**

Sexy, skimpy clothes are still clothes. I enjoy wearing them and looking good in them. But I don't think there's any real reason for nudity. Most of the time, it's just vulgar, and I don't go for that. David should have known I won't do it.

—BEYONCÉ KNOWLES, who walked out on a photo shoot when *David LaChapelle* **asked her to pose nude in honey**

There are two kinds of women. The ones who want to sleep with me and the ones who want to slap my face when I try to sleep with them. The most offended ones are usually the ones around my age, who're too old for me anyway. **—JACK NICHOLSON, whose latest flame was thirty-seven-years-younger** *Kate Moss*

We met at the Spice Island restaurant [in New York City]. He was a lot more charming than I thought he'd be.

—KATE MOSS, on *Jack Nicholson*

Oh, you are a fool. It should be four times this size!

—JOAN RIVERS, upon viewing *Christine Baumgartner's* **diamond ring from fiancé Kevin Costner**

Leonardo [DiCaprio] is still like a little boy. He'd usually rather be out with his friends, partying with the boys, than committing to a mature relationship.

—On-again, off-again girlfriend GISELE BUNDCHEN

I go to bed every night with Martha Stewart. Have you ever tried her sheets? I think they're really nice. I hope she doesn't go to jail. They wasted time and money on some rinky-dink $45,000 case. She hurt no one, and they allow corporate crooks to go loose.

—Filmmaker MICHAEL MOORE

When a girl says she wants to have my body, that only makes my wife Jada [Pinkett Smith] proud that she's *got* my body and that no one else gets to use it!
—**WILL SMITH**

I will get married when I find a man who has more balls than me.
—**SALMA HAYEK, soon after her split with *Edward Norton***

Bruce Paltrow [father of Gwyneth] taught me something profound: that men need women even more than women need men.
—**STEVEN SPIELBERG**

My parents don't need [a marriage contract] because they're so truly married, so how would they be any more married if some guy stood in front of them and said he pronounced them man and wife or husband and wife?
—**KATE HUDSON, daughter of *Goldie Hawn* and stepdaughter of *Kurt Russell***

Clint [Eastwood] was still married, but even after, I didn't think we needed those [contractual] papers. A real marriage doesn't need those papers. But a real breakup does.
—**Longtime companion SONDRA LOCKE, who wrote a book about their breakup, *The Good, the Bad, and the Very Ugly***

Out of selfishness, Sonny [Bono] delayed marrying me, and out of fear, I delayed divorcing him. When I finally made a move, he sued me!
—**CHER**

I call her Dame Doom. She's a worrier. She worries about everything. If I began giving details, you wouldn't believe half of it.
—**MICHAEL DOUGLAS, on wife *Catherine Zeta-Jones***

Everyone knows I'm ambitious, but no one believes I can be humble sometimes. Especially if the guy's my husband.

—JENNIFER LOPEZ

There are two men in my life I've never fought with: my husband, Mark Consuelos, and my co-host, Regis [Philbin]. Otherwise, I can be a little feisty now and then! **—KELLY RIPA**

It was really out of character for me. But, yeah, I did it.

—SCARLETT JOHANSSON, on having sex with
***Benicio del Toro* in an elevator**

My boyfriend Arun [Nayar] is very sweet, for a millionaire. He could tell you that regardless of this almost bitchy image the media have created around me, I'm often kind and vulnerable.

—ELIZABETH HURLEY

The reason Madonna can't hang on to a man is she has no humility. I do. It comes with my [Hispanic] background. I know when to turn the testosterone off. **—JENNIFER LOPEZ**

Lots of females want to get close to Ozzy. Sometimes very close. But usually not for more than a few hours. I'm the one who's stayed close for years and years. No one else can do that.

—SHARON OSBOURNE

Can you handle the fact that I don't love you?

—Singer DAVID BOWIE, proposing to future wife *Angela*

Mother told a friend, "I don't care if Lee [Strasberg] remarries. He can bring someone into my bed, but I don't want anyone to use my kitchen things. Tell Susie to take them."

—Actress SUSAN STRASBERG

One look from her could destroy a whole hotel just by looking at it, but so far, I feel perfectly safe around her.

—MATTHEW BRODERICK, on wife *Sarah Jessica Parker*

Men most often leave their wives for another woman. Nowadays, women leave their husbands for themselves—and that's what I've done. **—JOAN COLLINS, after divorcing *Peter Holm***

I'm getting to be known as the Elizabeth Taylor of marriage.

—JENNIFER LOPEZ, referring to her various engagements and husbands

I'm not at all flattered by any comparisons between her and myself.

—ELIZABETH TAYLOR, on *Jennifer Lopez*

It was great with Anjelica [Huston], but one reason we didn't make it official—and a reason I stopped marrying a long time ago—is I wanted to have more Oscars than marriages. Beautiful women are my Achilles' crotch. **—JACK NICHOLSON**

I knew it wasn't gonna last. I used to introduce him as my first husband. Being from the South, that made him stop and ponder a bit. **—BRETT BUTLER**

My first marriage went from 1983 to 1985. Now I think I'm committed for life. Vanessa [Paradis] and I don't have a marriage license, but we have all the important things, including two kids.
—JOHNNY DEPP

I had too many husbands. I was optimistic, right up through the last one. Personally, I don't think marriage works for most heterosexuals. **—ELIZABETH TAYLOR**

Beer and TV.
—Ex-girlfriend KELLY PRESTON, on *Charlie Sheen*'s idea of foreplay

I felt betrayed—betrayed by the One to whom I had vowed my life and my future. **—Former convent postulant MARIA VON TRAPP, in her memoirs, on husband *Captain von Trapp* expecting her to have sex with him**

I married the children.
—MARIA VON TRAPP, explaining why she wed *Georg*

At home when we're alone together, we're nudists.
—DANNY MODER, husband of *Julia Roberts*

People often don't know how to judge me, because if they disapprove of Roman [Polanski] they think they should disapprove of me too—without knowing anything about me.
—Wife and actress EMMANUELLE SEIGNER

Vanessa is French. Her last name means "Paradise." I wouldn't want to change her last name. It's perfect as it is. **—JOHNNY DEPP**

When Susan and I married and she took my last name, I never guessed she'd make it more famous than I or some other relative would.
—Actor CHRIS SARANDON

Tim [Robbins] and I are, technically speaking, a nonlegal couple. But either way, it makes sense. It's a matter of logic and fairness that a woman keeps her own name, whether or not she's an actress.
—SUSAN SARANDON

I wanted a third child, but Michael [Douglas] doesn't. Of course, he was a father before we got married. **—CATHERINE ZETA-JONES**

She is my favorite of my harem. **—LUCIANO PAVAROTTI, on**
twenty-six-year-old secretary *Nicoletta Mantovani*

No wonder men like Jack Nicholson refrain from marriage. Or someone like that wrinkled rocker Mick Jagger. The press would be bound to point out the appearance of incest. It would look like fathers marrying daughters. **—SHARON OSBOURNE**

I'm looking forward to working with actors closer to my age, for a change. It'll help me seem not so young. But as for dates and all that, I like men of assorted ages. **—Nineteen-year-old**
SCARLETT JOHANSSON (*Lost in Translation, Girl With a Pearl Earring*)

There are age differences, and there are age differences. Joan Crawford was about a year older when we married, and unknowledgeable about many things, yet she was mentally older than me by about five or seven years. By the time we divorced, she was ten or twelve years my senior. **—DOUGLAS FAIRBANKS JR.**

Rex Harrison was never young. Always a pompous old man inside. An *elderly* soul, you know. **—RACHEL ROBERTS (*Murder on the Orient Express*), who tried to time her suicide to ruin her ex-husband's theatrical comeback in Los Angeles**

Bill [Murray] is fun when he's up, but he's tired so much of the time. He once said to me, "Stop being so energetic, it's wearing me out." No, we didn't seriously consider marriage. Not to each other. **—GILDA RADNER**

They say comedians are easily depressed. That's a wide generalization, [but] Gilda is overall very bright and up. She absolutely makes me feel younger. I think comedians *should* marry comedians, to cheer each other up. **—GENE WILDER (*Willie Wonka and the Chocolate Factory*), *Gilda Radner*'s widower**

I think [Michael] Jackson, in some part of his mind, wanted to marry me. Not for the usual reasons, but so we could be together with no one coming between us. . . . He talked a lot about Peter Pan and Wendy. . . . **—DIANA ROSS**

We started as husband and wife, but it ended like brother and sister. **—ELIZABETH TAYLOR, on her second marriage, to actor *Michael Wilding***

My friend Bobby De Niro has a son that he called Raphael, after the hotel in Rome where he was conceived. Good thing Bobby and his wife weren't staying at the Rome Hilton. **—Actor JOHN CAZALE (How about the Paris Hilton?)**

I wonder who's the sensitive soul who named the daughter "Chastity." What were they *thinking*? And was it Sonny or Cher?

—JON STEWART (*The Daily Show*)

My second wife, Zsa Zsa Gabor, has never been famous for her brainpower. But my first was dull and stupid. Therefore I didn't take her out in public, and therefore very few people know I had a first wife. **—GEORGE SANDERS (*All About Eve*)**

I thought it was very humanitarian of Sean Penn and Madonna to marry each other. That way, they only make two people miserable instead of four. **—CESAR ROMERO (TV's *Batman*, as The Joker)**

I left Sean Connery after he bashed my face in with his fists.

—First wife DIANE CILENTO

If a wife insults her husband and he don't put her in her place, he stops being the husband.

—Boxer MIKE TYSON, after he punched *Robin Givens*

One actor I would never work with is Jan-Michael Vincent. He's violent—to women and animals. One of his ex-wives or ex-girlfriends said he stomped her pet kitten to death. That's inexcusable.

—Oscar- and Tony-winner SANDY DENNIS

I have alcohol problem, and sometimes I think is not fair Jackie [Bisset] should have burden of my problem. But thank God for female sex! **—Ballet dancer ALEXANDER GODUNOV**

It's interesting to marry creative men in different professions. I've married a writer, a director, an actor—a few weeks with the actor [John Heard]. How much could I learn from another actor?

—MARGOT KIDDER (*Superman*)

I split up with my girlfriend as well as my wife to marry Margot [Kidder]. We had a good run—like three years—but we also had a daughter, so it's more than just a memory.

—Author THOMAS MCGUANE

An inveterate liar who lived in a fantasy world.

—Ex-model KELLY LEBROCK, on ex-husband *Steven Seagal*

Women who loved the book and the movie have said to me how wonderful [author] Robert Waller must be. They're assuming *Bridges of Madison County* is quite autobiographical. I know it's not.

—MERYL STREEP (*Waller* and his wife of thirty-five years divorced. He moved in with a woman twenty-three years her junior.)

James Woods thinks he's the world's best actor and the smartest man since Einstein. When he's wrong, he's wrong all around.

—SEAN YOUNG, former co-star and flame

A man likes [very] young girls for several reasons. One is that they don't remind him of his mother. **—CHARLES CHAPLIN**

Charlie [Chaplin] always said he wanted a daughter, but at first he kept having sons. People used to joke, though never in print, that since he couldn't have little girls, he married them.

—Silent-star BUSTER KEATON

Elvis liked them young. I was very attracted to him—what a package! It was the drugs and the entourage that ended it for me.

—CYBILL SHEPHERD

For a date, Elvis Presley would rent an entire restaurant or theater for you. He'd try and sweep you off your feet, impress you with his big spending. He felt he had to do that. He didn't know how personally devastating he was. He didn't realize it.

—JULIET PROWSE

Frank [Sinatra], when we were going together, well, he wanted to be Tarzan.

—JULIET PROWSE

Sinatra had a Bogart fixation. In the end, he behaved like a perfect $#!%.

**—*Bogart*'s widow LAUREN BACALL,
for a time engaged to *Sinatra*, who suddenly dropped her**

Someday I will look back and laugh about this. But I don't know if I'll ever laugh about *Gigli*.

**—BEN AFFLECK, whose relationship with *Jennifer Lopez*
definitely ended with the release of their megaflop *Gigli***

The men I married, I chose because they were intellectuals: Charlie Chaplin, Burgess Meredith, and Erich Maria Remarque. They were my second, third, and fourth. I don't count my first husband—it wasn't memorable, and he was *not* an intellectual.

—PAULETTE GODDARD (*Modern Times*, *The Women*)

Some of my girlfriends have chosen me because they like it that I like guys too. That turns on a lot of girls.

—ANDY DICK

I did not have a good time with Warren Beatty. He sees women as statistics. He told me his first job was frightening away rats in an alley behind a theater. I wonder if he did it by flirting with them.

—**ANOUK AIMÉE (***A Man and a Woman***)**

Madonna said she'll flirt with anyone from garbage men to grandmothers. Is that equal opportunity or promiscuity? In any case, I notice that, like a lot of famous, pretty women, she rarely goes for handsome men, doesn't want much visual competition.

—**Author ANTHONY BURGESS**

I got sort of a crush on Jodie Foster. I didn't *know*. I saw her jogging several times on Santa Monica beach with her girlfriend Cydney, and they wear matching wedding rings. And, you know? I got a crush all over again. Can't help it.

—**Actor CHRIS REBELLO (***Jaws***)**

It's about meeting somebody you think you could easily fall in love with . . . but they, ah, they in fact play for a different team.

—**RUSSELL CROWE, to Salon.com, about the platonic result of his friendship with actor-director *Jodie Foster***

She was twelve years old. She had sex with another girl in the neighborhood. I don't know if I would call that a lesbian affair. Roseanne has not been having lesbian affairs during our marriage.

—**Informative ex TOM ARNOLD**

Cary Grant wasn't homosexual around me.

—**Ex-wife DYAN CANNON**

I can say from my experience that Cary Grant was not heterosexual when he was around me.
—DICK SARGENT (*Bewitched*), who worked with and dated *Grant*

My friends Cary Grant and Randolph Scott shared at least five homes all over L.A. I dated both, but despite their marriages to women, the enduring pair was Cary and Randy. That relationship lasted to the end. But then, Spence and I have been together half a century.
—MR. BLACKWELL

Nonsex sells too. My books are best-sellers, and more women prefer romance to sex. I'd far rather see a well-dressed Cary Grant kiss a lady's hand than watch one of those topless "hunks" obscenely huffing and puffing away.
—DAME BARBARA CARTLAND (1901–2000)

Bob Fosse grew up around strip clubs. Women were his hobby. He'd even cheat on his mistress. Part of him felt guilty, another part was ecstatic. It helped lead him to an early death.
—Wife GWEN VERDON

Christian Slater's wife has taken him back. He had to promise to avoid visiting strip joints. I guess X-rated videos aren't enough for some guys.
—BILL MAHER

I later found out Clint [Eastwood] had been having another relationship altogether while *we* were together. I can't imagine how many lies he must have told me.
—SONDRA LOCKE (*The Heart Is a Lonely Hunter*)

Liberace wrote in one of his books that he'd lost his virginity to an older woman. Declined to give her name, called her "Miss Bea Haven." He finally admitted to me, as he had to friends, that his first time was with a football player on the Green Bay Packers.

—SCOTT THORSON, who eventually sued *"Lee"* for palimony

Of course, it hurt me when I found out, although I knew it would not destroy our marriage. But it hurt even more when the public found out. Even wives have pride. **—SIMONE SIGNORET, on**

Yves Montand*, who had an affair with co-star *Marilyn Monroe

I'm as sure of Brad as I could be of any actor, and more than 95 percent of them. **—JENNIFER ANISTON, on her husband's fidelity**

If you want a husband that has a fighting chance of being faithful, stay away from actors and musicians. Rock stars have groupies chasing them, and actors have love scenes—and erections don't necessarily end because the director yells "Cut!"

—COURTNEY LOVE, widow of rock-star *Kurt Cobain*

I once did a lunch interview with an actor named Albert Salmi, who said to me, on the record, that the marriage vow was sacred and that if a woman was unfaithful she deserved to die. What about an errant husband? His answer was that the Bible does not prescribe death for *him*. . . . Of course, we don't know *why* he [later] killed his wife. **—*Los Angeles Times* columnist PAUL ROSENFELD**

I think if you marry an actor he'll be more sympathetic to your schedule and requirements, and less prone to jealousy when you do a love scene or flirt. And in this business, harmless flirting is just part of business and public relations. **—CHARLIZE THERON**

Most of what was printed [during his affair with co-star Sean Young] was false. But all the rumors and stories were embarrassing. Like her supposedly Krazy Glue-ing my penis to my thigh. I felt like a laughingstock.　**—JAMES WOODS**

The more men you get involved with, the more chances of something like that happening. It's over and done with, and I'm not gonna name a name.　**—HALLE BERRY, one of whose past boyfriends hit her so hard she lost most of her hearing in one ear**

I thought since [first husband Al Jordan] was a musician we'd have so much in common. He was a sadist. He tried to kill me while I was pregnant with our son.　**—DORIS DAY**

Opposites do not attract, as a rule. Men and women are terribly different, but some women like to play nursemaid.

—KATHARINE HEPBURN, who nursemaided *Spencer Tracy* through his declining, alcoholic years

We're happy 'cause we got a lot in common, outside of our bodies.

—JUSTIN TIMBERLAKE, during his relationship with *Britney Spears*

Roger Vadim and I were too different to last. I don't mean nationality, I mean attitude. I think opposites only attract for a brief, intense period.　**—JANE FONDA**

Chris [Robinson, rocker] is so nonmaterialistic, and I am heavy into materialism! I love to dress up, he doesn't. . . . Some opposites last a real long time, 'cause they keep discovering new things about each other—like my mom and pa.

—KATE HUDSON, reared by *Goldie Hawn* and stepdad *Kurt Russell*

No, opposites do attract, at least on a chemical level. But if it's going to survive, the wife has to make an awful lot of adjustments.

—LUCILLE BALL, whose first husband was *Desi Arnaz,* whom the network didn't think would be believable as her spouse on *I Love Lucy*

For peace of mind, it's better if you think the same about important things. Jennifer [Lopez] and I share the same beliefs about family and our work and love and money.

—Third husband MARC ANTHONY

I didn't know really who she was.

—DENNIS RODMAN, on *Carmen Electra,* his wife of nine days

Twenty-nine days was *way* too long!

—DREW BARRYMORE, on her 1994 marriage to *Jeremy Thomas*

It's almost, like, erased from my mind by now.

—JAMES DEBARGE, on his four-month 1984 marriage to *Janet Jackson,* which her father reportedly had annulled

She wanted him to become a fashion plate. But at heart he's a slob, like me. That marriage—and I can say it now—it would not have lasted a week.

—MATT DAMON, on his pal *Ben Affleck,* formerly engaged to *J. Lo*

It's so lame when magazines start talking about your marriage and whether it'll last.

—NICK LACHEY, husband and co-star of *Jessica Simpson (Newlyweds)*

Everyone was saying that Desi [Arnaz Jr.] and I could never make a go of it because I was an older woman. Yet we were mentally compatible. I still acted like a child star. But his mother [Lucille

Ball] wasn't having any of it. She was determined to break us up, and she did. **—PATTY DUKE**

I guess if your witchy wife won't give you a divorce no-how, no-way, suicide's one option. **—Shock-comedian SAM KINISON, on the suicide of *Edgar Rosenberg, Joan Rivers*'s husband**

I grew up with a lot of boys. I probably have a lot of testosterone for a woman—and that intimidates men, some men—older men, no question.
—CAMERON DIAZ, involved with younger man Justin Timberlake

I used to tell girlfriends, when it became serious, "I'm no world-class Romeo, but I am fast." Until it turned into my reputation, and girls would giggle when I'd ride by. **—TV cowboy REX ALLEN**

A friend of mine was married to a doctor. One day he confesses to her that he's had sex with some of his patients. She says, "But Howard, you're a veterinarian!" **—Comedian TOTIE FIELDS**

Men will do anything, sexually. If it feels good, they'll do it. You gotta watch 'em all the time. It ain't worth it!
—ETHEL MERMAN, after her thirty-eight-day marriage to actor *Ernest Borgnine*

I'm happy to cuddle up with my daughter Ireland, instead of looking for a new man. To be honest, I like being alone. I have my daughter, and we have our own little world.
—KIM BASINGER, post–Alec Baldwin

Donald helped me realize that happiness can't buy money.
—Ex-wife IVANA TRUMP

Great laughter is even better than great sex, and you can laugh with anyone—a friend, a lover, a mate. . . . Looking back, I really think our marriage vow was "As long as we both shall laugh."

—BETTE MIDLER, married to a part-time comedian

I would kiss a frog even if there was no promise of a Prince Charming popping out of it. I love frogs. I'd lick him.

—CAMERON DIAZ

No, Quentin [Tarantino] did not suck my feet. I hear Cameron Diaz said he's pretty good at it.

—BRIDGET FONDA, on her *Jackie Brown* director

I can believe Charlie Sheen's a sex maniac—and also very rude and loves to shock for the sake of it. He has problems.

—ERIC STOLTZ, after *Sheen* said publicly he'd like to
have sex with Stoltz's girlfriend, Bridget Fonda

Brooke Shields and Andre Agassi's grounds for divorce may be irreconcilable height. He only comes up to her chest, and apparently he didn't come up there often enough.

—1999 item from columnist CINDY ADAMS

I've worshiped him for years. He's fantastic. I like George's smile too.

—RICKY MARTIN, on fellow singer *George Michael*,
in the *New York Daily News*, December 1999

There was a big rumor on the set of *Bonanza* that [Michael Landon] was having an affair with Hoss [Dan Blocker]. My dad would sort of play with it. They would sort of hang all over each other and nuzzle on the set just to stir the pot.

—*Michael*'s openly gay son, CHRISTOPHER LANDON

She smelled so nice. You kiss an actor and you don't know what they are going to smell like. But you kiss a girl, and she is going to smell good. And she's very soft. They're soft and they smell nice. Guys don't. **—JULIANNE MOORE to the *Sunday Mirror*, on kissing *Toni Collette* in *The Hours***

Ozzy would be the first to say he's coarse and often difficult. And I'd be the second. **—Wife SHARON OSBOURNE**

If you're going to break up, the Cannes Film Festival is as nice a place as any. **—CAMERON DIAZ, who temporarily split there with *Justin Timberlake* in 2004**

I always stayed away from starlets, actresses, and bimbos. I did marry and divorce actress Kay Lenz, although I realized never to do that again. **—DAVID CASSIDY (*The Partridge Family*)**

Men think money can get them anything they want. My first husband was offered ten thousand pounds if he'd let me sleep with a wealthy Arab. Of course, the offer should have been to *me*, but those were the old days, and the would-be purchaser was a wealthy Arab. My husband—bless his greedy, voyeuristic little soul—wanted to accept the offer. As long as he could watch! I was disgusted with both men, and that ended my marriage. **—JOAN COLLINS**

The best thing about getting out of the marriage is that now I can park my Harley in the living room.

—BILLY JOEL, upon divorcing *Christie Brinkley*

I'll never forget the night I brought my Oscar home and Tony [Franciosa, also an actor] took one look at it, and I knew my marriage was over. **—Two-time Oscar-winner SHELLEY WINTERS**

If I'd stayed with Sonny [Bono], I wouldn't be an actress, I wouldn't be a woman. God, I'd be dead. **—CHER**

I feel as though I'm sixteen. I have always felt sixteen. Hillary, on the other hand, has always been forty-five. **—BILL CLINTON**

. . . And there are times when the First Lady has the last word. **—PRESIDENT HARRY S. TRUMAN, on wife** *Bess*

Remember that there isn't anything more important than the sleep and rest of Elizabeth Taylor. **—Then-husband EDDIE FISHER**

Getting married is just the first step toward getting divorced. **—ZSA ZSA GABOR**

We met on New Year's Eve, 1994. He came up, grabbed me, and licked my face. I thought he was a nice guy and gave him my phone number. **—PAMELA ANDERSON, on then-husband** *Tommy Lee*

Bob gets embarrassed when I'm affectionate with him in public because I tend to start licking his face. **—SUZANNE PLESHETTE, on former co-star** *Bob Newhart*

The question of whether Ben [Affleck] and I are gay is so awkward in a lot of ways. There is no right way to answer it. **—MATT DAMON in** *The Advocate*

I had a boyfriend I was semi-engaged to. But then he went to Europe and met someone else. Finally he phoned me and said he wanted us to stay close friends. But I refused, and later I returned all his postcards unopened. **—CAROL WAYNE, Johnny Carson's "Matinee Lady" on** *The Tonight Show*

After my wife died—we were married over fifty years—I found out her real age. I thought all along she was younger than me. Then I find out she was an older woman! I loved her all the same.

—Film gangster MARC LAWRENCE

There have been at least two occasions on which Michael Douglas found out that [wife Catherine Zeta-Jones] was older than he thought. One was a White House dinner involving a security check of the couple. . . . It really doesn't signify, because Douglas is so much older and because she looks so good.

—Columnist JANICE REID

I've gone out with some girls that sure are pretty, and I can't believe it because some of the gals in high school I dated looked like me in a wig. **—Oversized CHRIS FARLEY**

Once you get on stage, everything is right. I feel—complete, fulfilled. I think that's why, in the case of noncompromising career women, parts of our personal lives don't work out. One person can't give you the feeling that thousands of people give you.

—Opera diva LEONTYNE PRICE

Well, it shocked the nation. After she [divorced] Charles, Princess Diana's credit card was rejected at a major store. And all she was trying to purchase were two lipsticks for about [$38]. That makes you wonder about your *own* credit. **—MICHAEL HUTCHENCE, INXS**

Errol Flynn died on a seventy-foot boat with a seventeen-year-old girl. Walter has always wanted to go that way, but he's going to settle for a seventeen-footer with a seventy-year-old.

—Wife BETSY CRONKITE

Here lies David Diamond—underneath Tom Cruise.
>   —Openly gay rock musician **DAVE DIAMOND**, of the rock group Berlin,
>   when asked what he would like his epitaph to read

He is embarrassed by his wide hips, yes.
>   —**SONDRA LOCKE**, on ex *Clint Eastwood*

The best thing would be just us alone together. But with two big careers, we're not together very often, and hardly ever alone.
>   —**BRITNEY SPEARS**, on her relationship
>   with then-boyfriend *Justin Timberlake*

It was real simple then. In a way, I kind of miss it.
>   —**CAMERON DIAZ**, on the five years she lived
>   with video producer *Carlos de la Torre*

Woody [Allen] wasn't rich then. He really counted his pennies. I told him a penny saved is a girl lost, and just believe in your future—the big money will come. And he did loosen up a bit on his spending.
>   —Ex-wife **JANET MARGOLIN**

Susan [Anton] wanted us to marry. I liked things as they were. That's a luxury my parents never knew. Wasn't it Mae West who said, "Opportunity knocks for a man, but a girl expects a ring"?
>   —**DUDLEY MOORE**

I was in a car once with a boy I kind of liked and thought was attractive, and we were going to kiss—no petting above or below the waist, he just wanted to kiss me. Then he told me that he thought Richard Nixon was America's hope for the presidency. This was 1958, and I simply said, "Take me home."
>   —Novelist **ERICA JONG** (*Fear of Flying*)

Women are like elephants to me—I like to look at 'em, but I wouldn't want to own one.
—W. C. FIELDS

Do you know that all those years I was between marriages, I never had the guts to go to a gynecologist and ask him for a diaphragm? Never! You were just embarrassed about any sexual feelings you had—they were all supposed to be bad.
—JOAN RIVERS, on the 1950s

George Hamilton and Dolores Hart made a beautiful on-screen couple, and some of us [in *Where the Boys Are*] thought it might be for real. We were wrong. Men and acting were not her priorities. I guess she decided to keep the faith, instead of the face.
—Co-star JIM HUTTON (Timothy's father),
on the actress who became a nun

I'd done two movies with Elvis Presley, I'd been around Hollywood for a while—and saw how needlessly competitive and negative it could be. It never held my interest.
—DOLORES HART, now a mother superior

My husband is a sculptor, and we practice Zen, in our lives and in meditation, to increase serenity and fulfillment. It's not in the nature of Zen to preach it or to coerce others, but within our marriage it also helps keep us together.
—KATHERINE HELMOND (*Soap, Who's the Boss*)

The man I've married is Latin. He's, like, "You can see through that dress," or, "Is there going to be a love scene in that next movie?" It's sweet, but I go, "Look, the love scenes, the see-through dresses—all that stuff is good. As long as people like you, they're going to keep coming to see your movies. Do you want that house in Miami—yes or no?" I mean, this is what it's going to be. It's part of the business. **—JENNIFER LOPEZ, during her first marriage**

I *have* said that in my opinion the word "marriage" seems one which finishes a relationship—it doesn't start it. Reporters will ask, "Did you *really* say that?" I not only said it, I believe it. And as for children, in all good conscience I couldn't do what I do and have children. **—JACQUELINE BISSET**

A silly little thing. **—SADIE FROST's assessment of husband *Jude Law*'s on-set flirtation and fling with *Alfie* co-star *Sienna Miller*, which, however, eventually led to their divorce**

Lauren Holly and her soon-to-be-ex-husband Jim Carrey recently got together for a romantic dinner that reportedly turned ugly, ending in a screaming match when Lauren started to cry and left. Carrey ran out after her. Who says love is easy? **—Beverly Hills (213) in 1998**

An ugly trend has emerged of late, with husbands and wives airing their dirty linen in public. Frequently in restaurants. It's the lack of self-control I object to, and the general lack of maturity. Jim Carrey and [Lauren Holly] got together for dinner. The version I read said it became a screaming match after she began to cry and got up to leave. Then he runs after her. See, such episodes did *not* take place in times past, flawed as they were. Stars wouldn't behave in that way in public. They *cared* enough not to. **—KIRK DOUGLAS**

Political blacklists are wrong, but I don't see how or why extreme public misbehavior is condoned. Take Christian Slater. At a party, he punches his girlfriend. Then he bites the stomach of a man trying to defend her—apart from his cocaine and other drug abuses.

All right. He's sentenced to ninety days in jail. Fine, good. But under the studio system, such misbehavior would have ended a career. It's so extreme—and ongoing. Today, instead, it's just extra publicity. Most of the public and all the producers condone it, and he goes right back to work.

—Former teen heartthrob TROY DONAHUE in 1997

Christian Slater is easily one of the best patrons of a trendy strip joint in London where he came in wearing a Richard Nixon mask— tired of all the photos of him taken entering and leaving the club. . . . Asked to remove the mask, Christian refused and was eventually shown the door. In the future, he might find it easier, not to mention cheaper, to stay home and play house with his wife.

—Columnist ARLENE WALSH in 2004

If my boyfriend [Jordan Brotman] goes to strip clubs, I go with him. I don't mind if he enjoys watching—he can watch, but not touch! I'm open-minded, but when I tried to join in and do a mock strip, he wasn't too happy. I think women are definitely more open-minded than men.　　**—CHRISTINA AGUILERA**

It seems to me girls like her are more into settling down and having kids. If I do that, I think she might be the one. We met in Miami, and she already has a daughter. I do want kids. You can devote yourself to them.

—MATT DAMON, dating Hispanic *Lucianna Barroso*

From thirteen to eighty-three, sex is never far from men's minds or intentions. If there's a relationship, and a man's in it, don't be surprised if he cheats. You want fidelity above and beyond the usual norm? Try a lesbian relationship. Not that I have, mind you.

—Actress JANET MARGOLIN, who was married to *Woody Allen*

The only person who has anything to say about what happens to my body is me and Michelle Pfeiffer.
—ROSIE O'DONNELL, at a pro-choice fund-raiser

I find Michelle [Pfeiffer] fantastically attractive. I'm always kind of running up to her and kissing her on the mouth because she's so delicious. She's soooo delicious.   **—EMMA THOMPSON**

Who cares if a woman who once loved men now loves women? Who cares if someone's love fluctuates between men and women? What's the big deal? Let's stop being so judgmental of everyone who doesn't fit into our boxed-in perception of what love is.
—GILLIAN ANDERSON (*The X-Files*)

I had a teenage crush on Leif Garrett, because he looked like a chick.
—JAY MOHR

I'm not homosexual or anything, but you're gorgeous! You should get [breast] implants, John, then I'd be with you. We'd finally be together.   **—HOWARD STERN, to *John Stamos***

I'll probably grow old with Ben [Affleck], rather than the woman of my dreams. My longest relationship with a woman lasted two and a half years. That's short when I consider how long Ben and I have been pals.   **—MATT DAMON**

I have a potbellied pig named Max. He's sort of a watchdog. But he was no help during the [1994 Los Angeles] earthquake. He woke me up, and it was happening. I was naked. I had a buddy who lived downstairs in the guesthouse, and he was naked, but he brought his gun. Max was squealing real loud—my buddy thought it was someone breaking in. It was a wild scene, but not what you might think: two naked guys, a pig, and a gun. **—GEORGE CLOONEY**

George Clooney made enough suggestive comments about himself and close pal and co-star Mark Wahlberg that pressure was brought to bear for him to give over, and to start being seen again with a female on his arm. Pity that whatever the truth of a relationship might be, Hollywood's marketing police always interfere, to maintain the narrow status quo.

—London columnist AVIVA MEYERSON in 2001

George Clooney and his buddy Mark Wahlberg may be aging a bit, but that doesn't mean they have to grow up completely. The two recently bought matching go-carts and now race around George's sprawling Beverly Hills property. **—*Beverly Hills (213)* in 2004**

Speaking of Jerry [Brown, governor of California], I wonder where his Indian friend is living now that Jer's Laurel Canyon home went down the hillside during the big rains of two years ago? Just asking! **—Columnist BILL DAKOTA in 1981, in *The Hollywood Star***

I'm crazy about George [Michael], and I think he is about me too.

—BROOKE SHIELDS in the 1980s (In 1998 after he came out, she stated she wasn't surprised and was "relieved," since she hadn't heard from him since a few publicity dates.)

Will [Geer] suffered enough in his lifetime during the [political] witch hunts. So I didn't out him during his lifetime. Much of America wasn't ready to hear that Grandpa on *The Waltons* was bisexual. But Will's wife Herta and I used to joke that although she had him longest, I had him first.

—Actor-turned-activist HARRY HAY

He was AC/DC. **—ANN MILLER, on Judy Garland's director husband *Vincente Minnelli* (The quote was censored from an A&E *Biography* program on Miller's friend Garland.)**

Women fake orgasms because men fake foreplay.
—Talk host and author VIRGINIA GRAHAM

Okay, so now and then we fake a climax that isn't really there. But men can fake complete relationships! **—JOY BEHAR (*The View*)**

What can I do? I'm hot. **—JACK NICHOLSON, when longtime gal-pal *Anjelica Huston* discovered he'd been having affairs with younger women**

Howard Hughes offered me $10,000—a fortune in those days—to pose nude for a rubber dummy he wanted to have made and sleep with. I asked him why not sleep with me for free? He said because I was too good for him. **—Screen siren HEDY LAMARR**

I love feet. They talk to me. As I take them in my hands I feel their strengths, their weaknesses, their vitality, or their failings. As I take these feet in my hands, I am consumed with anger and compassion: anger that I cannot shoe all the feet in the world, compassion for all those who walk in agony.
—SALVATORE FERRAGAMO, shoe magnate and compassionate soul

I don't mind if a girl I go with is taller than me, because it means she has long legs, and that's *it* for me. **—ROD STEWART, five inches shorter than three-year girlfriend *Penny Lancaster***

When Howard Hughes was courting me—and I think he preferred that to anything more strenuous—he did mention a preference for oral sex. Frankly, that offended me at the time, and I let him know it—politely; he was quite powerful. That didn't seem to bother him. He'd come to my house just to sit and talk with my mother.

—LANA TURNER, on the bisexual tycoon and eventual recluse

I have this thing about wanting to marry him. I like these older guys. I have this weird nurturing sense.

—CHARLIZE THERON, admitting her weird crush on *Ozzy Osbourne*

The most romantic thing I've ever heard is something said to me by my co-star Robert Davi: "You're a hell of a guy, for a girl."

—ALLY WALKER (*Profiler*)

I told him to stop looking for love in all the wrong public places, and now he's settled down. We live in a sixteenth-century home in England, on the River Thames, with our Labradors Meg and Abby.

—*George Michael*'s partner of eight years, KENNY GOSS, who bailed him out of a Beverly Hills jail in 1998

Colin Farrell and Salma Hayek's not-so-secret affair had tongues wagging [on] the South African location of their film *Ask the Dust*. . . . They are inseparable. Hope this news wasn't too shocking for Salma's guy back home, actor Josh Lucas.

—Columnist CATHY GRIFFIN

Nothing to it. I was out of town making a movie, and Barbra is cheap. She hates to buy her own meals. Sharif was just somebody to pick up the tabs. **—ELLIOTT GOULD, on wife *Barbra Streisand* dining with *Funny Girl* co-star *Omar Sharif* (Most of the dinners were consumed in Sharif's suite in the Beverly Wilshire Hotel.)**

Nonactors have the occasional convention. Actors have locations—frequently. What it boils down to is, absence doesn't make the heart grow fonder, it just makes the libido grow stronger. Stick close to your mate, don't be too long apart. Only the saintly and the senile are immune to temptation. **—HALLE BERRY**

I had to worry if she was faithful . . . the guys on [Julia Roberts's] sets. And always the media, being in the eye of the hurricane . . . I wanted someone more ready to commit, to settle down, someone I could trust. **—BENJAMIN BRATT,** *Roberts*'s half-Hispanic fiancé,
who instead married Latina and former Bond girl Talisa Soto

I liked them both, but I was really with Hilary [Duff]. I was too young or—like out of my mind or something. But Hilary's the one I still love. It's just her. **—AARON CARTER, whom** *Duff* **dumped**
after he also began seeing *Lindsay Lohan*

We'll be very happy. . . . We're in love.
—Producer ROBERT EVANS (*Love Story***), on his fifth marriage, to far**
younger *Catherine Oxenberg* **(***Dynasty***). (It lasted twelve days. She**
claimed she'd been brainwashed into it after attending a spiritual
retreat; he attributed it to "irrational behavior caused by my stroke.")

I care about being with my husband. I take marriage seriously.
—SHANNEN DOHERTY, four months after wedding actor *Ashley Hamilton*
(son of George) and three months before filing for divorce

I'm so lucky to have met this person. I've never met anyone so supportive. **—DREW BARRYMORE, on marrying a bar owner (Two**
months later she filed for divorce, calling it "a green card situation"
and him "the biggest schmuck I've ever met in all my
years of existence.")

I didn't want him or anyone telling me what to do and how to live my life. **—BRITNEY SPEARS, on firing her manager *Larry Rudolph* because he objected to her marriage to Kevin Federline**

Maria is very capable. . . . She's independent. **—ARNOLD SCHWARZENEGGER, on his wife, *Maria Shriver*. (But like his father, he forbids her to wear pants, especially at home.)**

It's assumed Larry, thanks to his talent, was free of professional insecurity. Not so. Before going on stage, he would recite a little "pep" speech to himself: "That is my space. All of that space. I deserve to be there. No one else fills it the way that I do." **—JOAN PLOWRIGHT, widow of *Laurence Olivier***

I never stopped loving him. **—CHER in 1998, on late ex-husband *Sonny Bono*, whose estate she sued later that year for $1.66 million in unpaid alimony**

A nice thing about getting older is that kissing becomes more important. There may or may not be less sex, but there's more kissing. And a nice thing about being married to an actor [Hal Holbrook] is they've been exposed to love scenes, and *how* to kiss. **—DIXIE CARTER (*Designing Women*)**

The last man I'm going to marry is a man in show business. They're selfish, unreliable, and make lousy husbands . . . I'm going to take a good long look before I get married. I'm not going to jump into it. Certainly not to a showbiz character. **—SANDRA DEE, to *Parade* magazine in 1960 (Months later, after barely knowing him, she wed movie co-star Bobby Darin.)**

Marry a star. They're richer and less talented. With a good actor, how will you know if he's lying to you? **—AUDREY MEADOWS** (*The Honeymooners*), who married an airline president

Looking back, most of what we had in common was sex and glamour. Nice, but fleeting. What kept us together, while we were, was our son. **—BOBBY DARIN, ex-husband of *Sandra Dee***

Robert [Silberstein] and I are as happy as anyone could possibly be! We want to have more children—soon. We want a big family! **—DIANA ROSS, on the birth of her first child, which was by Motown chief Berry Gordy (She had two more daughters by *Silberstein*, and two sons by her second, Norwegian husband.)**

I like garage sales—you even find good clothes there. But my wife's asked me not to go to them anymore, 'cause I went to one where I found all these cool toys and clothes for Coco, our baby daughter. She didn't want them anywhere *near* Coco, wouldn't let me bring them into the house. So I said, "Yes, Mommy." **—DAVID ARQUETTE, married to *Courteney Cox***

As parents, it's important that we be consistent and not hypocritical. As Stephen Sondheim's song "Children Will Listen" points out, they pick up very easily and will call you on it. . . . It's *so* important to give our kids, always including daughters, the confidence to try and become whatever they dream they can be. **—BARBRA STREISAND**

To marry a senator and settle down in Georgetown.

**—Seventeen-year-old HILLARY RODHAM's ambition,
as noted in the future senator's high school newspaper**

My mother's been married ten times now. She says to me, "Sweetheart, settle down and marry a rich man." I said, "Mom, I *am* a rich man."

—CHER

There's not a lot of love in [show business]. Probably because there is so much money in it. So much acting too. If you want to be happy in this business, it helps to like yourself and to like others. As my dear friend Peter Finch says, "Most unhappy actors were unhappy before they became actors."

—VIVIEN LEIGH, a.k.a. Scarlett O'Hara

Haing Ngor was a fine, instinctive actor. More than that, the most positive and friendly, kindhearted, and selfless individual I've known in this business. He was a doctor first, and he was a Buddhist, and he came from Cambodia—a great human being.

**—SAM WATERSTON (*The Killing Fields*, which earned an Oscar
for *Dr. Ngor,* later murdered on a Los Angeles street)**

Don't postpone kind words if they're sincere, Monty used to say. In his life, he said more loving things than many people do who live to a so-called ripe old age.

**—ELIZABETH TAYLOR, on friend
Montgomery Clift, who lived to forty-six**

Love—the more you give, the more you get.

—HUGH JACKMAN, Tony-winner for *The Boy from Oz*

DEEP-DISSING

Arnold Schwarzenegger looks like a condom full of walnuts.

—Author CLIVE JAMES

A fellow with the inventiveness of Albert Einstein but with the attention span of Daffy Duck.

—Author TOM SHALES, on *Robin Williams*

She's not an actress. I wouldn't think she'd do street theater in Poland, would you? Do you think [Liz] Hurley really loves her craft? A lot of people I've met just want to be famous, and they don't care how they do it or what they do.

—SAMANTHA MORTON ("In America")

Val Kilmer loves the public eye, but not discipline on the set. Nowadays it's more about putting your face on the screen than putting your art or best effort into your work.

—Director JOHN FRANKENHEIMER (*The Manchurian Candidate*)

I'd let my wife, children, and animals starve before I'd subject myself to working with her again.

—Director DON SIEGEL (*Dirty Harry*), on *Bette Midler*

They told us to buy duct tape and portable radios so that if the world does end we can all listen to Rush Limbaugh blame it on Clinton.
—TV host (*Politically Incorrect*) BILL MAHER

He's the type of man who will end up dying in his own arms.
—Blonde bombshell MAMIE VAN DOREN,
on then-bachelor *Warren Beatty*

It's today's ideal couple. Demi Moore's in love with Ashton Kutcher and so is he, and their true love—both of them—is all the attention and career opportunities their twoness gives them.
—ALAN KING

Vin Diesel is said to shave his head so we'll have to guess what race he is and he won't be "typecast" in white roles. . . . I know *I'm* still guessing: Is he or isn't he in the human race?
—REX REED

It sounds strange, but it's a practical name. If he wasn't "Boy George," you might assume he was an overpainted lady in a hat and caftan.
—Rolling Stone KEITH RICHARDS

Somebody should clip Sting around the head and tell him to stop using that ridiculous Jamaican accent.
—ELVIS COSTELLO

So Madonna is into Kabbalah. Fine. But what about that [English] accent that comes and goes? She must believe she's a reincarnation of [Prime Minister] Disraeli.
—HUGH GRANT

Poor little man, they made him out of lemon Jell-O, and there he is. He's honest and hardworking, but he's not great.
—Veteran Hollywood writer ADELA ROGERS ST. JOHN, on *Robert Redford*

As easy as it would be for me to nail a custard pie to the wall.

—SHIRLEY MACLAINE, when asked how easily she could deal with having *Madonna* for a sister-in-law (The singer was dating co-star Warren Beatty while filming *Dick Tracy*.)

He couldn't ad-lib a fart after a baked-bean dinner.

—JOHNNY CARSON, on talk-show host (very briefly) *Chevy Chase*

Sarah Brightman couldn't act scared on the New York subway at four o'clock in the morning.

—JOEL SEGAL

I'm less fearful now. . . . There's nothing I wouldn't say to Richard Gere's face—both of them.

—DEBRA WINGER, on her *Officer and a Gentleman* co-star

Ewan McGregor has flashed his pole on screen more often than anyone since Richard Gere. Being a modern young European, he brags about it, and says his father brags about him too. Ewan, for gosh's sakes, put it back in your pants and keep it there!

—TV host DENNIS MILLER

I can say personally that George Clooney's codpiece will have to be significantly larger than those of his [Batman] predecessors Michael Keaton and Val Kilmer.

—Director JOEL SCHUMACHER

I think Mick Jagger would be astounded and amazed if he realized to how many people he is not a sex symbol but a mother image.

—Androgynous singer DAVID BOWIE

If Justin Timberlake's a sex symbol, then so's every punk kid in America. But I still hold there's a difference between horny and famous and sexy and celebrated.

—DREW CAREY

Jane Fonda had the best body in the whole world—and her husband left her anyway. Thank you, God. **—JOAN RIVERS**

She says things like, "Uh, what did you think about my last phone call?" **—Columnist LIZ SMITH, on *Raquel Welch***

I once told a story to my dear friend and protégée Marilyn Monroe, and afterward I added that it was probably apocryphal. She said to me, "Oh, Sidney! You mean you can't tell if it's properly punctuated?" **—Columnist SIDNEY SKOLSKY**

Who can forget Mike Myers as the Cat in the Hat? I know I'll sure try. **—TV host BILL MAHER**

Have you seen Erik Estrada lately? He's all over the TV. That's not surprising in terms of desperation, but it is in terms of how awful he looks . . . from hunk to chunk, and his face looks like it's melting. Sad, sad. **—DANNY BONADUCE (*The Partridge Family*)**

Unpleasant man. No one has yet worked out what really makes him tick. **—Director ROBERT ALDRICH, on *Frank Sinatra***

Mother Carey **—FRANK SINATRA's nickname for co-star *Cary Grant* (from the then-famous story *Mother Carey's Chickens*)**

Frank Sinatra, when I contacted him to appear [at the first AIDS fund-raiser], he did not want to be associated with this. I don't know what he was afraid of. **—ELIZABETH TAYLOR**

People say I remind them of Liz Taylor only because I'm not skinny. **—CHRISTINA RICCI**

The hair is now something like the wig of a fop in Restoration comedy. The speaking voice continues to sound like Rice Krispies if they could talk.

—Critic JOHN SIMON, on *Barbra Streisand* **in** *A Star Is Born*

. . . John Malkovich, the bald, cross-eyed actor with a voice like an unbroken dial tone.

—Critic REX REED

Michael Jackson is not a star. He's got no business being on stage. He's too fat, he wears underwear on the outside, and he's been accused of abusing children.

—NASH KATO of Urge Overkill in 1993

In his three-hour lie [*J.F.K.*], Stone falsifies so much he may be an intellectual psychopath.

—Commentator GEORGE WILL, on writer-director *Oliver Stone*

It's great to be with Bill Buckley, because you don't have to think. He takes a position and you automatically take the opposite and you know you're right.

—Super-economist JOHN KENNETH GALBRAITH

My boy, when I want to play with a prick, I'll play with my own.

—W. C. FIELDS, after MGM chief *Louis B. Mayer*
suggested a round of golf

If I'd lost to Donny Osmond, I would be living in Tibet so nobody would recognize me.

—DANNY BONADUCE, on a charity
boxing match against Marie's brother

Marie Osmond looks like a wax dummy. The middle of her face looks weird, as if she has had too many injectables, and her eyebrows arc unnaturally.
—Plastic surgeon Z. PAUL LORENC, in his book *A Little Work*

She has a big heart, anyway. She said to me, "I think being homeless is un-American. You can never get very successful that way. Because if opportunity knocks, you're never home."
—JOHNNY CARSON, on his *Tonight Show* "Matinee Lady," *Carol Wayne*

Remember when sleaze was wholesome? You know, like Johnny Carson's occasionally racy jokes? Now you have people, even on TV, that personify and exude sleaze, joking or not, racy or not. Like Chris Rock. I think he crawled out from under one.
—Radio host KEITH MICHAELS

Howard Hughes, who owned the studio [RKO], once asked me a rather foolish question. He knew I was born in Japan, and he asked me why on earth I was born there. What could I say? "Because I wanted to be near my mother." **—JOAN FONTAINE**

Stephen Sondheim is a virtually peerless composer but an unusual person. He didn't come out of the closet until his sixties, even though everyone on Broadway *knew*. They say it's because he didn't want his mother to know, so he waited till she died.
—Tony- and Emmy-winner MICHAEL JETER

Redundant? Lily Tomlin's lived with the same woman for thirty or more years, but she was able to mask it by saying Jane [Wagner] was her collaborator, which is true. Still, why did she wait until sixty or so to finally admit what everyone knew and had been pressuring her to say? It's not like she was a beauty and did movie love scenes with men. Half the women in comedy are lesbian. Is this a surprise? —Columnist **MICKEY BARNETT**

Cameron Diaz was this delightful neophyte when we did *The Mask*. Toward the end of filming, she asked me where she and her family could see the movie when it was all done. —**JIM CARREY**

(*Diaz* became the second actress to earn $20 million for one film.)

It would be medieval not to approve of female priests, as we now have [in the Anglican Church]. However, in the United States, anyone can become a minister by mail. . . . It isn't a calling, it's something one *sends* for, "plus postage and handling." The latest American ordained minister is actress Sharon Stone, who plans to marry two friends—to each other—at her Beverly Hills manse, come November [2004]. —**London radio host DWIGHT POPOVICH**

For her follow-up to her Oscar-nominated *Lost in Translation*, director Sofia Coppola plans to star the unprepossessing Kirsten Dunst as Marie Antoinette. . . . This is akin to casting Minnie Mouse as Mata Hari. Are there no *women* in Hollywood, only girls, chicks, babes, and clones? —Columnist **GEORGE BYINGTON**

Michelle Pfeiffer's roles are a lot less sexy than mine are.
—**SHARON STONE, who's also been Oscar-nominated less often**

I look for a good story. Why just do *Rambo*? I feel cheated when I see things like that. I feel like a fool. —**ESAI MORALES (*La Bamba*)**

I'm too *good* to play that role. —**SOPHIA LOREN, on Alexis in *Dynasty*, which then went to Joan Collins**

The first time my girlfriend and I were followed by street photographers, she wanted to bash them. But I said, "No, then you would be the lesbian Sean Penn. Just grin and bear it."

—CHASTITY BONO

All of a sudden I'm the celebrity of yesteryear, even on my own network. I'm not David Duchovny, I'm not Scott Wolf. I might as well be George Hamilton.

—JASON PRIESTLEY (*Beverly Hills 90210*)

I really like Warren Beatty, and I'd like to hang out with Warren Beatty, but the bottom line is I'm busy.

—Writer-director QUENTIN TARANTINO

[Michael Jackson] is the best friend you could ever have. He's gentle, not rough like the other guys.

—EMMANUEL LEWIS (*Webster*) in 1984

The subject of girlfriends is off limits. So is his friendship with Michael Jackson. **—*People* magazine in 1994, on**
**   *Emmanuel Lewis*, twenty-three and still living with his mother**

The D.A. has decided not to press charges against Michael Jackson. . . . He can stop pretending to be married to Lisa Marie [Presley] now! **—JAY LENO in 1994**

. . . that cunning little linguist.

—DAME EDNA EVERAGE, on *Jodie Foster*

I'm fine. How are you? **—Openly gay NATHAN LANE, to Tony Awards**
co-host *Rosie O'Donnell* (then not yet openly gay) when she pretended
to switch places with him and asked, "How's my beard?"

I wish Simon would just come out. He's one of the most repressed men I've ever met. He would enjoy his life a lot more if he would just come out. I reckon he's dying to.

—SHARON OSBOURNE, on *Simon Cowell*

I have to tell you, it feels very violating. This is one of the strangest experiences that's ever happened to me in my life, and I'm having to deal with it. **—Actor RICHARD HATCH (*Battlestar Galactica*),**

on the fame of *Survivor* champ *Richard Hatch*

I know that I am not alone in the opinion that all of Kathie Lee Gifford's orifices should be hemmed shut by Filipino immigrants for six dollars. **—Author CINTRA WILSON**

[Columnist] Liz Smith used to kiss my ass so much it was embarrassing. [She] disgraced the industry.

—DONALD TRUMP, who also dislikes negative coverage

Barbra [Streisand] executive-produced many films starring herself where the male protagonist had to look down at her as she was nestled coyly under the freshly dampened sheets and say, "God . . . you are so, so *beautiful.*" **—Author CINTRA WILSON**

One of the hardest things to endure was having a husband who was prettier than me.

—JOANNE WOODWARD, married to *Paul Newman*

Danny Moder has been wearing an empathy-belly around the house, so that his pregnant wife Julia Roberts wouldn't feel odd.

—*Beverly Hills (213)*

Not Normal: Tom Throws Like a Girl! This action hero has a wimpy pitch! Tom Cruise tosses a ball at a Tokyo ballgame on October 19, 2004.
—*Star* **magazine, stereotyping**

He no playa da game, he no make-a da rules.
—**U.S. Secretary of Agriculture EARL BUTZ, commenting in 1974 on *Pope Paul VI*'s opposition to birth control**

Richard Nixon impeached himself. He gave us Gerald Ford as his revenge.
—**Congresswoman BELLA ABZUG**

I can't possibly believe Jerry's a dumbdumb. . . . How many really intelligent presidents have we had?
—**First Lady BETTY FORD in 1974**

He [has] the least impressive record of any head of state in all our history. Oh, he's failed in many, many areas. His first reaction to a question about the death penalty was to burst out laughing. Soooo disgusting.
—**UMA THURMAN, on *George W. Bush***

Under his [governorship], Texas ranks first in toxic air pollution, first in water pollution, in total residents without health insurance, in number of gun shows, first in executions. . . . Bush accuses Gore of saying anything to get elected. But in fact it is Bush who will say anything to get elected—and say it in poor English.
—**BARBRA STREISAND, on *George W. Bush***

Interesting that Liberace, who created the phrase "I cried all the way to the bank," chose to lie all the way to his grave.
—**Director TONY RICHARDSON, who lied about not having AIDS (as did the closeted pianist)**

Michael Jackson is afraid to ever give the impression he might be gay. Maybe he's not. There are so-called gay-acting heterosexuals, besides straight-acting gays. What I think he really is, is a pedophile.

—BRAD DAVIS (*Midnight Express*), who was closeted about his bisexuality

If God dislikes gays so much, how come he picked Michelangelo, a known homosexual, to paint the Sistine Chapel ceiling while assigning [homophobe] Anita Bryant to go on TV and push orange juice?

—Chicago columnist MIKE ROYKO

As to Anita's fear that she'll be assassinated? The only people who might shoot [singer] Anita Bryant are music-lovers.

—Gay author GORE VIDAL

What entertainer turned anti-gay activist after discovering that his or her husband or wife is secretly attracted to his or her own kind?

—1970s *Hollywood Star* item

She demonstrated certifiable proof of insanity.

—JACK NICHOLSON, on his *Chinatown* co-star *Faye Dunaway*

If in ten years she is still walking around and allowed to make movies, I will be amazed.

—*Chinatown* director ROMAN POLANSKI, on *Faye Dunaway*

Talk about an odd couple! You know who Jack Nicholson has glommed onto now? And she doesn't mind that he's old enough to be her ancestor? *Kate Moss.* That skinnier-than-thou model! They're going out together! People call them Bitsy and the Beast.

—JOAN RIVERS

It was the war of the beauties when J. Lo and Kate Moss both showed up at the party for the one hundredth anniversary of Coty. Both were done up to the nines, Jennifer in a cream-colored outfit. . . . Her only accessory besides her jewels was her new husband, Marc Anthony. Supermodel Kate showed up in a dress by Chanel and stole the show. When it comes to fashion, she's the queen.

—Columnist ARLENE WALSH

You can get yourself a catchy first name and you can land on a hit daytime show [*The View*] and get most of the attention on it, and you can even be praised for being fat. . . . But if you insist on dressing like a clown, what's the point?

—San Francisco columnist ELLIE AZZOPARDI on *Star Jones*

Oprah Winfrey issued a statement that even though she appeared on the *Ellen* coming-out episode, she's not gay. Meanwhile, Ellen DeGeneres issued a statement saying even though she appeared on *Oprah*, she's not black.   **—CONAN O'BRIEN**

I feel just like Oprah, except my man married me and I let other people read what they want.   **—*Lovita (The Steve Harvey Show)***

Brad Pitt's a good friend and he's awfully cute, but I think he's afraid of commitment.

—JULIETTE LEWIS, after *Pitt* and *Gwyneth Paltrow* split up

Either I was too young for the part, or [Michael Douglas] was too old for it. I'm not surprised it flopped.

—Co-star GWYNETH PALTROW

She's better known for her love life than as an actress.
> —A miffed **MICHAEL DOUGLAS**, on *Gwyneth Paltrow,* shortly before she
> won a Best Actress Academy Award

Brad [Pitt] is a good friend of ours, but he did *not* donate the sperm for our baby.
> —**MELISSA ETHERIDGE**, co-parent with *Julie Cypher*

Me with a guy? Never happen! . . . Well, maybe Brad Pitt.
> —**RODNEY DANGERFIELD**

Brad Pitt is handsome but not that talented. And he admits he goes through four cartons of cigarettes a week. Need I say less?
> —**HELENA BONHAM CARTER**

We were [on location] in this little town on the edge of the Sahara, and there was nothing to do at night except go to this disco. But it was all men dancing with men because women weren't allowed out at night. So we're standing at the bar, watching all these guys dancing, when Sean [Connery] leans over and says to me, "Do you mind if I dance with your driver? Mine's too ugly."
> —**SIR MICHAEL CAINE**

Noel [Coward] and I were in Paris once. Adjoining rooms, of course. One night, I felt mischievous, so I knocked on Noel's door, and he asked, "Who is it?" I lowered my voice and said, "Hotel detective. Have you got a gentleman in your room?" He answered, "Just a minute, I'll ask him."
> —**BEATRICE LILLIE**, then known as "the funniest woman in the world"

The humongous Marlon Brando walked into a local coffee shop and asked to be seated. There was a long line, and he asked the hostess, "Do you know who I am?" She replied, "Yes, I do, but you will still have to wait your turn." With that, Marlon walked out in a huff.　　　　　　　　　　　　　　**—Columnist RICHARD GULLY**

Don't you *know* who I am?!
　　　　—DENZEL WASHINGTON at an L.A. eatery, before yelling at a
　　　　　　　maitre d' who stated he didn't have a free table

I did dedicate my memoirs to my mother. Without her, I might have been somebody else.　　　　　　　　　　　**—MAE WEST**

All I can say is that when I'm trying to play serious love scenes with her, she's positioning her bottom for the best-angle shots.
　　　　　　　—STEPHEN BOYD, on co-star *Brigitte Bardot*

William [Hurt], in his soul, is a truly conflicted, turbulent human being. And he has a rage in him that is really scary to a lot of people.　　　　　　　　　　　　**—Co-star MADELINE STOWE**

How would you feel about a co-star who earns so much more than you, for no discernible reason, and feels he's worth it? No, we are *not* close, except when the camera's running and we're doing our job. That's when I like him—'cause that's when I'm acting.
　　　　　　　—GILLIAN ANDERSON, on *David Duchovny* (*The X-Files*)

Val Kilmer isn't impressed with Brad Pitt's macho. The hotheaded star has taken some shots at his better-liked and better-paid rival. When speaking of *Troy*, he says, "I like those pictures of Brad Pitt.

They're all airbrushed. He's a nice guy, but he's a wimp." With this attitude, Kilmer will never make the good-ole-boys' club.

—Columnist ARLENE WALSH

Don't ask *me* what's going on here, because Tom [Cruise] is dating Penélope Cruz, or at least it is made to look that way.

—Columnist CATHY GRIFFIN

Tom Selleck and Paulina Porizkova did have a feud while making *Her Alibi*. But I can't tell you why she had antipathy for him. In Hollywood, you can get sued for telling the truth. After all, it's Hollywood where the truth lies. **—ANTHONY PERKINS**

J. Lo was supposed to be the most difficult star to satisfy, but you've got to make room for Ricky Martin. He demanded forty rooms at the five-star Piatra Mare Hotel in Bucharest, Romania. Ricky travels with his own pillows and insisted he get an endless supply of his favorite mineral water. During his stay, he was guarded by members of the Romanian National Guard, who are usually employed taking care of visiting dignitaries.

—Beverly Hills (213)

Is there not something unnatural, not to mention spoiled rotten, about nonfat famous fathers with already-fat wannabe sons? Not just greedy for the inherited limelight, these boys don't seem ever to eat on an empty stomach . . . and, unlike daughters of the rich and famous, seem to have no interest in presenting an attractive aspect to the world. *Latest* example: Donald Trump Jr. Message to Donny: Stop chowing down! Give it a rest, and give us a break.

—Columnist SUSAN STANLEY

Back in the 1920s, the "set" had a style, élan, and dash about them. The Hiltons have the dim and glazed eye of a dead mullet.

**—Actor STEPHEN FRY, filming *Bright Young Things*,
about London's past aristocratic party set**

Big Ben is no longer. . . . The view in Tinseltown is that, after several film flops, after Jennifer Lopez, and as a fading pretty face, he can no longer carry a movie. He isn't getting offers for top roles now. Rumor says he visited a psychic to learn if things would turn around for him. She gave him the thumbs down. At least he still has poker. . . . **—*The Westwood Villager,* on *Ben Affleck***

Whatever happened to *Welcome Back, Kotter* alumnus Lawrence Hilton-Jacobs? You'll recall he played Freddie "Boom Boom" Washington. The dismal news is that the last time he made the news it was for wife-battering. Sometimes, you'd almost rather not know. **—Columnist GEORGE BYINGTON**

You know you're asking essentially bulls**t questions. I'm giving you bulls**t answers, but I'm doing it because there's a movie opening and the studio expects me to do it.

—RICHARD GERE, being uncooperative with a *Movieline* interviewer

After trying and failing to flag down a cab, one well-known New York gossip columnist reportedly ran after the taxi and punched out the driver through an open window.

—*Allure* magazine (alleged initials: AJB)

[Andrew] Lloyd Webber's music is everywhere, but then so is AIDS.

—British musical authority MALCOLM WILLIAMSON

She is always complaining "I'm not happy." She married one of the richest men in the world. His mother owns England, Ireland, Scotland, Canada, New Zealand, Australia. By sleeping with Prince Charles, one day she will own—listen to the verb, *own*—England, Ireland, Scotland, Canada, New Zealand, and Australia . . . I would screw a duck for Rhode Island. What does she want?

—JOAN RIVERS, on *Princess Diana*

They've said [Louis B.] Mayer's his own worst enemy. Well, not really. Not while I'm around. **—Fellow mogul JACK L. WARNER**

I felt a special relationship to Elvis Presley because he was from Mississippi. He was a poor white kid . . . he sang with a lot of soul. **—PRESIDENT BILL CLINTON**

President Clinton is a seafood man. He sees food, and he eats it.

—JAY LENO

You get all the french fries the President can't get to.

—AL GORE, on one of the perks of being Vice President

Ms. Oprah Winfrey was dining in a San Francisco eatery, and when the waiter came by to offer dessert, she declined, explaining, "I'm on a diet." After all, she'd just ingested crabcakes, tuna tartare, a dozen oysters, stuffed calamari, risotto with truffles, and salmon with mushrooms. A true seafood diet.

—Columnist RICHARD GULLY

You look disgusting! **—DANNY BONADUCE to former**
***Partridge Family* co-star *Susan Dey*, upon seeing her in a bikini**
when she'd dieted down to eighty-nine pounds

She projects the passion of a Good Humor ice cream: frozen on a stick, and all vanilla.

—**SPENCER TRACY**, on actress *Nancy Davis*, later *Nancy Reagan*

I was proud to be a part of this industry when Marilyn was fired. I don't think she has a friend in this town, because she hasn't taken the time to make any. And the same with Liz [Taylor]. She's a taker, not a giver. She deserves the same as Marilyn, but nobody has guts enough to fire her. But she'll get it. Liz can get what Liz wants only for so long. —**JOAN CRAWFORD**, railing against two younger competitors in 1962 (*Monroe* died weeks after Fox fired her.)

Well, darling, I thought one more bitch wouldn't matter.

—Actress **HERMIONE GINGOLD**, with a canine in tow, joining guests *Zsa Zsa Gabor* and columnist *Pamela Mason*, after talk-show host Merv Griffin exclaimed, "Hermione, you've never brought a dog on before!"

It's surprising how some people will [complain about] Ellen [DeGeneres] for no good reason. Like Chastity Bono saying the sitcom was "too gay." No one ever said *L.A. Law* was "too straight." . . . Or people who criticize Ellen for not coming out till her sitcom needed better ratings. She wouldn't have *had* a sitcom if she'd come out before it. —**K. D. LANG**

Christian Maelen in *I Think I Do* was great. He's straight, but he was very generous about not being obvious about his discomfort with kissing a guy. Whenever we did it he was into it 100 percent. He even slipped me the tongue a little now and then.

—**ALEXIS ARQUETTE**, on his best kisser on-screen

She grabbed that lip and just ripped it right off. —**JOHN CUSACK**, on *Julia Roberts*'s kissing technique in *America's Sweethearts*

When I got the chance to do a love scene with Clark Gable, I couldn't help remembering Vivien Leigh's famous comment about the smell of his dentures when they made *Gone With the Wind*.

—SUSAN HAYWARD

I'm not the only one to have had this experience. . . . But when I was new to Hollywood and had to go to the dentist more often than I ever dreamed, he told me Clark Gable was a patient and asked if I'd like to see Clark Gable's smile sometime. Would I! When could he arrange it? "How about after we finish?" he said. "But I'm not dressed for. . . ." To bring the story to a close, afterward he took me into an adjacent room full of supplies, and in a cupboard in a jar was a set of Gable's teeth, soaking.

—ANNE BAXTER (*The Razor's Edge*)

Dean's original nose, it looked like he was eating a banana.

—ALAN KING, on *Dean Martin* (A rhinoplasty financed by Lou Costello of Abbott and Costello, plus a name change from Dino Crocetti, enabled the singer to become a matinee idol.)

Kate Beckinsale asked for her breasts in the ads for her new movie [*Underworld*] to be enlarged. But the artist made them too big. Kate complained that they look like Lara Croft's and demanded that they be reduced to a happy medium.

—Columnist ELLIE AZZOPARDI

Diana Ross is getting a little long in the yellowing tooth for that same Medusa hairdo she's had for lo these many decades. It's time for a chic, more modern, shorter cut. Otherwise she'll be like another Ann Miller, sporting the same outdated 'do to her grave. Once a woman enters middle age, long hair looks grizzly.

—Columnist MARK SENDRAK

Jerry Lewis, when he was a movie star, came on our dumb little morning show like the big king, demanding everything. He arrived late, full of being Jerry Lewis. He wanted a bigger dressing room. He wanted champagne. He wanted flowers. Two-thirds of the way through the show, he looked at his watch and said, "I've got to go," and walked out.

—JOAN RIVERS

Sinatra's behavior was unbelievable. There was an old lady playing the slot machines nearby, and this annoyed him. He kicked a couple of bottles of champagne toward her and said, "Get away, you're bothering me." . . . We weren't given any choice. He chose wieners and sauerkraut for everyone. And there was more trouble. Sinatra decided he didn't like the pianist. So he tossed a handful of coins at him and told him to take off. That did it. My friend and I got up and left.

—VALERIE PERRINE

If anything positive comes of the dreadful behavior of some of the big, very angry stars, it's that they may choose to engage in charity events to try and clean up their reputations some. Unfortunately this doesn't mean the behavior changes much.

—Screenwriter STEVE TESICH (*Breaking Away*)

Most men are so weak, and to cover it up they act like they don't care and are macho because they don't want to show their true feelings. They're too fragile inside.

—SALMA HAYEK, after breaking up with *Edward Norton*

I was [Elvis Presley's] favorite actor. . . . I did create a project [*Thunder Road*] that was meant to star him; I tailored it for him. But his greedy old manager, Colonel Parker, pulled him out of it, shoved him into another crummy musical. Elvis was more obedient to that old cuss than any son would be to a father.

—ROBERT MITCHUM

[Joan Crawford] even had a special outfit for answering her fan mail.

—ANTHONY PERKINS

We didn't want to work together, because it might spoil our marriage. It's like wearing an article of clothing that's special too often. You get to taking it for granted.

—BRUCE WILLIS, whose marriage to *Demi Moore* ended anyway

George [Stephanopoulos] married me thinking I was Gwyneth Paltrow and ended up with Phyllis Diller. . . . I don't exactly ask him how to punch up a joke, nor does he ask me, you know, anything.

—Comedic actress ALI WENTWORTH

Women are never satisfied with their looks. Remember when actresses used to lipstick way over the lipline? Like Joan Crawford. You'd see a rare photo of her sans lipstick, it didn't look like her! Now, you see Oprah or Naomi Campbell, and they lipstick well within the lipline, to make their lips look smaller. The cosmetic grass is always greener.

—Beauty columnist FONTAINE ROCHEFORT

It is so ridiculous when you try to be what you're not, when you want to appeal to some demographic. Like Mariah Carey when she hangs out with black rappers and does her hair a certain way. It looks so desperate and calculated. Some singers will do anything for attention.

—SANDRA BERNHARD

In some lighting, Beyoncé Knowles looks light black, in others she looks white. There are lots of mixed-race people in America, but it's like you have to choose sides. Pick one team or the other. It shouldn't be teams. It should be people. And preferably individuals.
—London radio host DWIGHT POPOVICH

You have Ashanti, Vivica A. Fox, Thandie Newton, Tyra Banks—all African-American. Right. It's about *sales*. It's also about making black women who aren't part white feel self-conscious and less desirable.
—Nigerian-born Chicago writer PETER ODALAPO

Call me an ass, call me a blowhard, but don't call me an African-American. Please. It divides us, as a nation and as a people, and it kind of pisses me off.
—WHOOPI GOLDBERG

I'm not an African-American actor. I'm an actor.
—MORGAN FREEMAN

One of my role models has been Eartha Kitt. Same for one of my relatives, whose name I won't say. She's half-white too, and beautiful. She could be an actress. I offered to help. But she knows if she went out to Hollywood, they'd typecast her and she'd be paired with black actors—only. Now, that's racist too. She wouldn't be allowed to play opposite white actors, and even for publicity she'd be expected to preferably not date them. They're still segregating!
—Singer MINNIE RIPPERTON

I call her Yoko Oh-*no*. I can't stand her—even if she weren't the Jap who broke up the Beatles.
—Writer TRUMAN CAPOTE (All four former Beatles eventually said that *Yoko Ono*, who married John Lennon, did not break up the quartet.)

At an audition once, a casting executive smiled at me condescendingly and said, "So, you're Latino, eh?" I kept my supposed Latin temper in check and said, "No, I'm female." I broke the bewildered silence by explaining, "A female cannot be *Latino*." But I am Hispanic—it's a less sexist word. As a Hispanic or a Latina, I get double bias from Hollywood. **—Actress MARGA SAUCEDO**

I did move from Los Angeles [to New York City]—several factors, earthquakes not least among them. I do think the intellectual level is lower there. It can get you down, and it's not good for kids. And today's young movie executives—puhlease! I saw one staring at a can of orange juice. "Why're you doing that?" I asked. He said, "It says *concentrate*." **—BETTE MIDLER**

Privately, I called him Deep Throat, because he blew so many musical notes before we got it all recorded and perfect.
—Producer ALLAN CARR (*Grease*), on *John Travolta*

The poor thing looks so frail that an ejaculation would blow him sky-high! **—IRENE RYAN, "Granny" on *The Beverly Hillbillies*,**
on guest star *Wally Cox*, whose roommate Marlon Brando
said Wally was stronger than he was

If I wasn't in a relationship [with Christina Applegate] and he [Tom Cruise] wasn't married and he wanted to have sex with me, I would have sex with him.
—JONATHON SCHAECH in 2000 to Britain's *Hello* magazine

I haven't got a chance. I'm up against two Orientals, one an amateur, and one black guy, and Sir Ralph Richardson, who's dead.
—Undiplomatic JOHN MALKOVICH, on his Oscar competition
(The "amateur," *Dr. Haing S. Ngor*, won.)

Kevin Spacey discovered Colin Farrell in a Dublin theater, was very taken with him, and made introductions. Farrell is now a major movie star, while Spacey's star has slipped considerably. One wonders if he regrets his move, for the handsomer, more virile Irishman is now getting roles that would have gone to Kevin.

—Columnist GEORGE BYINGTON

If it ever gets out about Dr. Seuss, the publishing world will cook my goose.

—The secretly gay children's-book author's literary agent JED MATTES, to *Entertainment Tonight* head writer Wayne Warga

Does fetus count? I guess I've always known. I can remember as a kid watching television that Scott Baio totally did it for me.

—WILSON CRUZ (*My So-Called Life*), when asked how long he'd known he was gay

[James Michener] has never written anything that would remotely interest me. Why on earth would I be interested in reading a book called *Chesapeake*? **—Fellow author TRUMAN CAPOTE**

She needs strong direction. She's such an intimidating individual that the only way to direct her would be to grab her by the balls, so to speak. **—GUY RITCHIE, who eventually directed wife *Madonna* in the flop *Swept Away***

She's such an icon to so many of us. We grew up on her, we worshiped her. I met her one time at the Academy Players screening of something. She was wearing a big hat, I was standing three steps below her, thank God. If I had been taller, she probably would have pulled out a gun and shot me. I was totally nervous, but I worked up the balls to say, "Uh, hi, Barbra." Not a word. She just looked down at me from her perch. She froze me out!

—Former *Streisand* fan SANDRA BERNHARD

I introduced myself to Tom Cruise at the Golden Globes party, and he didn't give me the freakin' time of day.

—NEIL PATRICK HARRIS

He's like a junkie, an applause junkie. Instead of growing old gracefully or doing something with his money, be helpful, all he does is have an anniversary with the president looking on. He's a pathetic guy.   **—MARLON BRANDO, on *Bob Hope***

[Marlon Brando] has preserved the mentality of an adolescent. It's a pity. Speaking to him—it's like a blank wall. In fact, it's even less interesting, because behind a blank wall you can always suppose that there's something interesting there.   **—BURT REYNOLDS**

We had an earthquake here in L.A. over the weekend. They said it's the first time Kathie Lee Gifford's CD actually flew off the shelf.

—JAY LENO

I think Dolly Parton's a celibate in slut's clothing.

—Writer-director COLIN HIGGINS (*Nine to Five*)

She is humorless and uncomfortable being a woman.

—Screenwriter ARTHUR LAURENTS, on *Katharine Hepburn*,

with whom he worked and socialized

Actually, my mother got along with Whoopi [Goldberg] beautifully, because my mother's a dyke.

—**TED DANSON (*Cheers*), at a 1993 Friars roast**

My boat's bigger than yours!

—**What director FRANCIS FORD COPPOLA yelled from his yacht at Cannes in the late seventies at producer *Sir Lew Grade* aboard his (Grade yelled back, "Yes, but I own mine!")**

He never has to worry [financially] again in life. He could have told General Motors, "I've got an obligation to a union I belong to. Let's work something out." But he didn't, deciding to make big bucks on the short term. We have members . . . losing their homes, not working over principles. How much money does Tiger Woods need?

—**Screen Actors Guild member KENT MCCORD (*Adam 12*), on the golfer who crossed a picket line in 2000 to make a commercial**

Anyone who believes that Tom Cruise and Penélope Cruz have "found each other" must be from another planet. They share the same publicist. They co-starred in *Vanilla Sky*. Even when Nicole Kidman was told about them, she said she didn't put much credence in it.

—**Hollywood columnist ARLENE WALSH**

I don't know if I believed that one.

—**Co-star EVA MARIE SAINT, on *Cary Grant*'s claim that the twenty-five cents he charged for every autograph went to charity**

My mother couldn't believe I wanted to be an actress. She said, "They're tramps, but they're *pretty*." My high school drama teacher also wouldn't let me in because of my looks. So I became a comedienne, and later—aha! —a comedic *actress*. So *there*.

—**KAYE BALLARD (*The Mothers-in-Law*)**

I drink too much because my parents were both actors: she, alcoholic; he, indifferent.

—JAMES KIRKWOOD, who co-wrote *A Chorus Line*

My husband David [Craig] is a vocal coach, so I tend to overenunciate.

—NANCY WALKER (*Rhoda*)

My mother fell out of a porthole and landed on her head. She was all right, but she lost much of her hearing. I therefore developed a very concise, clear way of speaking. Unkind persons sometimes label it "prissy." Rex Harrison, who made a hit in one of my plays, is one of them.

—SIR NOEL COWARD

People often have such unthinking preconceptions. Some people find out I have a Jewish mother and behave like that's so rare, so odd, so unusual. Jesus had one. . . .

—HARRISON FORD

Woody Allen used to talk about never joining a club that would have him as a member. Who knew then that he was talking about the P.T.A.?

—BILL MAHER

They say when O.J.'s jury visited his house to see for themselves, his lawyers got there first and took down all the photos of O.J. [Simpson] with white people and replaced them with photos of black people. Is that tampering, or what? My opinion is that if that was really so, then the jury was had. And either way, the country was had.

—HOWARD ROLLINS (*A Soldier's Story*)

O.J. Simpson is now undoubtedly the luckiest man alive. He is a brutal double-murderer who doesn't have the good sense to keep his mouth shut. He's an arrogant man who doesn't love anyone. Not his children. Not his slain wife. Nobody but himself. I only wish that, in a different context, we could settle it man to man, because he's a creep and he needs to be punished.

—GERALDO RIVERA, in *Playboy* magazine

I'm terribly vindictive. If somebody ripped me apart in the press, I'd kill them. I would *have* them killed, and no one would ever know. I mean, I haven't done it, but I'm ready. There's this stuff in Australia, it's for pest eradication. It's odorless, colorless, tasteless, and one teaspoon will give you an instant brain hemorrhage. And it doesn't leave a single trace. It's perfect!

—MEL GIBSON in 1991, publicizing *Hamlet*

Mel Gibson played Hamlet. Mel lost.

—British actor HARRY ANDREWS (*Gibson* said of Shakespeare's masterpiece, "I mean, it's a great story. It's got some great things in it. I mean, there's something like eight violent deaths.")

There's only one thing Rod cares about, and that's Rod. Despite constant requests from charities, I never saw him dip into his pocket once. **—Music publicist KEITH ALTHAM, on *Rod Stewart*, whom he nicknamed the Tartan Tightwad (Mick Jagger, another ex-client, reportedly tips cab drivers no more than twenty-five cents.)**

Chuck Heston thinks the mere fact of your serving him is privilege enough. . . . Mel Gibson thinks if he smiles at you, that's your tip.

—Columnists THE HOLLYWOOD KIDS, after interviewing waitresses at celebrity restaurants

Big Spender: Wesley Snipes may be cheap about paying a 20 percent tip on a bottle of champagne, but he has no problem dropping $24 million for a three-story Big Apple townhouse.

—Columnist ARLENE WALSH

When a billionaire gives dozens of millions but makes it a condition that his name goes on the buildings . . . or when an actor makes a major charitable donation, remember that it behooves both these Tinseltown bigwigs taxwise and also reaps sensational publicity. But it *is* a tax break, and often a needed one.

—Financial columnist HOWARD DELMUTH

The late Princess Diana's brother, Lord Spencer, now seems to make a career of her memory and takes a strong line against the tabloids. It bears remembering that he turned against them, originally, because they wrote of his marital infidelities, and that he has sold photos of his infant son [to a U.K. tabloid]. He has also been employed as a "royal commentator" by [Britain's] *Today* on television . . . and is making money from the Diana cult by transforming her burial site into a new Graceland.

—"Royals expert" and columnist ALFRED CLUCKIE

I'm proud of my education. A lot of singers and actors never went to college. That's why I didn't much flinch in the old days when certain parties criticized me for publicly admitting that my mother was a maid for a rich family, a rich family that endowed several colleges and offered me a scholarship. Yes, and my dad was a valet-chauffeur. It's all good, honest work.   **—JOHNNY MATHIS**

Joan Collins is a commodity who would sell her own bowel movement.   **—Ex-husband ANTHONY NEWLEY**

She keeps putting so much makeup on during the day that by nightfall she looks like she's in drag.

—Actress-turned-writer CARRIE FISHER, on *Joan Collins*,
who co-starred in a telemovie Fisher wrote

She was the girl next door—if you live next door to a self-centered, insecure, untruthful phony.

—EDDIE FISHER, on ex-wife *Debbie Reynolds* (Carrie's mom)

Yes, son, and now you bore me. **—Director *William Wellman*'s mother at a 1945 party he threw for her (During the party, he drank too much, made a long speech, then finally proposed a toast: "To my mother, who bore me. . . .")**

With my hands, stupid. **—MINNIE MALDEN, who lived to 104, when actor son *Karl* asked her how she felt**

I've got to don my breastplate once more to play opposite Miss Tits. **—RICHARD BURTON, on *Cleopatra* co-star *Elizabeth Taylor*, before they fell in love**

I loved *True Romance*. It's one of my favorite films. I've seen it about twenty times. Patricia Arquette, to me, is one of the sexiest women on film. I just love her. It's like you look at her and you just want to touch her. **—MADELINE STOWE (*The Last of the Mohicans*)**

He doesn't get along with anyone. He's a miserably unhappy man, unhappy that he hasn't become a Hollywood-type star. Most of us in this country become actors for the love of acting, not for hoke and glory.

—TREVOR HOWARD, on pre–Hannibal the Cannibal *Anthony Hopkins*

The most obnoxious actress I've ever worked with.

—ANTHONY HOPKINS, on *Shirley MacLaine*

Wasn't Dennis Hooper [*sic*] in *Easy Rider*? I hated that movie. I wouldn't work with any of the miscreants in it. Never have, never will!

—JOHN WAYNE, who did work with *Hopper* in *The Sons of Katie Elder*

The Specialist. It was horrible. [Sylvester Stallone] has to take it to another level. It's called acting class. The action thing just ain't working for him.

—LL COOL J

They always want to know: Who do I like better, Tom Wopat or John Schneider? Why do you always have to choose? They're different personalities. I'll just say this: If it was real life, I'd rather have Wopat for a nephew. He is a bit of a nicer fellow, not quite so agitated-like.

—DENVER PYLE (*The Dukes of Hazzard*)

Sidney [Poitier] just picked and chose when he wanted me to come to dinner. He still does it now. Even if I'm a guest in his house, there are some things he just will not invite me to—situations where he feels it will just make it uncomfortable for the people he's going to be with.

—HARRY BELAFONTE, on his fifty-year friendship with *Poitier*

I was discussing Faye Dunaway with a mutual associate, who said she's so terribly aloof to most people. I disagreed. I said, "Not really. Not all the time—oh, maybe half the time." He winked and said, "Half aloof is better than none."

—WILLIAM HOLDEN (*Network*)

Poor Julie Andrews. Once *the* biggest movie star; now she smiles too often and too widely—*very* un-diva-like—and makes it painfully clear she's *so* happy to have been asked to attend. . . . And those

Princess Diaries movies—what a royal comedown. Movies only a nondiabetic teenage girl could stand.

—Columnist ELLIE AZZOPARDI

I guess she'll say anything to try and make herself interesting on a talk show. She was on *The Tonight Show,* this was in the late sixties. She said I'd died! In Vietnam. So people believed it. But I was serving in the National Guard at the time.

—JERRY MATHERS (*Leave It to Beaver*), on *Shelley Winters*

I was staying at a hotel in San Francisco. I went to my drawer to get some underwear and found Tony Bennett's heart.

—Comedian HENNY YOUNGMAN, at ninety-one

You know, Madonna just bought a home—with nine bedrooms. You know what that means? No waiting! **—JAY LENO**

I'm sick of her, because I have no respect for the way she utilizes her talent. She could do so many things that are more constructive.

—JENNIFER JASON LEIGH, on *Madonna*

She is the worst possible Italian-American role model, at least since Al Capone and that ilk. **—DON AMECHE (*Cocoon*), on *Madonna***

A crass social-climber and a tramp.

—JACKIE ONASSIS's assessment after son J.F.K. Jr. brought married woman *Madonna* home (She warned him to stop seeing her.)

She's a *cochon* [pig, in French]. **—MADONNA, on *Zsa Zsa Gabor***

Warren [Beatty] is a wimp. I know I have a much bigger following than Warren does, and a lot of my audience isn't even aware of who he is.   **—MADONNA, on her former co-star and serial beau**

[Antonio Banderas] probably has a really small penis.
    —MADONNA, after his then-wife scared her off a potential affair with him

He paid me lots of compliments, which is about all he ever paid.
    **—HATTIE MCDANIEL (*Gone With the Wind*), on her first husband
(She added, "The rest didn't even bother with compliments,
after the honeymoon!")**

James Caan has talent. But not for kissing. He's a slurpy kisser. He slurps too much!   **—SALLY KELLERMAN, on her *Slither* co-star**

English girls are not always straitlaced. There's been a time or two, doing kissing scenes with Joely [Richardson], who plays my wife, that I thought she was using her lips like a suction pump!
    —DYLAN WALSH (*Nip/Tuck*)

It was fun to kiss Elvis, but the girl had to do most of the work. I certainly don't think he felt his tongue was any kind of a sexual instrument.   **—JULIET PROWSE**

Elvis had the *most* dynamic lower lip. Working with him, it was a perk to get to kiss that lip!   **— SHELLEY FABARES**

Cameron's an aggressive kisser. I got used to it, now I love it!
    —Eight-years-younger JUSTIN TIMBERLAKE, on *Cameron Diaz*

One day [producer] Hal Wallis approached me with a $5,000 bonus if I could make Joseph Cotten have an erection during a scene. Wallis said, "Joe is such a gentleman. He's made no approach to his leading ladies." During our love scene I leaned against him, but I could not feel any swelling. My tongue intensely searched Joe's mouth. I could see him react with shock. When I separated from our embrace, suddenly teeth flew out of his mouth in my direction. In my ardor I had dislodged his partial bridge!

—French actress CORINNE CALVET

One reason our love scene plays so well on screen [in *Another Country*] is we couldn't abide each other. He hated me, and it was therefore mutual.

—RUPERT EVERETT, on *Cary Elwes* (*The Crush*)

When the participants in a kissing scene or love scene are slightly nervous or antagonistic or competitive, it typically comes out better than if they genuinely like each other. Real affection feels good, but it often photographs wimpy.

—Director JOEL SCHUMACHER

She thinks she doesn't get old. She told me once it was her cameraman who was getting older. She wanted me to fire him.

—Producer JOE PASTERNAK, on *Doris Day*

I have everything Gwyneth Paltrow has, but I've had it longer.

—Mother BLYTHE DANNER

The handsomest actor in pictures was [Mexican] Gilbert Roland. He had the sexiest bedroom eyes, a killer smile—he was drenched in "It." He married Constance Bennett, and when they went out together, even though she was the bigger star, he became the center of attention due to his great looks. I love those Latin looks!

—LUCILLE BALL, who married a Cuban

In a way, I'm proud. In a way, I can't stand it. I think I was the first Australian actress to work consistently in American film and TV. Now it's a whole influx of Aussie actresses with talent—*and* with great beauty! Rose Byrne [*I Capture the Castle*] is just the latest one.

—JUDY DAVIS, who's played Judy Garland and Nancy Reagan on U.S. television

He once played Attila the Hun. The man is frightening! If there really were a Dracula, he'd be it. **—DAME JUDITH ANDERSON, on the looks of *Jack Palance* (*City Slickers*), who did play Dracula**

She does affect a pale—some might call it ghoulish—complexion and image. Partially, only it's for her fans. It also is from within, an outer reflection of what she feels, writes, and has gone through.

—STANLEY RICE, husband of vampire novelist *Anne*

Paris Hilton has this hatchety nose to go with her hatchety tongue and sharp ambition. You *know* that nose is real, because *no* plastic surgeon would have left it that way. **—JON STEWART**

She has a face that belongs to the sea and the wind, with large rocking-horse nostrils and teeth that you just know bite an apple every day. **—SIR CECIL BEATON, on *Katharine Hepburn***

Too thin is too thin, especially when you get older and all the veins show. Audrey Hepburn thin was lovely as a girl, but now she looks pained, with that scrawny chicken neck, and I do love her. . . .

Mia Farrow nowadays just looks bedraggled. The same with Diana Ross—she looks like she just arrived from Ethiopia.

—**DAME JUDITH ANDERSON**

A former friend said that "Miss Ross" disliked Princess Di from the first—on account of her "taking" the pop star's name and going further with it.

—Columnist **AVIVA MEYERSON** (*Ross*'s given name was *Diane*)

Diana Ross doesn't want to do this movie because she wants to be white. —**RYAN O'NEAL, on** *The Bodyguard*, **eventually filmed with Kevin Costner and Whitney Houston**

It is puzzling that a popular and attractive singer like Whitney Houston should have, and increasingly display, so much anger. Does a poor self-image tie in with her increasingly publicized drug problems? —Columnist **RICHARD GULLY**

He's an idiot, like a big cheesecake on legs.

—**BOY GEORGE, on** *Andy Warhol*, **who habitually wore a platinum wig**

Fred Astaire was almost as concerned with his toupee looking right as he was with perfecting each dance number.

—*Astaire*'s choreographer, **HERMES PAN**

Nobody's seen what Tina looks like without her wig—not in years, baby. She moved to Europe to get away from those inquiring eyes.

—**IKE TURNER**

Jude Law's hair is thinning on top, little tiny bald spot coming on, gonna grow bigger, and then bigger. You notice it's these handsome *blond* guys that start balding first? Isn't it sad? *No*. There *is* some justice in the world. **—Comedian RICHARD JENI**

John Carpenter directs mostly horror films, modern horrors. He's still slender, but he's bald up top, with long hair on the sides—not a great look. I don't understand why, unless he wishes to resemble a movie creature, he doesn't go off to [hair restorers] Elliott and True.
—CHRISTOPHER HEWETT (*Mr. Belvedere*)

It's true, as "ageless" divas like Joan Collins say, that a waist is a terrible thing to mind. If you don't watch your weight, no one will watch *you*, and I admire the gals who fight fat and gravity. But face lifts can be taken too far—when an actress looks like she just escaped a wind tunnel, or her eyebrows are halfway up her forehead and at forty-five-degree angles.
—Plastic surgeon DR. ZAHI BADUNIS

Zsa Zsa [Gabor] didn't appreciate it when I informed her in a sisterly way that if she has one more face lift she's going to finally have a beard up on her chin.
—PAMELA MASON, columnist and wife of actor James

Barbra Streisand had a face lift but did not have her eyes done, and now they look out of sync. **—Author DR. Z. PAUL LORENC**

Any celebrity has the money for cosmetic surgery. Those who avoid having it are invariably either cheap or scared. . . . Some have only a minor procedure or two done, usually the eyebags, sometimes the nose . . . and may or may not admit it. The older actress on *Judging Amy* [Tyne Daly] makes a moral issue out of it, which it is not. She's simply self-serving—and, I wonder, is becoming fat "aging gracefully"? **—DR. SYLVIA B. C. CORRAL**

Jennifer Grey had a distinctive nose. She had it bobbed. It was a terrific nose job. But, as she has admitted, she literally became unrecognizable. No one believed she was the same adorable actress from *Dirty Dancing*. And there was nothing Jennifer could do to replace her lost nose. **—DR. Z. PAUL LORENC**

'Tis said Michael Jackson preserves pieces of his old nose from past operations in jars filled with formaldehyde, at his Neverland Ranch. These he shows to good friends. Wonder what he shows his enemies? **—HENRIETTE MANTEL (*The Brady Bunch Movie*)**

[Raquel Welch] will only admit to a nose job. She says she corrected what she calls her "Latin nose." What the hell is a Latin nose? I am myself a Latin, and my nose is most decorative!
—Argentine FERNANDO LAMAS (*Welch*'s father's surname was Tejada.)

Dean Martin, the Gabor sisters, Dana Wynter, Carolyn Jones, Peter O'Toole, Stephanie Powers, Suzanne Pleshette, Rita Moreno, George Hamilton, Joel Grey [Jennifer's father], Sissy Spacek, Carole Landis, Marie Wilson, Nanette Fabray, Joan Hackett, Jill St. John, Raquel Welch, Talia Shire, Marlo Thomas, Annette Funicello, and Barbara Eden. **—Hollywood historian PENNY STALLINGS's list of older celebs who have had nose jobs**

Dinah Shore, Lee Grant, Vera-Ellen, Al Jolson, Cameron Mitchell, Bobby Van, Alan King, Mitzi Gaynor, Rhonda Fleming, Juliette Gréco, Jan Sterling, Fanny Brice, and Milton Berle.

—PENNY STALLINGS's list of celebs who had nose jobs *after* becoming famous, not including Michael and several other Jacksons

The tie for the biggest shoulders in Hollywood history has to be between Joan Crawford and Anthony Perkins. Both of them psychos!
—Actress JOAN HACKETT

Reliable rumor has it that one *big* reason Jennifer Lopez kept returning to Marc Anthony between marriages, and finally married him herself, was that he has more covert talent than any man she's wed or romanced.
—Columnist TONY BEEMAN

Forrest Tucker [*F Troop*] has a daily ritual at his country club. He falls asleep, or pretends to, with only a towel around his middle, after a shower. Club members go into the locker room, they take their guests—I have personally seen this—and they quietly lift the towel. It is an awe-inspiring sight, because Mr. Tucker is more than well-endowed. They say that one of the guests had been traveling in Arizona but was more impressed by what he saw at the country club. He is supposed to have shouted, "$#@% the Grand Canyon!"
—FERNANDO LAMAS (a.k.a. Mr. You-Look-Mahvelous)

Word gets around. . . . I once shook hands with a starlet who said, "Oh, Mr. Berle, I've heard so much about yours!"

—MILTON BERLE

Brigitte Bardot never became a Hollywood star. . . . She has a boyish ass. Most American men do not like boyish asses.

—SAMMY DAVIS JR.

You can always tell gay actors. They're the ones who have the plain or ugly wives. Or live with an ugly girl. Besides, most of the gays in Hollywood are good-looking. They don't let themselves go to pot or fat, like Chevy Chase or Dan Aykroyd. Gay actors prize their looks, and so do their easily fooled public! **—ANNE BAXTER**

In his own way, Ashton [Kutcher] is romantic. We were apart for awhile, and he phoned me and said he'd shaved his leg. One leg. Because then at night, in bed, he said, it's like sleeping with a woman when he rubs against himself. **—DEMI MOORE**

Drew Barrymore and Lucy Liu, co-stars in the big-screen *Charlie's Angels,* are very close off-screen buddies. Together they posed suggestively in scanty lingerie for photos that Drew thought might amuse her latest boyfriend-of-the-moment. The photos were transmitted to his cell phone, and he chose to share them with various pals. When she found out, Drew was fit to be tied—excuse the expression. **—Columnist SUSAN STANLEY**

Calvin Klein wanted [Orlando Bloom] in his underwear ads. You can be a serious actor and do such things, now. It'll be great exposure for Orlando. Some people who see undies ads don't go to many movies. . . . We're not engaged, and I'm not sure if we were married whether I'd let him do those ads—some fans take them too seriously.

—*Orlando*'s girlfriend KATE BOSWORTH (Sandra Dee in *Beyond the Sea*)

John [F. Kennedy Jr.] once confessed that if his family weren't political he'd have liked to be an underwear model. He liked how it brings a guy sex symboldom so easily and generously, without the assorted emotions actors have to go through.

—*George* magazine aide HEATHER SCOTT

Politics is for people who are too ugly to get into show business.

—BILL CLINTON

Sorry, Rush [Limbaugh], Newt [Gingrich], and Jesse [Helms], but the artist as citizen is here to stay. **—BARBRA STREISAND**

Arnie long ago tired of being seen as just a body, or a body with an accent. **—Kennedy family member MARIA SHRIVER, on husband *Arnold Schwarzenegger*'s move into American politics**

IDOL CHATTER

Donald Trump's hair is to coiffure what Ashton Kutcher is to dramatic acting.
—Beverly Hills hairdresser TONY VITALE

Replacing Tom Snyder as a talk-show host with Craig Kilborn is like sending Ali MacGraw into the ring to replace Muhammad Ali.
—Author DOUG MCCLELLAND

Julia Roberts makes sure she is the only Pretty Woman in any movie scene by ensuring that any female extras are a plain-Jane bunch. Recently in Amsterdam, Julia stopped filming cold on [the sequel] *Ocean's Twelve* when she demanded that the director change the extras because they were all drop-dead gorgeous. . . . This was done, and she gave her okay to go on shooting.
—Columnist ARLENE WALSH

Nicole Kidman proved the shallowness of Academy voters. She was nominated for Best Actress, but in a supporting part [in *The Hours*]. In a scene together, Meryl Streep would have blown her away, fake nose and all. Do you think if an actress who looked like Virginia Woolf had played her, with her own nose, and as well or better than Kidman, *she* could have won the Oscar? No way.
—Australian radio host DEXTER JEFFERS

Diana Rigg is built like a brick mausoleum with insufficient
flying buttresses. —Sexist critic **JOHN SIMON**, on a
stage nude scene in *Abelard and Heloise*

Tom Cruise is still sensitive about his height, or lack thereof. . . .
At premieres, his contract calls for a ramp to be installed under the
red carpet so that photographers shooting pictures will have to
aim their cameras up at Tom as he passes by.
—Columnist **CATHY GRIFFIN**

She was good at being inarticulately abstracted, for the same
reason that midgets are good at being short.
—**CLIVE JAMES**, on *Marilyn Monroe*

Tom's character [in *Minority Report*] has to break down and cry. He
worked on that scene for two days, and the final take turned out
quite well. But the poor guy was so exhausted from actually having
to really act that he had to take the next two days off.
—Columnist **JACK MARTIN**, on *Tom Cruise*

Years ago, John Malkovich told *Vogue* magazine that he'd gladly
leave acting behind if someone would offer him a decorating job
instead. However, no philanthropist ever stepped forward to make
the offer. . . . Despite its title, the film *Being John Malkovich* is not
a horror movie. —**REX REED**

Whitney Houston's friend Sharon Osbourne has convinced the
singer, fresh out of rehab, to do a new reality-TV series with her
husband, just released from prison. It's called *Me and Bobby Brown*—
wonder who chose the title? —and promises to out-scare Ozzy and

Sharon's long-running series or, for that matter, Liza and her fourth and former husband's non-running reality series. . . . Whitney and Bobby may bring TV to a new low—and a new high, if you know what I mean.

—Columnist MARK SENDRAK

To show you how far back she went, when Redd Foxx came along, they nicknamed him the male Moms Mabley. On my show, she gave one of the most honest answers I *never* expected. I asked her, "How does a lady make it in show business?" She answered, "Well, honey, it involves not being a lady for a little while." **—JOHNNY CARSON**

When Courteney Cox, wearing no makeup, spotted paparazzi hovering outside an L.A. eatery, she sent hubby David Arquette on a makeup run [to] a cosmetic shop a couple of blocks away—she gave him a shopping list. He ran and got them, then the former *Friends* star hopped in the loo to apply the beauty buys, and then happily faced the photogs. **—Beverly Hills (213)**

The twenty-two-year-old popster needed to tone herself up before dancing around in lingerie on her current [2004] tour. The sight of her in her underwear on stage . . . I would have gone to the gym a bit more before I did that.

—British music producer SIMON COWELL, on Britney Spears

Jodie Foster recently sold her two kids' old toys and clothes off in a garage sale. [She] loaded everything up and drove it over to her pal's Beverly Hills house, where the sale was taking place. At the end of the day, Jodie turned up to collect the $300 that the stuff had sold for. **—L.A. City Beat (Foster had earned a reported $15 million for one film.)**

Without the peroxide, Jennifer Aniston, though very likable, might well be a salesgirl somewhere. But thanks to the bottle, *Friends*. Thanks to *Friends*, Brad Pitt. . . . And now she's in one nonhit movie after another—a true Hollywood luck story.

—E! Entertainment host STEVE KMETKO

In an interview, the unlikable rap star's ex-girlfriend Brazilian manicurist Kesia Alvarez said, "He has a very tiny thing, nothing to tell your girlfriends about, and when we were together he sometimes suffered from premature ejaculation. The first night, it was all over in twenty seconds. He wasn't even a one-minute man that time. Sometimes I had to work really hard to get him to perform. He was mortified."

—Editor-columnist ANN ROSTOW, on *Eminem*

It's not often discussed, but some of the angrier men—actors, politicians, and so forth—are angry because they have small endowments. John Wayne, according to several who knew, for instance. Hence his vendettas during the [political] witch hunts. With short men, you *see*; with *little* men, you don't. . . . Now, Napoleon was both short *and* small, and nearly conquered all of Europe.

—Historian-author MARTIN GREIF

He certainly doesn't publicize it now, but in the 1950s John Wayne was one of the biggest Hollywood supporters, financially, of the Ku Klux Klan. **—RALPH BELLAMY (*Trading Places*)**

The first thing he said to me on the set [of the film *Jinxed*] was, "I want you to know, I hate niggers and faggots." I had no idea why he said that, because we had neither of those in our picture.

—BETTE MIDLER, lamely explaining in
Rolling Stone about co-star _Ken Wahl_

Kevin Spacey was playing a crime chieftain named Mel Profitt on *Wiseguy*. Ken Wahl, the star of the series, took an instant loathing to him for no reason. Wahl's antagonism was much commented on by the cast and crew, and soon, all over town. Wahl disliked most actors, but he hated Spacey.　**—Actor RON VAWTER (*Philadelphia*)**

Donald Trump's TV show *The Apprentice* is largely about contempt. And Trump is full of it. . . . Money corrupts as surely as power. Some people can't get enough money, but Trump can't seem to get enough coverage. He ran for President, remember? Money was his qualification. He didn't win—maybe 'cause he didn't have a rich, famous father or the Supreme Court behind him—so TV was the next logical step.　**—Columnist MARK SENDRAK**

Trump felt he and his show "was robbed" of the 2004 Emmy Award, of course never pausing to notice that the competition was higher quality.

—Monte Carlo columnist and radio personality DELPHINE ROSAY

Jane Fonda seems to like to shock and conform—seesawing. A self-described feminist, she never employed a female director in her more than thirty movies, nor wishes to direct herself . . . and then willingly abdicated her movie career to marry a billionaire [Ted Turner], rarely opening her mouth in his presence. Now she wants to donate millions of dollars to fund gender-studies programs in colleges, but she's also supposedly found religion. She should stick with one side or the other.

—Anonymous editorial in *The Villager*

In their anticipated screen comebacks, Jane Fonda and Barbra Streisand play harridans, mothers-in-law—Fonda in *Monster-in-Law* and Babs in *Meet the Fockers*, taking up where Robert De Niro left off in *Meet the Parents*. . . . May we suggest a teaming titled *What Ever Happened to Babs and Jane?*

—Hollywood columnist JACK MARTIN

You can't count on anything these days. Robert Redford doesn't even look like Robert Redford anymore [in *The Clearing*]. . . . His eyelids no longer meet his eyeballs. His ruddy, mottled skin needs sanding. His face looks like the map of Argentina. In the close-ups, there's a sore on his lip.   **—Reviewer REX REED**

He's already burly, but he'll be a little more beefy when he appears onscreen as a New York City boxer in *Cinderella Man*. While standing with some real-life cops on a street, [Russell] Crowe was spotted woofing down a Subway sandwich, a Burger King whopper and a hot-fudge sundae from Baskin Robbins within the space of an hour.

—Beverly Hills (213) columnist CATHY GRIFFIN

On the Spanish set of *Solomon and Sheba*, Yul Brynner has hired a man whose function is lighting his cigarettes while the star sits in his chair between takes. This one's for Ripley's Believe It or Not!

—1958 column item by HEDDA HOPPER

The woman was nasty and brainless. My friends and I called her Hedda Lettuce.   **—GENE KELLY, on *Hedda Hopper***

Filming *The Cinderella Man* with Renée Zellweger, word is that Russell Crowe has hired a human cigarette holder, since the boxing gloves he has to wear most of the time keep him from doing it himself. The aide lights the cig, puts it between Russell's lips, lets him take a puff or two, and then removes it. He even uses this aide when the gloves are off.   **—THE DUPONT TWINS, columnists**

Friends of Madonna are now supposed to call her *Esther,* her Hebrew or Kabbalah name. The Material Girl has become the Mystical Girl. What next? **—Radio host KEITH MICHAELS**

Jeers to Paris Hilton and Carmen Electra for their kiss at the MTV Movie Awards. After Britney Spears and Madonna locked lips at the MTV Video Music Awards, such a display doesn't seem provocative—just predictable.

—July 4, 2004, *TV Guide* (Less predictable if two *guys* did it. . . .)

David Caruso arrogantly ditched the small screen for the big screen, finding small success there. He's back on the little screen, arrogant as ever, on *CSI: Miami*. In fact, insiders on the set say his arrogance is growing as the show's ratings increase.

—KEITH MICHAELS

At the AD club in L.A., an eyewitness reports that Leo DiCaprio and Tobey Maguire stood looking on in amazement as Drew Barrymore and Heather Graham spent the evening locking lips while sitting together in a cozy booth.

—ARLENE WALSH, in her February 13, 2002, column

If Leonardo DiCaprio ever does get around to wedding Brazilian bombshell model Gisele Bundchen, he'll have to clear it with best bud Tobey "Spiderman" Maguire so he can fit the honeymoon into his schedule. **—In *L.A.* magazine**

Rudolph Valentino could not have been gay, because he had a sense of humor. **—Author-filmmaker KEVIN BROWNLOW,**
on the apparently bisexual silent superstar

They named Sheik condoms after Valentino's most famous role. As to whether Rudy was *gay*, I couldn't say, but I know most of his boyfriends were.
—Designer NORMAN NORELL,
who did costumes for one of his films

Did you hear about Pete Rose? . . . Admitted he bet on baseball, but he still denies he took his hairstyle from a lesbian.
—CRAIG KILBORN on *The Late Late Show*

The thing is, Andrew McCarthy—from some of those Brat Pack movies—makes a sort of comeback in Stephen King's *Kingdom Hospital* on ABC-TV, but you never really knew he'd been away, or much cared.
—*Fab!* newspaper

Movie star Greg Kinnear enacts late TV star Bob Crane in a steamy biopic of the *Hogan's Heroes*' lead, without a quarter of the flash or personality of the small-screen star. Yesterday's TV was *bigger* than today's movies!
—Reviewer HAROLD COSITZ

Take away Julia Roberts's wild mane of hair and all those teeth and those elastic lips, and what've you got? A pony!
—*L.A. Times* columnist JOYCE HABER

It seems not everybody is totally taken with Ben Affleck's looks. The roommate of his latest girlfriend told friends, "He has really ugly hair on his back and lots of hair on his belly and they end up all over my furniture. I had to leave and go to my mother's house because I didn't want to see that. He obviously thinks he's big stuff, but he sure isn't to me."
—Columnist ARLENE WALSH

I won't use her. We have a no-a**holes clause.
—Designer TODD OLDHAM, on supermodel *Naomi Campbell*

Matt Damon popped into Starbucks on Sunset Boulevard to smell the coffee. Smelled ten different varieties before an irate customer waiting in line piped up and said *some* people were on their lunch breaks and had ordinary-paying jobs to get back to.

—*Out and About* columnist **TONY BEEMAN**

When the four stars of *Will and Grace* go out for lunch together on their breaks, as they frequently do, they always go dutch, pulling out their individual credit cards. The bill is almost always under $20 each.

—Radio personality **MELINDA LEE**

My Three Sons' patriarch Fred MacMurray didn't become rich by throwing his money around. Oh, no. At a Van de Kamp's restaurant in Hollywood, he left wearing a frown—or is that his habitual expression? The only tip he left the waiter with was, "Next time, don't wait for me to ask for a coffee refill!"

—Item from 1968 *Modern Screen*

Ashley Olsen may be a teenage zillionaire, but when she's out on the town with pals, she goes dutch. Recently she and four girlfriends stopped by the West Hollywood eatery Mix, and when it came time to pay the bill all five dug into their pockets to pay for their own food and drink. Ashley may be loaded, but everybody paid their share.

—Columnist **CATHY GRIFFIN**

Warner Bros. studio was so insecure and bullying that they considered suing the Marx Brothers for calling their movie *A Night in Casablanca*, because of Warner's own *Casablanca*. Ridiculous. But Groucho wasn't fazed, and told Jack Warner he would then sue the studio for use of the word "Brothers." So the studio backed down.

—Film historian **CARLOS CLARENS**

She never says anything kind about anyone unless first you cross her tongue with silver.
—**JOYCE HABER, on fellow gossip columnist *Rona Barrett***

What drove John F. Kennedy Jr. to argue so angrily with his *George* magazine co-founder, Michael Berman, in February that security guards had to be called in? . . . Why would Raquel Welch furiously scissor a costume and fling a mirror backstage [the] summer during her Broadway run in *Victor/Victoria*? . . . What spurred Val Kilmer once to burn a camera operator's face with a cigarette?
—***Allure* magazine, September 1997**

Kevin Spacey made a fashion faux pas at the [2004] premiere of his new film in Toronto. The perennial bachelor is still trying to look like a leading man. He is reported to have tried to hide his balding spot by resorting to spray-paint on his scalp.
—***Beverly Hills (213)***

I wrote four scripts, and all of them were optioned. One, *Cynara*, got pretty famous. But it was a lesbian love story. Everyone shied away from it. . . . Jodie Foster loved it, said she'd do anything to help get it made, but she couldn't play the lead.
—**Filmmaker NICOLE CONN (*Claire of the Moon*)**

A reporter asked me, "Wasn't Tom Hanks brave to do *Philadelphia*?" I said, "I think he's great, but I don't think he's brave. I think a gay man playing the part would have been brave." . . . Robin Williams has the number-one film [*Mrs. Doubtfire*] in the country by wearing a dress, and when Divine wore one, they wouldn't even show it on the airlines. So, things have changed, but not really—because everyone knows Williams has a wife.
—**Director JOHN WATERS (*Hairspray*)**

Kevin Kline as the [aged] Cole Porter has a bald head, liver spots, and wrinkles for days, but he doesn't remotely resemble Kevin Kline or Cole Porter. He looks like Carl Reiner.

—**REX REED** reviewing *De-Lovely*

I was in a department store in Beverly Hills, and this little old lady came up to me and said, "You're Dolly Parton." I said, "No, ma'am, I'm not. I'm Barbara Mandrell." She seemed puzzled, then looked at my chest as discreetly as she could and said, "I think you're right."

—**BARBARA MANDRELL**

What's Mick Jagger's girlfriend's name? I did four parts [a four-part interview] with her. *You* try that sometime. It's like talking to a window. —**BRYANT GUMBEL, on *Jerry Hall*, Mick's future wife**

You walk out of the Amphitheatre after watching the Rolling Stones perform and suddenly the Chicago Stockyards smell clean and good by comparison. —**TOM FITZPATRICK**

Michael Bolton sounds like he's having his teeth drilled by Helen Keller. —**JEFF WILDER**

Bob Geldof is a loss to the road-sweeping profession.

—**JILLY PARKIN**

He plays four-and-a-half-hour sets. That's torture. Does he hate his audience? —**JOHN LYDON, on *Bruce Springsteen***

Her voice sounded like an eagle being goosed.

—**RALPH NOVAK, on *Yoko Ono***

. . . Like an illustration for a bird-seed commercial. Maybe those wide-eyed one-liners and pregnant pauses work on television, but if Miss [Goldie] Hawn is to have any kind of future in movies, she needs to learn something about the rudimentary techniques necessary to sustain a comic scene without putting the audience to sleep.

—REX REED

I'm tired of all that Pamela [Anderson Lee] crap. She attracts a very tacky press line. It was starting to turn off viewers.

—DAVID HASSELHOFF, _Baywatch_ star and producer

[Helen] Hunt is one of those who [do] not suffer fools well, which makes her particularly ill-suited to participate in press junkets. Colleagues tell me that Helen was not in the best of moods as she faced likely silly question after silly question, [which] is par for the course. If there is an Oscar campaign in her future, she is simply going to have to learn to better play along.

—Columnist SAM RUBIN (_Hunt_ won the Oscar anyway.)

Hal Wallis the producer told me that [playwright] Lillian Hellman had invited him to the opening night of her latest play. She would send two tickets for him. "Bring a friend," she added, "if you have one." Hal said he couldn't make it that night. Instead he requested tickets for the second night, and added, "If there is one."

—Actor-director PAUL HENREID

I turned down _Kramer vs. Kramer._ I thought it was middle-class bourgeois horse***t. Later I heard [Meryl] Streep rewrote the courtroom scene herself! Even if it's only half true, I wouldn't have put up with it. She was hired to act, not write. No chick's ever gonna rewrite any scene I'm in!

—JAMES CAAN

When I got [to the set], I walked in thinking I was a star, and then I found I was supposed to do everything the way [Faye Dunaway] says. Listen, I'm not going to take temperamental whims from anyone. I just take a long walk and cool off. If I didn't do that, I know I'd wind up dumping her on her derriere.

—ROBERT MITCHUM

I told Mia Farrow to title her memoirs *Mama Mia*. Great title, catchy. You can remember it. Somebody said her book is wonderful, you should read it. But he couldn't remember its name. See? Stars don't want to listen.

—LARRY KING

I hope the next time she crosses a street four blind guys come along driving cars.

—FRANK SINATRA, on his biographer *Kitty Kelley*

When movie stars fade and they're brainy, they write books. Take Lilli Palmer or Dirk Bogarde. When dumb movie stars fade, they paint—Tony Curtis, Anthony Quinn, [Sylvester] Stallone. . . .

—PETER COOK (*Bedazzled*)

Just ignore what I'm placing between you. She's very beautiful. Very stupid. She's just arrived from England. So Jack will want to have first crack at it.

—Writer GORE VIDAL, reportedly quoting *Jackie Kennedy* as she seated him near *J.F.K.* at a White House dinner

[John F.] Kennedy's only complaint about Jackie in all the years I ever knew him was that she spent too much money. "That Jackie," he'd yell. "She's unbelievable. She absolutely does not appreciate the value of money. Thinks she can keep on spending it forever. God, she's driving me crazy—absolutely crazy. I tell you, George, she's run through all the government funds and is drawing on my personal account. If the taxpayers ever found out what she's spending, they'd drive me out of office!"

—Former U.S. Senator GEORGE SMATHERS

They call Ronald Reagan the great communicator. Well, any man that can call a nuclear missile "Peacemaker" is free to call his son "Butch."

—Comedian turned San Francisco politician TOM AMMIANO

When I began calling him gay publicly, I got a call from my agent, who was also Ron Reagan Jr.'s agent. "Ron wants to write to you." So he sent me a very long letter [saying he wasn't gay], and I wrote back to him saying that my sources told me he was gay. And indeed I was acquainted with someone who'd been in his class at Yale who maintained that they had slept together. And there were other stories from other people. I said that if he was prepared to deny these specific allegations I would stop making them. I never got a reply.

—Playwright (*The Normal Heart*) and activist LARRY KRAMER

When Hitler's favorite director, Leni Riefenstahl, came to Hollywood during the Nazi era, every studio head refused to welcome her, including the Gentile Darryl F. Zanuck [of Fox], but not including Gentile but very right-wing Walt Disney, who treated her most warmly. **—Blacklisted GALE SONDERGAARD, first actress to win a supporting Academy Award**

I was advised by my agent not to discuss the fact that I was Jewish.

—LESLEY ANN WARREN (*Cinderella*), on making her film bow for *Walt Disney*

I don't belong to any political party, and certainly not the Republicans. I'm more liberal than Kristin's old man.

—RON REAGAN JR. in 1997, about his new TV show
with Kristin Gore, daughter of then-V.P. Al Gore

TV remunerates those already famous or with famous relatives. Also amoral extremists who rant, rave, and twist facts. TV enshrines controversy, real or artificial, and conservatism. Look at Bill O'Reilly, who used to be a moderate, till he found out being a zealot pays off better.

—California state senator
SHEILA JAMES KUEHL (former *Dobie Gillis* co-star)

One of the media's worst failings is the buildup it gives to people who do wrong. And then patting them on the back for not doing it anymore. . . . Carol Burnett had three daughters. One became a drug addict, and it was hell for her parents. And that is the one whose name became known, who got so much coverage, who went on talk shows, then got a chance at an acting career. . . . Meantime, the two other daughters—well, who's ever heard of them?

—CLEAVON LITTLE

I read where O.J. Simpson said he wasn't going to lower himself to read any of the latest books about him. "Lower" himself? To do that, he'd have to *climb*.

—Director-producer GEORGE SCHAEFER

Call me innocent, naïve, whatever. But I did hang out with [madam to the stars] Heidi Fleiss three times before I caught on what her profession was. It's not like she handed out business cards or anything.

—DAVID LEE ROTH

Photographer John Rutter was ordered to stand trial for attempted grand theft, attempted extortion, perjury, and forgery after trying to blackmail [Cameron Diaz] with topless shots he had of her from a 1992 shoot.
—*Internet Movie Database* **on "20 November 2003" (So why'd she pose for them?)**

You don't see many [male] actors nude in the movies, but by now probably everyone's seen the nude photos of [Arnold] Schwarzenegger and [Sylvester] Stallone. Not too impressive. Big muscles, is all. . . . They say little pitchers have big ears. Seems to me big stars have little—you-know-whats.
—**Director DON SIEGEL (***Dirty Harry***)**

If you detect a certain frostiness between Stallone and Schwarzenegger, still, it's because years ago Arnold discovered that Sly was secretly financing an author's very unflattering book about the foreign newcomer that he thought was encroaching on his territory.
—*Star* **columnist JANET CHARLTON**

When it comes to ultra-conservatives, it's usually like father, like son. Arnold Schwarzenegger's father was a Nazi—*fact*. I don't say the son is, but he has, for *a fact*, publicly expressed admiration for Hitler and he *did* invite the ex-Nazi president of Austria to his wedding.
—**Playwright BOB RANDALL (***The Magic Show***)**

I think Mel Gibson's father had eleven or twelve kids. If you want to know what he's like, they used to call him the Catholic Jerry Falwell. He took his brood from America [to Australia]—thought [America] was getting "too liberal." . . . Most people say Gibson is very like his father. Though I believe he has only six or seven children.
—**PATRICK WHITE, Australia's sole Nobel Prize writer**

It is very unfair, and amounts to cultural imperialism, that today Australian performers like Judy Davis and Russell Crowe, and Brits from Cary Elwes to Joely Richardson, have to use American accents to work in U.S. television or in most feature films. Diversity of nationality is at an all-time low, not to mention one billion Indians and one and a quarter billion Chinese not represented at all.

—Radio host DEXTER JEFFERS

How's this for a rumor? You can't confirm anything. Stanley Kubrick's keeping a completely closed set [on *Eyes Wide Shut*]. But it's been reported that Kubrick has hired a sex therapist to counsel Tom Cruise and [Australian wife] Nicole Kidman on enacting the relationship between their characters, who are married.

—Historian-archivist JIM KEPNER

There's something sleazy about Robert Blake. His wife Bonnie was sleazy too, but you almost feel sorry for her. Did he kill her? Have her killed? Will he go free, like O.J.? You look at photos of him as a child actor, with that angelic face and beautiful, vulnerable eyes, and you wonder, What the hell went wrong?

—PAUL WINFIELD (*Sounder*)

Carmen Electra must have wanted to clobber hubby Dave Navarro when the rocker announced she was looking "a bit worn out." The sexy siren, thirty-two, was humiliated [by] "Delicate Dave," as he's known not so lovingly. "Carmen went ballistic," says a friend. "She was absolutely livid that Dave would make disparaging remarks about her once-perfect body."

—*Beverly Hills (213)*

A visit to Thailand has left an indelible mark on Angelina Jolie. After a two-day visit to Cambodia, the twenty-nine-year-old stopped in Bangkok to have a thirty-centimeter-long tiger tattooed on her lower back. Last year she had an image featuring Cambodian script applied to her back to ward off bad luck.

—*The Japan Times,* **July 23, 2004**

Colin [Farrell] may be a sex maniac, but he's also considerate. Stars with tattoos generally expect us to cover them up for them, but Colin has his own very expensive airbrushing machine that he's known to bring to every movie set.

—**Makeup artist DALE ALYSON**

I miss the old Woody Allen. The one who didn't look like your most boring or preoccupied uncle. The one who got involved with girls more or less his own age.   —**WILLIAM HICKEY (***Prizzi's Honor***)**

Why did Dick Nixon watch *Deep Throat* three times? So he could get it down Pat.   —**SAM KINISON**

Opera singers are trained to open the back of their throats. They can control the glottis, open or close the back of their throats. It is for muscle purposes, for the music, but is very handy for fellatio. Rumor had it that's why Aristotle Onassis stayed so long with Maria Callas.   —**Disc jockey STAN MARTIN**

You ain't going nowhere, son. You ought to go back to driving a truck.   —**Grand Ole Opry manager JIM DENNY in 1954 to *Elvis Presley*, whom he fired after one performance**

With his womanly voice, stark white skin, and Medusa hair, his gash of red lipstick, heavy eyeliner, almost nonexistent nose, and lopsided face, Michael Jackson was making this appearance to scotch all rumors that he is not quite normal. **—CRAIG BROWN**

John Hensley, who plays the son on *Nip/Tuck,* did a guest role on another nighttime drama, as a Michael Jackson-like child-molester. . . . When somebody on set noted that Hensley is Caucasian, a production assistant explained, "Michael is not Caucasian, but he is white." **—Columnist MARK SENDRAK**

Paul Hogan, the *Crocodile Dundee* actor, was a golden flash in the pan from Down Under. Everything he's done since has turned to tin. **—*Movieline* magazine**

Aussie-born Rupert Murdoch has almost single-handedly lowered the level of U.S. television with his low-concept shows, tabloid TV, assorted knockoffs, the most tacky and tawdry "reality" shows, and of course his not at all "fair and balanced" Fox news channel. **—JAMES GREGORY (*Barney Miller*)**

Those aren't reality, but gimmick, shows . . . things like *Joe Millionaire.* They're substitutes for good writing and don't require trained actors. **—Reviewer HAROLD COSITZ**

You know, if anybody—any of my dancers—got their hair cut like yours, they couldn't be in my show. Because it's tired. . . . These couches have to go! When you drive down the street, these couches are in the window—it always says Half Off. **—MADONNA, to *Arsenio Hall* while guesting on his Fox-TV show**

Yes, it's wonderful that Carol Channing is still touring [in 1997]. Even if it's still *Hello, Dolly!* You know what they've nicknamed it? She's seventy-five, I believe, so some of them are calling it "the death tour."
—Actor-coach BOBBY LEWIS

That is a fake, made-up story. Barbra would never be that superficial, and she'd be the first to say that it's a sexist and ageist false story.
—Hubby JAMES BROLIN, denying a rumor
that the sixty-two-year-old *Streisand* had
removed all the mirrors from their Malibu home

Jake Gyllenhaal and Kirsten Dunst had a big bash at their L.A. home recently. But before they let anyone drive home, they had them take a breathalyzer test. The caring couple hired help to do the honors to each departing guest, and if they didn't pass, they were given rides home in town cars by specially hired drivers.
—Beverly Hills Today

Look, Molly, there's the man who killed all of Daddy's friends.
—AIDS activist and former screenwriter LARRY KRAMER,
to his dog, when Kramer, who blames the ex-mayor for the
spread of AIDS there, bumped into his Manhattan neighbor *Ed Koch*

Bill Clinton was willing, able, and set to host *Saturday Night Live* when word came through that Hillary was adamantly opposed. Mr. Clinton, who had written some of his own comedy material, reluctantly deferred to his wife's insistence that the gig was undignified and might hurt her future political career . . . as governor or as president?
—Columnist DELPHINE ROSAY

Melanie Griffith has a reputation of being frighteningly jealous of any woman who looks at her husband Antonio Banderas. Her last big jealousy attack happened when she accused poor Antonio of having an affair with co-star Emma Thompson. Banderas tried to tell his wife how insecure she was and how she was embarrassing herself. At the same time, he had to ask himself how much more of her tantrums he could take before they would destroy him.

—Columnist JANET CHARLTON

Psycho? This hot stud is heavily into being dominated by women, but the word is he doesn't have sex with them. He is rumored to swing in a very different direction, and he's innocent enough that he doesn't realize that everytime he "plays," there are more and more witnesses and the story builds up steam.

—Blind item from ARLENE WALSH

Jennifer Lopez was hoping to transform fiancé Ben Affleck into a big spender like herself. No such luck. However, new husband Marc Anthony plays right along, even if he's less flush than Affleck. Marc just bought his bride a pair of eighteen-karat gold flipflops. Insiders say he thinks Jenny has the prettiest tootsies anywhere.

—*Fab!* newspaper

I've always thought breakups should be civilized, not fly-away-by-night things. Two weeks' notice should always be given, and depending on who's richer, severance pay might be involved.

—DUDLEY MOORE

The reason publicity was next to nil after Barbra Streisand fired Dudley Moore after a day's work on her [1996] movie *The Mirror Has Two Faces* is twofold. One, Dudley couldn't perform, due to his brain-related illness, and thus had to be replaced. Two, the publicity could have been distorted to make Babs look like a heartless ogre. Besides, the small role was filled by George Segal, who was once Streisand's leading man but now works in support.

—ED MARGULIES, *Movieline* editor

Her three co-stars aren't talking, but I can. Kim Cattrall has behaved like a &*@&# on and off the set, and she's the one who scuttled the movie version of *Sex and the City* by asking for too much money, ruining it for everyone. It'll be interesting to see what kind of work she gets after that. **—Co-star WILLIE GARSON**

I got this doll that was a replica of my mother [Tippi Hedren] that was in a coffin from Alfred Hitchcock for my birthday. Nice, huh? I think he was very strange. That's a strange thing to send to anyone, much less a five-year-old little girl. I never played with it. I just put it away. **—MELANIE GRIFFITH, whose mother worked twice for the director-producer**

He is the least weird man I've ever known.

—ELIZABETH TAYLOR, on *Michael Jackson*

People often wonder what keeps Missy Black Star married to her bad-boy husband, especially as she's long-rumored to be gay. Gay? No way! But she is bisexual—and *so is he*. That, plus their kid, plus love, will keep them together.

—Blind item from columnist ARLETA P. CAIN

In [his book] *My Prison Without Bars*, belatedly confessed gambler Pete Rose gripes about being banned from baseball while Robert Downey Jr. and other naughty celebs still get to work. Dude, just apologize already! **—*Entertainment Weekly***

Mel Gibson's father, Hutton, has never apologized for printing anti-Semitic brochures in Australia, and now [in 2004] declares in the *New York Times Magazine* that the Holocaust was exaggerated. The man is without reason or shame, and his son does nothing to distance himself from his crackpot propaganda.

—Former New York mayor ED KOCH

Anna Nicole Smith may be lacking taste or *pudeur,* but she's not without willpower. The girl who never met a billionaire she didn't like has Lost the Weight, and looks terrific again. . . . The question is, what will she do with her new looks and energy? Hopefully she won't waste them on more tasteless E! Entertainment programs, or on unsuspecting rich old fools.

—Columnist TONY BEEMAN

I wonder how many Chinese had to go bald to supply Elton John with his latest hair? **—Fellow Brit PETER COOK**

Somehow, Farrah Fawcett's led a hard life. Or so it looks on her face. It's gotten thinned out and sad-looking. Even her hair is kind of straggly and sad now. Blonde beauties don't generally age too well. **—Designer BILL BLASS**

Lucille Ball scared the hell out of me from the beginning, when I worked with her on a Danny Thomas special. She walked around with that low voice and a cigarette hanging out of the side of her mouth. She was already in her fifties then, and she always called me Mackie. "Hey, Mackie!" **—Designer BOB MACKIE**

I'll hit him when I see him. I'll punch him right in the nose, and I hope I have these rings on!
**—LUCILLE BALL, at sixty-three,
to *People* magazine, on *Marlon Brando*,
who starred in the X-rated *Last Tango in Paris***

There was the time Tom Arnold and Roseanne signed a deal with Slim-Fast that would net them $10 million if Arnold, then a whopping 325, lost forty pounds, and Roseanne, a petite 270, dropped thirty. They each gained twenty-five pounds instead.
—*Gentleman's Quarterly*

Yes, he had a profound influence on me [as a child] by being so goddamned awful. The hideous spectacle of Gene Autry on a horse, giant buttocks bouncing up and down, wearing that ten-gallon hat, and that dreadful voice singing some dreadful song—it was horrifying.
—Author JOHN RECHY

What has she ever done apart from abolish cellulite? Does that really deserve admiration?
—Writer-politician EDWINA CURRIE, on *Elizabeth Hurley*

Whoopi Goldberg brought production on *The Rat Race* [2001] to a halt when she decided she couldn't live without her preferred French bottled water and Tootsie Rolls. The film company was shooting on location in Ely, Nevada, so a production assistant had to drive to Las Vegas, *six* hours away, to stock up on purified H_2O and candy so the show could go on!
—Columnist CATHY GRIFFIN

Leonardo da Chintzy: Seems Leo DiCaprio doesn't belong to a gym, but likes to use gym facilities, *but* doesn't like to pay, *and* thinks his stardom entitles him to *not* paying. Gym members reveal that he enters on the tails of guest passes, then expects trainers to work out with him for *free*.
> **—Columnist ROMEO SAN VICENTE (The L.A. gym is named Crunch.)**

Carlos Leon, who became semi, momentarily famous by fathering Madonna's daughter, no longer works at Crunch, but occasionally works out there as a nonemployee—the Material Girl apparently left him well provided for. . . . Some gym buddies confess that Carlos won't discuss mother *or* daughter, because he feels like a disposable parent.
> **—*Frontiers* magazine**

I felt it was a snub. . . . I said, "You gotta go for the team. The consequences of not going [to the Oscar ceremonies, on behalf of *Titanic*] will be that you're gonna look like a spoiled punk." [Leonardo DiCaprio said:] "It just ain't me, bro." Apparently, getting $4 million to do a juice ad that only airs in Japan is him; going to the Oscars is not.
> **—Director JAMES CAMERON**

That afternoon the news was out that Joan Crawford had passed away. I was talking to a movie critic . . . when I noticed a slight commotion in the room. Then suddenly people parted, as they did when Bette Davis came into the room, and as always this tiny woman made a beeline for me. "Well, the &*@&# died today," Bette said. "Uh, Bette, I don't think you know this gentleman. He writes for *Playboy* magazine." Bette immediately said, "But she was *always* on time."
> **—BURT REYNOLDS, in his memoirs**

Everyone has always been really civil to me. The only person who ever was not was Arnold Schwarzenegger, who was phenomenally stupid, in my opinion. He could have deflected the question so easily, and he didn't. Instead, he had his bodyguards push me around.
—Interviewer TED CASABLANCA

The damn southerners.
**—North Carolina native
ANDY GRIFFITH's reaction when informed
that President Kennedy had been shot in Texas**

Don't worry, my psychic told me I would never die in a plane crash.
—GOLDIE HAWN, comforting co-star *Diane Keaton* on takeoff

Well-heeled model and Brazilian beauty Gisele Bundchen has offered to sell posters of herself in a revealing red, white, and blue designer bikini to help the World Trade Center survivors. Amazingly, the relief committee said "Thanks, but no thanks."
—*Westwood Villager* columnist SUSAN STANLEY

So how much have the queen of England—estimated wealth, $2 billion—and Prince Charles—$550 million—given to the [WTC] disaster fund? The Q. has made a personal donation of $3,500 and the prince $15,000, according to the *London Daily Telegraph*.
—*Toronto Star*

Liza Minnelli's desire to have Liz Taylor for her matron of honor at her wedding to promoter David Gest won't come cheap. Taylor travels only first class, with an entourage of ten—secretary, masseuse, her dog Sugar, etc. —and Liza will have to supply a private plane, not to mention deluxe accommodations.
—*Westwood Villager* columnist MICKY BARNETT

No dog is an actor. It takes seventeen years to be an actor. Most dogs don't live that long.

**—KELSEY GRAMMER, reportedly jealous of
the attention his *Frasier* co-star *Eddie* was getting**

Acting is the most minor of gifts. After all, Shirley Temple could do it when she was four. **—KATHARINE HEPBURN**

If you can't do anything else, there's always acting.

—STEVE MCQUEEN, to his karate teacher *Chuck Norris*

If Bo Derek got the part of Helen Keller, she'd have trouble with the dialogue. **—JOAN RIVERS**

Besides having dirty minds, censors can be quite stupid. An example was the Lord Chamberlain, England's chief censor. Before World War I, there was a famous singer whom my relatives much enjoyed and whose name I have forgotten. In any event, she introduced a song entitled *She Sits Among the Cabbages and Peas,* which highly offended the L.C. So she shrewdly changed the lyrics to *She Sits Among the Lettuces and Leeks,* and he was satisfied.

—SIR JOHN GIELGUD (1904–2000)

Michael Jackson's supporters are the same people who let him whittle down his face to the proportions of Bambi, allowed him to purchase the bones of the Elephant Man, stood by as he wrapped his children's faces in silk veils that would have them blend in at a Kabul bazaar, and stayed calm as he dangled his infant son out a window in Berlin. These are not friends or supporters. They are enablers. . . . It's still a sick and twisted way for a forty-five-year-old man to live. **—Columnist A. J. BENZA**

If he'd have lived, they'd have discovered he wasn't a legend.

—HUMPHREY BOGART, on *James Dean*

Sinbad was an Arab sailor. Your American TV actor who takes that name, he is not a sailor or an Arab, and he is black. Egyptians and other Arabs are not black. . . . Yes, Egypt is in Africa. Many younger Americans need geography lessons.

—Egyptian ambassador AMIR AL-SAID

Luis Valdez, the director [*La Bamba*], is either blind or sexist, or both. He said that Rita Hayworth, who was born Margarita Cansino [from a Spanish father], was "passing for white." First, she was white. So was her father. But second, her mother was from Ireland, and her mother's last name was Hayworth. Some people try to twist facts to suit their agenda.

—Actor-coach JAIME YBARRA

Shall We Dance?—an arthritic remake of the delightful 1996 Japanese film of the same title—is a big mistake. It's not a Halloween movie, but it can be bloodcurdling watching Jennifer Lopez try to act. . . . It doesn't go for any feelings at all, and Richard Gere doesn't supply any. . . . The great and wasted Susan Sarandon must be slumming to accept not only a nothing role [as Gere's wife] but second billing to J. Lo! . . . Lopez is reportedly asking $12 million a picture just to shake her ass; she makes one flop after another and they pay it. Can you wonder why the movies are headed for hell in a Hollywood hot tub?

—REX REED

Christian Bale, the usually hunky actor and stepson of Gloria Steinem, is either more desperate for an Academy Award nomination than anyone in living memory or has gone too far for his art. In *The Machinist* he will not be seen by a wide audience, unless his stunt is widely publicized or he gets an Oscar nomination in 2005. For the role, he has lost nearly one hundred pounds of body fat and now looks shockingly cadaverous.

—Reviewer ANGELA THORNE-BARDRY

[Jodie] Foster's publicist was planting stories that she had a live-in boyfriend, the better to appeal to AMPAS voters after her Oscar nomination for *Nell*. She already had two of the statuettes but obviously craved a third. . . . Several columnists ran the item but scoffed at it; others declined to run such a fantasy and were validated when later in the year the young man in question came out as homosexual in the pages of the national les-bi-gay magazine *The Advocate*.

—Columnist MARK SENDRAK

We had to sew the fly on his pants shut. We were finding that every time we went past Bill Clinton, the zipper was undone.

—VICKY BROWN, spokeswoman for Madame Tussauds Wax Museum, regarding the *Clinton* mannequin that inspired familiarity from too many visitors

Being in the public eye, as Monica [Lewinsky] will be for the rest of her life, is like being the lady with the mustache at the circus. You're a curiosity, and you will never stop being one.

—Former call girl CHRISTINE KEELER, whose sexploits helped bring down Britain's Conservative government in 1963

He had polyester sheets, and I wanted to get cotton sheets. He discussed it with his shrink many times before he was able to bring himself to make the switch.

—MIA FARROW, on former lover *Woody Allen*

Joan [Crawford] was the only person I have ever known who could sip vodka or any whiskey and tell you its exact proof.

—Columnist JAMES BACON

Antonio Banderas and Catherine Zeta-Jones are making a *Zorro* sequel and sharing beauty secrets. Specifically, each swears by an age-retarding eye cream that they apply before bedtime. Cath and Tonio trade lotions and skin creams regularly; both are older than they so beautifully look!

—*Youth & Fitness* magazine

Yesterday's socialites had more class and breeding and didn't automatically head into acting. Or favor sexcapades that brand them as debutramps. . . . The Hilton girls and Cornelia Guest are just uninteresting. . . . You know, socialites and cockroaches are the only creatures that can stay up all night and eat anything.

—Palm Beach columnist RICHARD VANDERBILT

Other day at the [Malibu] market, Pamela Anderson kept those in line behind her waiting the better part of five minutes while she explored in her purse for coupons. Our natives were growing restless, but Pam stood her ground and finally produced all the coupons that saved her an awesome—we won't say buxom—$3.40!

—*Malibu Courier*

Lee Radziwill, so tired of being Jackie O's kid sister, was determined to marry rich and famous and very publicly. The groom was movie director Herb Ross, who'd had many hits and who was gay—as Jackie commented-questioned to a guest at the reception. . . . Well before his death, Ross tired of Lee's imperious ways and the affluenza she shared with Jackie. It was said she nearly drove Herbie broke, as well as nuts.

—Author DON DALEROI

She's a gay man trapped in a woman's body.

—BOY GEORGE, on *Madonna*

Her body has gone to her head.

—BARBARA STANWYCK, on former co-star
*Marilyn Monroe***'s not seeking more challenging roles**

It's not about acting, technique, or art. It's about effects. I wouldn't become an actor again if I could change. I'm too bright for a career that runs out. I thought I'd spend my life telling good stories to an intelligent public. I must have been out of my mind.

—KATE NELLIGAN (*The Prince of Tides, The Eye of the Needle***)**

I liked working with Chris Reeve and others, and the attention and pampering were nice. But I'm glad I don't have to play lead roles anymore. That's one of the rewards of not being the hot young babe. In L.A. they think they shouldn't embarrass older women by making people watch them on screen, and that's why I've played all these odd roles in independent movies.

—Former Lois Lane MARGOT KIDDER in 1997

With television, you can be on top and in the pits at the same time, thanks to reruns. . . . I never thought I would reach the age where the audience wouldn't let me or want me to work anymore.

—LUCILLE BALL, after her final series, *Life With Lucy*

Julie's been number one in the world, a box-office joke, and in between. I told her her career's had more ups and downs than a lavatory seat in a coed dorm.

—Director BLAKE EDWARDS, husband of *Julie Andrews*

"She's been throwing fits," says a *Victor/Victoria* insider about the play's star. Not to mention objects—a hairdresser was wounded in action when [Raquel] Welch reportedly flung a handheld mirror at him. **—*Allure* magazine, September 1997**

Woody Allen was shocked by my language. I guess he'd only seen me in *Cheers*. But one of the reasons I got into acting was to express myself, let it all out . . . and use my favorite four-letter word, which starts with an *f*. **—KIRSTIE ALLEY**

Around eight, I discovered that I fancied other boys, and I later found emotional release on the stage. There you are on the stage, free with your feelings, with people sitting there admiring you. If I'd not been gay, I wouldn't have become an actor.

—SIR IAN MCKELLEN

Actors are very sensitive people. I remember how crushed I was when I went to Broadway and had a hit but then received a clipping that read "British Actress Mildly Welcomed in America." Even though I knew it was a typo—I'd been *wildly* welcomed.

—GLENDA JACKSON

Basically, I became an actor to meet women.

—Irish star COLIN FARRELL

The thing about Maggie Smith, who is a great performer, is that she never allows you to forget that she is performing.

—JEREMY BRETT (TV's Sherlock Holmes)

For an actor who's appeared in a famous film, once the offers dwindle down to a precious few, you can turn to being an acting coach. It draws young people who long to be in a famous movie.

. . . What aspiring actors are never advised is that in Hollywood movies acting talent is tertiary to looks and personality, *and* that actors, as opposed to actresses, don't have much acting to do. The main task is always memorization.

—FREDERICK COMBS (*The Boys in the Band*)

After acting, I was too egotistical to become a drama coach. So I became an author.   **—TOM TRYON (*The Cardinal*)**

He has never been known to use a word that might send a reader to the dictionary.   **—WILLIAM FAULKNER, on *Ernest Hemingway***

I don't want to read a book by some guy who's on TV every night. Do these guys even write *part* of their books? . . . A friend sent me a copy of Jon Stewart's book. To be polite, I sent back a thank-you note, said I'd waste no time reading it.

—Columnist A. J. BENZA

I've given up reading books. I find it takes my mind off myself.
—Actor-pianist OSCAR LEVANT

Céline Dion filled in for Barbra Streisand on the Oscars. She sang Streisand's Oscar-nominated song. Barbra was there that night, but she didn't feel like singing, I guess. While Céline was singing—beautifully—Barbra just happened to be taking a bathroom break.
—FRAN DRESCHER (*The Nanny*)

All those musicals—a thing of the past. If we remade *Singing in the Rain* today, Gene Kelly would be looking around on that rainy street to make sure he wasn't going to get mugged.
—Director STANLEY DONEN

A phenomenal career turnaround. . . . In 2000 Halle Berry was fined $13,500 and given three years' probation for the hit-and-run accident that left another woman with a broken wrist and additional injuries. Berry's movies, besides, were bombs. Then she copped the Oscar. . . . However, all her films since have also been bombs, even *Catwoman* and excepting the James Bond film in which she played the chief Bond girl. **—Columnist MICKEY BARNETT**

It's often difficult for people with a prison record to get a job. But not to get into show business. Lots of celebrities have seen the inside of a jail, some *before* they become famous, the most notable and wealthy example being Tim Allen.

—TV critic SHAWN GOLDHAMMER

See, it makes no sense. Actors are not automatically what they portray . . . but Tim Allen [*Home Improvement*] has his own line of tools. Now, by this logic, if I break my leg, should I check into St. Elsewhere or make an appointment with Doogie Howser, M.D.?

—Comedian CATHY LADMAN

Nowadays it's usually considered negatively to change your name as an actor, but stop and think. Some names, you wouldn't *want* them to have. Our Diana Dors, sex symbol, was Diana Fluck. The petite American Sandra Dee was Alexandra Zuck. And TV star Tim Allen was born Tim Dick. **—British columnist DEREK DAVENPORT**

Calling the O.J. Simpson trial "the trial of the century" is a farce and an insult. The trial of the century was the Nuremberg Trial [of World War II Nazi criminals]. **—JOAN RIVERS**

I've bailed out Robert Downey Jr. and Gary Busey. Stan Kenton, drunk-driving. Keenan Wynn, many times. . . . And who's the little guy I bailed out? The Englishman? Dudley Moore. The night of the Academy Awards a few years ago, his car was blocking his wife's car in the driveway, and he hid her keys. They had a fight. It was stupid stuff.

—HARRY FRADKIN, bail bondsman to the stars ("Don't Wait in Jail, Call Harry For Bail")

When I was making *The Wizard of Oz,* [studio head] Mr. Mayer told me he was giving me a perk that no other star on the lot—not even Garbo—was getting. My own cook in my dressing room . . . the sweetest old lady—we got along famously. I never suspected any deceit until years later when this kind old grandmother came to me and confessed that Mr. Mayer had hired her to chop up speed pills [for appetite suppression] and mix them in with my food.

—Columnist JAMES BACON, quoting *Judy Garland* explaining the start of her drug dependency

When Belushi and John Candy and Roseanne and me say we're happy being fat, we're just being stubborn. Or defensive. Or tired of being nagged. *Obviously* we'd rather lose weight, for our own best interests—socially, aesthetically, sexually, professionally, and healthwise too.

—CHRIS FARLEY, who died prematurely

Good wine and good food render conversation unnecessary. I was at a party. . . . A young lady at my side kept trying to start a conversation. Without success. Finally she said, "Mr. Barrymore, I've made a bet with my mother that I can get you to say three words to me during dinner." I smiled and said, "You lose."

—JOHN BARRYMORE (Drew's grandfather)

Meg Ryan suddenly appeared one day with visibly altered lips. I'd say she had Gore-Tex put in her lips. You can tell because her face is smiling while her lips remain immobile. . . . Sharon Stone is an example of too much Botox, injected badly. Proper application is based on a strong knowledge of anatomy. If you totally deactivate the forehead, the result is a mask, not a mobile, expressive face.

—N.Y.C. plastic surgeon Z. PAUL LORENC, author of *A Little Work*

I'm proud of *Queer Eye for the Straight Guy* because it's about how to *live* better. Sure, grooming's important too, but ours isn't like one of those *swan* or *makeover* shows that prey on people's insecurities, particularly women's, and tell them that to be happy they have to change their looks. That is so superficial. And mean, really.
—CARSON KRESSLEY (the blond one)

What is it about blonds that the media so adore? . . . The one star to emerge from *Queer Eye* is the blond—all the other guys have dark hair. And I guess they couldn't find a gay black who was out of the closet or articulate enough. I guess the visualness of blond hair standing out is a tremendous plus for those in show business. Blond hair shows better and clearly attracts more. Unfair, but a fact.

—Radio host BILL RUMSEY

Blond men aren't thought to be dumbbells, so why are we? A lot of girls aren't naturally blonde, and they don't all of a sudden lose IQ after dyeing their hair. It's a vicious stereotype. It limits all blonde actresses, except Meryl Streep. **—JESSICA SIMPSON**

Who could possibly object to doing a love scene with Catherine Deneuve? **—SUSAN SARANDON, on her blond co-star in the vampire film *The Hunger***

Susan [Sarandon] is the ideal woman for me. I'm secretly in love with her. If anything ever happens to Tim [Robbins], I'm more than willing to step in.   **—JULIA ROBERTS, on her *Stepmom***
co-star, quoted in Australia's *Woman's Day* magazine

It's been written that the most "cursed" Hollywood film is *Rebel Without a Cause*. Its stars—James Dean, Natalie Wood, Sal Mineo—all died before their time. But *The Boys in the Band* has lost most of its [nine] stars and several behind-the-scenes people, especially to AIDS.
—Film historian DAVID SHIPMAN

Damon Wayans used to do humor based on physical gay-bashings. He still uses homophobia as humor. But just let a gay or straight diss blacks the way he does gays. . . . In 1998 at the Laugh Factory in Hollywood a male couple got up and left after having to listen to his bigoted jokes. That's when he said, "I don't think there's no faggots in the room now." And his younger Wayans brothers just laughed.   **—CAROLYN G. HEILBRUN,**
Columbia University professor and mystery novelist

I went on the Internet once. Found something called the Society to Annihilate Bette Midler. I didn't go on it again.   **—BETTE MIDLER**

Repeated dogging by the paparazzi on his honeymoon with Téa Leoni made [David] Duchovny so boiling mad he hurled a cup of coffee at a photographer.   **—*Allure* magazine, September 1997**

There was an up side to playing a nymphomaniac on TV. I'm not married anymore.   **—TÉA LEONI**

Someone handed me cocaine at a party in a disk with a gold spoon. I thought it was Sweet'n Low and put it in my coffee.

—SHIRLEY MACLAINE

I do feel it's too easy for an actress to be overshadowed by her hairdo.

—JENNIFER ANISTON

A certain standard of living is necessary for someone to be taken seriously as a player in Hollywood. **—Director PETER BOGDANOVICH, after declaring bankruptcy, when a lawyer questioned his still paying $250 to have his hair cut**

I hate interviews because I do not get paid for them. I hate to give autographs and never do. I am always rude to people. I am not a sweet person. I am a disagreeable person. I am a hateful person. I like to be hateful.

—GEORGE SANDERS, in his *Memoirs of a Professional Cad*

I was in a family situation with my baby, in a resort area. Someone came up to me, spat at me, and called me a Commie @^%&. I was very, very frightened and completely upset. I was happy my baby was so small he didn't understand what was going on. . . . I then followed him into the bar and asked him *why*. He explained that he was a Marine, as if that explained it all. I can't believe every Marine is that stupid and that cowardly. He didn't even confront me.

—Liberal activist SUSAN SARANDON

My only regret is that my apology might come off like I was apologizing for being against the [Vietnam] war. I didn't apologize for that, just for the things that hurt the soldiers, because I never blamed the war on the soldiers. **—JANE FONDA**

I do not regret one professional enemy I have made. Any actor who doesn't dare to make an enemy should get out of the business.

—BETTE DAVIS

I'll do anything for money. Even associate with my agent.

—VINCENT PRICE

People don't believe it yet, but right now I'm very underpaid.

—JENNIFER LOPEZ, on her $2 million salary for *Out of Sight*,
for which George Clooney got about $10 million
and for which she'd asked $5 million

First of all, Oprah did not buy those cars for her audience. They were given to her by Pontiac/GM. Second, and most important, the audience is responsible for the taxes on the "free" cars, which average around $7,000. Before we crown Oprah a saint, let's remember that this publicity stunt put people in debt; it didn't help them.

—JIM THATCHER's letter to the editor of *TV Guide*, October 31, 2004

After you're famous, all your bills go up. There's more to buy, what you buy tends to be of higher quality and higher in cost, and service people almost always charge you more because they know how rich you are. . . . The one expenditure that does go down—has to go down, particularly for a successful actress—is your food bill.

—DEBORAH KERR

I am of the philosophy that it's always wise to be nice to working-class people because they're the ones who can make you or break you—your mechanic, electrician, gardener, plumber. For example, the morning of the big earthquake in L.A., my water heater sprung a leak. This is six in the morning, and I call Gary Bergantino, my plumber, and get through. He's over in five minutes and has the damn thing fixed in fifteen. Now, as much as I like to hang with the beautiful people, I can't imagine Naomi Campbell showing up with a wrench at my house first thing in the morning.

—SANDRA BERNHARD

Police caught an airline security guard at Los Angeles International Airport stealing items from [Cameron] Diaz. Diaz reported her passport and a large sum of cash missing.

—*Los Angeles Times* item, December 1999

Many people or fans do, but most don't *think*. . . . If they stare and I'm shopping, are they making me feel like a shoplifter? If it's in a restaurant, are they making me self-conscious about how I chew or how much I eat? And if you're at a urinal— do I need to complete this sentence?

—CHRIS FARLEY

I don't get pissed off about the bad stuff, but I milk it for everything it's worth because you have to have some balance in your life. If there are free seats to the baseball game, you bet I'm there.

—MEL GIBSON

I only know the rear entrances of the hotels I stay in. I always have to climb over garbage cans and hampers full of dirty linen and sneak up to my room on foot or in the service elevator.

—GRETA GARBO, on a legend's unglamorous life

My biggest sacrifice for success as an actor has been privacy. You sacrifice the ability to be left alone if you want to be and the ability to know if someone is being completely honest with you. . . . To find someone you can get along with in life is hard enough, but when you're an actor it's even harder.   **—ESAI MORALES**

Once, while a new acquaintance was telling me about the year he spent watching his wife die of cancer, four people shoved paper in my face asking for autographs. In situations like these, it takes longer to turn people away than to give in and sign. **—JOAN RIVERS**

The worst was when my [late] sister was in the hospital and she saw a magazine cover [revealing] her inoperable brain tumor. They actually found out her condition from her [medical] records. She called me and said, "I hate you." It was devastating.

—LINDA GRAY (*Dallas*)

If one is a celebrity who does not become obnoxious, and still there is resentment, bitterness, then probably it is jealousy. Especially within the family. A celebrity who is a stranger, that is usual; a celebrity who is a relative, that is often insupportable.

—Writer FRANÇOISE SAGAN

When I got accepted into an acting school, that confirmed to my parents that I was really going to be an actress, as I'd already said. My mother fell to her knees and wailed, "If you become an actress, it will kill me!" What else could I say but, "Well, then you'll have to start arranging your funeral"?

—ELIZABETH PEÑA (*Down and Out in Beverly Hills*)

I think most of the hardness or pretentiousness I have seen in actors is from being hurt. I think it is their defense. They would rather be first to hurt someone else.   **—DR. HAING S. NGOR**

As I look around the world I am frightened. I am Jewish [and have] had fantasies of, Gee, what happens if my plane is hijacked. . . . I thought of all those things. A lot of Jewish people have. . . . I thought of going abroad, going to Paris. Think of the anti-Semitism that has been shown around the world. It's frightening. I don't remember feeling this way when I was younger. It's just getting so strange around the world. **—MICHELE LEE (*Knots Landing*)**

The camera saved my life. If I hadn't gone in front of the camera, I'm sure I would have been a terrible criminal. I was a criminal in my teenage years, but I would not have survived. My father wanted me to be a movie star, and he was nuts. The only decent thing he ever did was kill himself back in the fifties. He wanted my brother to be a movie star. They hated the fact that I was a successful [child actor] and wanted to kill me for it. I stayed in front of the camera in spite of my family, not because of them. **—ROBERT BLAKE**

Kevin Spacey is one lucky man. He was photographed canoodling with another man in a car, in a Los Angeles park. The pictures appeared in a national tabloid, yet still the media count him officially straight. . . . Usually when you state somebody is gay, someone who wishes it weren't so will say, "Where's the proof?" Rarely is there photographic proof—either way. **—Radio host KEITH MICHAELS**

The way it works is they won't *out* someone admired, someone real famous, someone non-freakish. . . . The *Wall Street Journal* saw fit to out David Gest, of Liza Minnelli fame, after he visited a gay men's sex venue. But had it been one of the above types instead, that paper would have ignored the situation. **—Writer MICHELANGELO SIGNORILE**

Back in 1995 Leo[nardo DiCaprio] did *Total Eclipse*, [as bisexual poet] Arthur Rimbaud. The film has some graphic sex scenes between DiCaprio and David Thewlis [as Paul Verlaine]. . . . In the past few months, rental copies of *Total Eclipse* have been pulled from the shelves of video stores around the country. . . . My sources say a "major studio" bought the rights and is trying to bury it. "In the interests of Leo's career, it's best that this film never happened" is how it was described to me.

—Columnist BILLY MASTERS in March 1998, after *Titanic*

Post-2000, Hollywood's Judeo-Christian filmmakers still decline to be honest about who in history was gay or bi, or about the acceptance of bisexuality in polytheistic cultures like Greece and Rome. . . . And so, an Alexander [the Great] or Leonardo [da Vinci], as well as twentieth-century figures from Howard Hughes and Cary Grant to Amelia Earhart and Katharine Hepburn, still are depicted as heterosexual, . . . erasing and ultimately denigrating gay people.

—Reviewer ANGELA THORNE-BARDRY

Elvis used to brag about his manager, called "The Colonel," . . . and how he came up from working in carnivals. He had an act of some renown called The Dancing Chickens. Later I learned it was far from benign. The young chickens seemed to dance when they were put atop a sawdust-covered hotplate.

—Girlfriend and actress JULIET PROWSE (*Can-Can*)

I wasn't surprised that Elizabeth Dole tried running for president. She was trying to get out of the house, away from the horrors of Viagra. They never actually tell you about the other side, about the person who is on the receiving end.

—BETTE MIDLER, on the wife of Viagra spokesstud Robert Dole

California governor Arnold Schwarzenegger may seem like a big, tough guy, but you wouldn't know it by some of his more feminine habits. He gets a manicure and pedicure weekly, has a full-time hairstylist on payroll, and gets regular Botox injections to smooth out the wrinkles in his fifty-six-year-old face. Friends tease him that he's more vain than wife Maria Shriver, which is saying something!

—Columnist CATHY GRIFFIN

Jackie Gleason stole my material—when he was real young, working . . . at a dump so lousy the rats went next door to eat. So I got the tip-off and went from Broadway to Newark, and it was awful. Not only was he doing my act, he was funny doing it. I confronted him, and he was arrogant as hell, and a nobody, but I didn't prosecute. I just warned him it was one thing for him to do *my* act in Newark, but if he ever went big-time, he'd better steal from someone else.
—MILTON BERLE

Bela Lugosi was treated shabbily by Hollywood. He was foreign, he was poor. . . . In one film, he played a deaf-mute, and complained to the director that someone else had "taken" all his lines! . . . When his stardom was past, he still couldn't believe it.

—VINCENT PRICE

I basically was sexually harassed by [Warren Beatty]. This kind of thing wasn't news to anybody. What *was* news was I blew the whistle on it. I talked about it . . . and boy, oh boy! He didn't like *that*. . . . There is one rule in Hollywood you don't break—you don't tell the truth about people in the press. And I broke that rule, and I paid a very, very big price. **—SEAN YOUNG (*Blade Runner*)**

Conrad Nagel was a leading man through the 1920s and part of the thirties. . . . And then [MGM chief] Louis B. Mayer decided to ruin his career due to Nagel's involvement with labor. He was pro-union. . . . He helped found the Academy of Motion Picture Arts and Sciences; he'd wanted it to be more of an actors' union than a committee handing out awards. However, he was overruled, and Mayer hated him ever after. . . . After Nagel was washed up in pictures, he ran an acting school.   **—Journalist RUTH BATCHELOR**

Because of the [political] blacklist, I wasn't able to work in film or television for five years, for signing civil rights petitions. . . . I was in a Lillian Hellman play. That was also on my list. The first thing on my list was attending a world peace conference at the Waldorf Hotel in 1947 or 1948. I supposed there were some Communists there, but there were four hundred American sponsors, including Albert Einstein.
      —KIM HUNTER (*A Streetcar Named Desire, The Planet of the Apes*)

John Wayne and his drinking buddy Ward Bond went around wrecking careers with their gung-ho willingness to blacklist anyone who politically disagreed with them during the 1950s.
                    —Two-time Oscar-winner MELVYN DOUGLAS

Elvis was the kind of white-trash-turned-star that when the Beatles came along he called them sissies or Communists because they knocked him right out of the limelight.   **—Singer JOHNNIE RAY**

I had to appear before a Congressional committee and explain that I wasn't a member of the Communist Party. . . . I was cleared then, but I hadn't worked in three years. . . . John Wayne and Ward Bond

weren't happy with my testimony because I hadn't named anybody. So Dore Schary, the head of MGM at that time, a wonderful liberal guy, broke the spell for me and gave me a part as Spencer Tracy's first mate in *Plymouth Adventure*. I had worked on the picture for about a week when they got a call from Ward Bond, who said, "He's going to have to clear himself." . . . So I went and convinced him, apparently, so that I was able to go back in the picture. It wasn't a very good picture, but I had at least broken the spell.
—LLOYD BRIDGES, film and TV actor and father of Jeff and Beau

During the blacklists, many good writers had to write movies under pseudonyms, as with *Roman Holiday*, which won an Oscar that its writer couldn't collect. . . . It was therefore a time when many amateurs tried writing scripts, and I recall one who asked a director friend of mine to read his, then asked him if he should put more "fire" into his pages. The director answered, "No, the other way round."
—Director SIR CAROL REED (*Oliver*)

I heard Burt Reynolds misspelled his own name in cement [at Grauman's Chinese Theatre]. It may be true, but the point is it didn't surprise me.
—Co-star JACK WESTON

Men who claw their way to the top don't get chastised for it. But look at all the grief they gave Joan Rivers for clawing her way to the middle.
—TV reporter RUTH BATCHELOR

Rosie Perez? I don't think I could spend eight or ten weeks on a movie set with her. Her voice would drive me back to heroin.
—CHARLIE SHEEN

I have seen her on many occasions, and she is quite simply in need of a shower or bath.
—DONALD TRUMP, on *Daryl Hannah*

She's got this gold tooth in her mouth and all this $#!% around her eyes. She looked like Beetlejuice or something.

—MARK WAHLBERG, on *Madonna*

First, Ashlee [Simpson] goes brunette . . . doesn't look natural, more like daughter-of-Dracula. Then she attributes her lip-syncing debacle [on *Saturday Night Live*] to acid reflux. . . . Is this any way to launch a non-Jessica career?　**—TV critic SHAWN GOLDHAMMER**

Grace Kelly told enough white lies to frost a cake.

—Columnist HERB CAEN

Anyway, going against [closeted] Michael Bennett's stern advice—"Have a girl on your arm, even if it's [oversized] Pat Ast!" —Michael Stuart and I inched our way into the Shubert Theatre: the tall [Tony] nominee and his boyfriend. We were seated on the last row—me on the aisle, then a support column between us, then Michael's seat—so if the camera should need to land on me, you the viewer wouldn't see that I didn't have a girl date.

—TOMMY TUNE, Tony winner

Chen came to me and asked if I knew of any rich men who'd be willing to donate money to Elizabeth's charity. I knew that Malcolm was looking for a beard. Chen hooked them up.

—An ex *Forbes* magazine editor, quoted in the book *Dish*, on publicist *Chen Sam*'s stage-managing of the "romance" between AIDS activist *Elizabeth Taylor* and closeted gay tycoon *Malcolm Forbes*

It became Barbra Streisand's *Yentl*. . . . She should never have opened her mouth to sing in this picture.

—ISAAC BASHEVIS SINGER, author of the short story on which the film musical was based

As an actor, I appreciate research, but she's making me nuts with that instrument!

—RYAN PHILLIPPE, on wife *Reese Witherspoon*'s practicing at home with an autoharp for her movie *Walk the Line*

Yeah, we're real good friends now. The only thing about her I can't stand is her chain-smoking.

—ZACH BRAFF, on co-star *Natalie Portman*

There was a lot of creative tension. Well, I don't know how creative it was. **—KATIE COURIC, on working with *Bryant Gumbel***

There's a lot of nervous stress between a couple, until they're married. When they are, it then shuttles between exasperation and being taken for granted. Or so I found with most of my husbands.

—VIVIAN VANCE (*I Love Lucy*)

A model's own career typically lasts ten or twelve years. However, if she snags a star—whether movie or rock—she'll have a showy career that lasts much longer . . . with tremendous alimony at its conclusion.

—Former movie executive and columnist RICHARD GULLY

Brazilian model Gisele Bundchen wised up and got rid of Leonardo DiCaprio. Gisele arranged a modeling assignment in L.A. so she could hang out with Leo in his home. But Leo found it more interesting to run off to Las Vegas with his pals.

—Columnist ARLENE WALSH, December 12, 2001

Gisele Bundchen must have gotten tired of being taken for granted. . . . She and Leonardo DiCaprio have had an on-again, off-again relationship for the past few years. Recently the Brazilian beauty said that most of the time they went out, she pays. While Leo is out of town [filming], she's been seen around town with tennis star Gustavo Kuerten, and they seemed to be having more than a good time. **—Columnist ARLENE WALSH, September 10, 2003**

Gisele Bundchen gave Leonardo DiCaprio his walking papers. The supermodel spent the past four years of her life waiting for Leo to pop the question. . . . Luckily, she's found great comfort in her new friendship with Josh Hartnett. The two met at a party, and he's been very attentive to Gisele.

—Columnist ARLENE WALSH, October 13, 2004

While Gisele Bundchen was spotted getting hot and heavy with Lenny Kravitz in New York, and while she was seen out with Josh Hartnett, she was still trying to quash rumors that she and Leonardo DiCaprio were kaput.

—Columnist ARLENE WALSH, November 3, 2004

Stars are pretty private people—unless they want [you] in a movie theater seat or tuned into their television show. Then they're out on talk shows pretending to be ordinary people.

—Novelist BEN TYLER

Movie stars get millions of dollars for nothing, so when someone asks them to do something for nothing, they go crazy. They think that if they're going to talk to somebody at the grocery store, they should get fifty dollars an hour. **—ANDY WARHOL**

I think the saddest question one could ever be asked is, "Didn't you used to be famous?" The next saddest would be, "Why don't you get some plastic surgery?" when you already have done so.

—DENHOLM ELLIOTT (*A Room with a View*)

Half the people in Hollywood are dying to be discovered. The other half are afraid they will be. **—LIONEL BARRYMORE**

There is not a reporter in Hollywood who could not rock the country by sitting down at his typewriter and recording merely a portion of the things he knows.

—Publisher-editor DOUGLAS CHURCHILL in 1935

Because it is so unbelievable, the truth often escapes being known.

—HERACLITUS (540–480 b.c.)

SLUGFESTS!

She's angry because I have a natural nose and she doesn't.

—MADONNA, on *Janet Jackson*

I could take off all my clothes and stand on the freeway, but would that make me an artist? **—JANET JACKSON, on *Madonna's* book *Sex***

[Bill] Murray exemplifies an actor who makes millions off movies but gives nothing back to his art. He's a taker.

—British producer and former studio chief DAVID PUTTNAM

Everybody's worked with a jerk in their lives, and I'd work with David Puttnam tomorrow—if he had a script. **—BILL MURRAY**

I don't need gimmicks or multi-hour marriages. I have a voice.

—CHRISTINA AGUILERA, on *Britney Spears*

People who listen to her at concerts must have a high tolerance for boredom. **—BRITNEY SPEARS, on *Christina Aguilera***

This arrogant, sour, ceremonial, piously chauvinistic egomaniac.

—ELLIOTT GOULD, on *Jerry Lewis*

Oh, him. Isn't he the guy who was married to Barbra Streisand?

—JERRY LEWIS, on *Elliott Gould*

She's an incredibly nasty person and goes around bad-mouthing me all around the world. She blames me for the end of her marriage. I know Martha too well to believe she's innocent.

—Novelist ERICA JONG, on former Barnard classmate and neighbor *Martha Stewart*

She'd rather be a celebrity than a writer. Reviewers say that she compensates for lack of talent with hot sex scenes.

—MARTHA STEWART, on *Erica Jong (Fear of Flying)*

I was not impressed, and he treated the rest of the cast like peons.

—JENNIFER LOPEZ, on former co-star *Jack Nicholson*

I think from early on, Miss Lopez was a diva-in-training.

—JACK NICHOLSON

This is desperation. She's definitely had a tit job.

—MADONNA, about *LaToya Jackson*'s appearance in *Playboy*

She climbed the ladder of success wrong by wrong.

—LATOYA JACKSON, on *Madonna*

Bruce [Willis of *Moonlighting*] used to moon us all the time. He had a very hairy bottom but was always concerned with the thinning hair on his head. One day I suggested he might get a transplant from his [bottom] to his head. At least that kept him from mooning us for several weeks. **—CYBILL SHEPHERD**

Cybill wasn't terribly easy to work with. She had big mood swings. She loves food, but she was always on some diet and trying to look young.
—BRUCE WILLIS

It's kind of really sad how she went from being a fairly successful TV actress to hosting some reality show that the critics all dump on.
—PARIS HILTON, on *Shannen Doherty*

I'm not sure. I think she hopes to be an actress. But her whole résumé is having an ancestor who [founded] a hotel chain.
—SHANNEN DOHERTY, on *Paris Hilton*

I was a fan of hers, back when she was popular.
—MARIAH CAREY, on *Madonna*

This is the same country that buys Mariah Carey records. It has nothing to do with art.
—MADONNA

Hugh Grant has two expressions: confused and trying to crack a joke. He's the token Englishman that Hollywood still uses opposite a bigger female star.
—ROBERT DOWNEY JR.

He showed some early promise but has since binged on downers, uppers, and other assorted drugs—in and out of jail. He chose tragedy over comedy.
—HUGH GRANT, on *Robert Downey Jr.*

I think he finally wanted to experience an old, I mean older, woman.
**—BRITNEY SPEARS, on ex *Justin Timberlake* (twenty-three)
going with *Cameron Diaz* (thirty-one)**

She made a movie. It came and went—right? It at least proved she can't act, either.
—CAMERON DIAZ, on *Britney Spears*

I don't think the remake [of *Freaky Friday*, starring Lindsay Lohan] was as good as the original. Don't ask me about Lindsay Lohan. I don't want to criticize my elders. **—HILARY DUFF, age sixteen**

I didn't see [*The Lizzie McGuire Movie*, starring Hilary Duff], even though I'm not diabetic. **—LINDSAY LOHAN, age seventeen**

Understand . . . there's no feud, and I don't give a twig about Michelle Branch. **—HILARY DUFF**

This time I'm rooting for the wicked stepsisters. **—MICHELLE BRANCH, on Hilary Duff, star of A Cinderella Story**

Her ambition is *showing* on her face. **—COURTNEY LOVE, on Madonna**

Whatever I did early on, I was never a stripper. **—MADONNA, on Courtney Love, who was**

In one scene, I have to hit [Bette Midler] in the face, and I thought we could save some money on sound effects here. **—KEN WAHL, her leading man in Jinxed**

[Ken Wahl] is such an angry man, so full of bile . . . [with] a skinhead mentality. **—BETTE MIDLER**

Nobody wants to admit these great icons are killers. When I dared cross Johnny Carson to go to Fox [for her own talk show], he came on like a gutter-fighter—and let his representatives do the talking. . . . To succeed in this rough business, we all have to be killers. Myself included. **—JOAN RIVERS**

She has no class. **—JOHNNY CARSON, on *Joan Rivers***

She played my daughter, but we did not socialize. We're too different. She's off the wall, even for me. **—SHIRLEY MACLAINE, on her *Terms of Endearment* co-star *Debra Winger***

I was actually grateful when [MacLaine] won [an Oscar], because I thought that would shut her up for a while. Imagine my dismay when she just kept having fiftieth birthdays and doing interviews. Jack Nicholson called me up for her second fiftieth and said, "Didn't we celebrate her fiftieth birthday in Texas?"

—DEBRA WINGER

He has become a very greedy actor. It is his big chance, and he is trying to take [the producers] for all he can.
—RICARDO MONTALBAN, on *Fantasy Island* co-star *Hervé Villechaize*

They wanted to put a female regular in *Fantasy Island*, so they hired one [Wendy Schaal] to play Montalban's goddaughter. . . . Suddenly I found myself doing, "Eh, boss, what's *this* fantasy?" and "Goodbye," and that's it. I was a glorified extra.
—HERVÉ VILLECHAIZE, who left the series the following season

He is infatuated with himself, and he's not a very good actor.
—VILLECHAIZE, on *Montalban*

She should stick to singing, which she does as well as a lot of people. But she can't act.
—MADONNA, on *Jennifer Lopez*'s movie career

Even in [*Evita*], a musical, Madonna can't act.
—JENNIFER LOPEZ, on *Madonna*

She's better known, even now, for her very public private life than for any movie she's been in. She did *Selena,* and then only flops, right?
—**MADONNA, on *J. Lo***

Did you see *Swept Away*? Did *anyone*?
—**JENNIFER LOPEZ, on *Madonna*'s latest flop**

It's all untrue, and I wouldn't lower myself to her level.
—**MADONNA, denying she'd dissed *Lopez*, who'd been calling the eleven-years-older star a has-been and untalented**

We called her Miss Cute because of all the cute tricks she pulled to get all the attention on herself.
—**GLADYS KNIGHT, on *Diana Ross***

I liked the Pips. They had some good songs. The lead singer was good too.
—**DIANA ROSS, on *Gladys Knight and the Pips***

Just another black guy looking for his fifteen minutes of fame.
—**CHARLTON HESTON, about *Ice T* in *Esquire*, 1997**

Yeah, what's *he* done in the last twenty years?
—**ICE T, on *Charlton Heston***

Barbra is too busy to have friendships or care much about people. She doesn't have much time for her own mother.
—**DIANA KIND, *Streisand*'s mother, in the 1980s**

Although she's lost some of her memory, the malice is gone.
—**STREISAND, on her mother's increasing senility**

He's just lucked out, and he's full of subterfuges, among other things.

—VAL KILMER, on Oscar-winner *Kevin Spacey*, his former pal and Juilliard classmate (Val's wealthy father loaned Kevin the $18,000 tuition, most of which Spacey allegedly didn't pay back.)

I wouldn't *think* to do the kinds of projects or roles he does.

—KEVIN SPACEY, on *Val Kilmer*

Childish and impossible.

—Director JOEL SCHUMACHER (*Batman Forever*), on *Val Kilmer*

I don't like Val Kilmer, I don't like his [lack of] work ethic, and I don't want to be associated with him ever again.

—Director JOHN FRANKENHEIMER (*The Island of Dr. Moreau*), on *Val Kilmer*

He likes to upset people, but I can see that inside he's upset himself. . . . He didn't really bother me.

—MARLON BRANDO, on his *Moreau* co-star *Kilmer*

Frankenheimer, for someone who'd been directing so long, was at times incompetent. . . . I'm not difficult with competent people.

—VAL KILMER

He has secrets . . . [and] a lot of self-hate.

—BRANDO, on *Kilmer*

He was okay. But I think he's overrated . . . very eccentric.

—KILMER, on *Brando*

She likes men. . . . I heard she never turns anything down except the bedcovers. —**MAE WEST**, on *Jayne Mansfield*

If I look that good at sixty-four, I'll have no problems . . . [though] I think most of Miss West's curves now are from overeating.

—**JAYNE MANSFIELD**, on *Mae West*

She is jealous that I should prefer a twenty-two-year-old girl to a woman of about seventy.

—Bodybuilder **MICKEY HARGITAY**, who was in *Mae West*'s nightclub act and who married *Jayne Mansfield*

It seems to me that when you reach the kind of acclaim that she's reached and can do whatever you want to do, you should be a little more magnanimous and a little less of a @^%&. —**CHER**, on *Madonna*

I think Madonna called [Cher] a @^%& once, but I'm sure she meant it in the nicest possible way.

—**LIZ ROSENBERG**, publicist for both *Cher* and *Madonna*.

It was like being in a blender with an alligator.

—Director **PETER BOGDANOVICH**, on working with *Cher*

He thinks the frigging director is God.

—**CHER**, on *Peter Bogdanovich* (*Mask*)

The face that [Doris Day] shows the world—smiling, only talking good, happy, tuned into God—as far as I'm concerned that's just a mask. I haven't a clue as to what's underneath. Doris is just about the remotest person I know. —Co-star **KIRK DOUGLAS**

Kirk [Douglas] was civil to me, and that's about all. But then Kirk never makes much of an effort toward anyone else. He's pretty wrapped up in himself. The film I made with Kirk, *Young Man With a Horn,* was one of the few utterly joyless experiences I had in films.
—DORIS DAY

Of all the people I performed with, I got to know Cary Grant least of all. He is a completely private person, totally reserved, and there is no way into him. Distant. Very distant. **—DORIS DAY**

Oh, yes. Miss Day—nice girl. Good singer . . . a good comedienne.
—CARY GRANT

I have eight gold records, and here I'm taking all this crap from a midget.
—SONNY BONO, guesting on *Fantasy Island*, on *Hervé Villechaize*

He's just the shorter, uglier half of Sonny and Cher.
—HERVÉ VILLECHAIZE, on *Sonny Bono*

What that kind of actor really wants is to be on screen every second of every day with no distractions, such as commercials or other actors—just limitless close-ups of his face. This is the person who envisions conquering everyone and forcing them to fix their attention on him and to worship him like a god—the ultimate screen hog. We all know what happens to hogs. They get slaughtered.
—BURT WARD, on his *Batman* co-star *Adam West*

Burt [Ward] had a lot of growing up to do when he came on the series. From what I've seen and heard since, he still has some growing up to do. **—ADAM WEST**

In thirty years, I can count on one hand the times I've actually witnessed [Adam West] open [his wallet] and part with money. The big dipper is a small tipper.   **—BURT WARD**

Sometimes he'd just get jealous because, despite his being taller, I'm the one who's—let's say, I have more *private* talent.
—BURT WARD, on *Adam West*

He has enough baloney in there to open a butcher shop.
—ADAM WEST, on *Burt Ward*'s memoirs, which stressed Ward's sex life

How many *Rocky* sequels can he make?
—ARNOLD SCHWARZENEGGER, on *Sylvester Stallone*

You need a knife for that thick accent.
—SLY STALLONE, on *Arnold Schwarzenegger*

I played his mother once—did it for the money. Movie bombed—good lesson. Don't take the money and run. . . . Girlfriend of mine said she's seen every performance Sly ever gave. She's seen *one* of his movies.   **—ESTELLE GETTY (*Golden Girls*)**

I think she was overwhelmed. She's better on TV.
—STALLONE, on *Estelle Getty* (*Stop, or My Mom Will Shoot*)

The older she gets, the lighter her hair gets. Which means that her hair is giving her [age] away!
**—GILDA RADNER, on *Barbara Walters*, whom she
impersonated on *Saturday Night Live***

I didn't find her to be a very talented impressionist.
—BARBARA WALTERS, on *Gilda Radner*

Ronald Reagan doesn't dye his hair. He's just prematurely orange.
—PRESIDENT GERALD FORD in 1974

Gerald Ford . . . was a fine Vice President.   **—RONALD REAGAN**

It's our own fault. We should have given him better parts.
—Studio mogul JACK WARNER, on hearing
***Reagan* had become governor of California**

Jack Warner was a born comedian. He never knew how funny he was.
—RONALD REAGAN

She nitpicks! She actually tries to correct me on international TV
[at the Oscar ceremonies] on how to pronounce Barbra Streisand's
last name.
—GOLDIE HAWN (who did mispronounce it), on *Bette Midler*

I'm ready, willing, and able. So is Diane [Keaton]. Ask Miss Hawn. . . .
—BETTE MIDLER, as to whether or not there would be a
sequel to their hit film *The First Wives' Club*

I had to teach [Erik Estrada] the basics you learn in the first year of
acting school. And that was just the beginning. He doesn't know
what gratitude is.   **—*CHiPs* co-star LARRY WILCOX,**
who eventually left the series in disgust

He couldn't handle how I was more popular than he was. But that
was the fans' fault. . . . And then I got a piece of the show. That
really rattled him.   **—ERIK ESTRADA, on *Larry Wilcox***

Tom Arnold's penis is three inches long. Okay, I'll say four, 'cause
we're trying to settle.   **—ROSEANNE, during her divorce**

Even a 747 looks small when it lands in the Grand Canyon.

—TOM ARNOLD, replying to *Roseanne*

I'm not upset about my divorce. I'm only upset I'm not a widow.

—ROSEANNE, post-*Tom*

I don't like Josephine Baker because of her radical politics, that's all.

—Columnist WALTER WINCHELL

[Walter Winchell] hates me because I am a colored woman who made good. . . . I left America to go to France, where I became famous and rich. **—Singer-actress JOSEPHINE BAKER**

Sometimes when I look at my children, I say to myself, "Lillian, you should have stayed a virgin."

—LILLIAN CARTER, mother of *President Jimmy*, also *Billy* and *Ruth*

You gotta take anything Miz Lillian says with a grain of salt. She's provocative, purposely. **—BILLY CARTER**

Zsa Zsa Gabor is a cop socker.

—DEBBIE REYNOLDS, after *Gabor* slapped a Beverly Hills cop

Is she making fun of me, darling? Is that really nasty? I think she looked better in her *old* movies.

—ZSA ZSA GABOR, on *Debbie Reynolds*

Back when Tab [Hunter] and Tony [Perkins] were real close, the story was that Tab told Tony, "Someday you'll make a fine actor." And Tony was supposed to have answered, "I already have. Several of them." **—SAL MINEO**

It's too bad. But his career was already dead.
—TONY PERKINS, on hearing of *Sal Mineo*'s murder (by a robber)

He's not aging well. The best thing to happen to his career is for him to die immediately.
—Director WERNER HERZOG, on actor *Klaus Kinski*

Herzog is a miserable, hateful, malevolent, avaricious, money-hungry, nasty, sadistic, treacherous, cowardly creep. His "talent" consists of nothing but tormenting helpless creatures and, if necessary, torturing them to death. . . . I absolutely despise this murderer Herzog. . . .
—Polish-German KLAUS KINSKI, who starred for *Herzog* in *Aguirre: The Wrath of God*, made in the Amazon jungle

I couldn't stand Chris O'Donnell when we met on the set of *Batman Forever*. He was such a jock, such a frat boy, the kind of guy who expects you to be impressed by the labels on his clothes.
—DREW BARRYMORE

I thought she was grungy. . . . She had a lot of attitude.
—CHRIS O'DONNELL, on *Drew Barrymore*

Raquel Welch was the star of the picture [*Myra Breckinridge*]. She could have been nice to somebody new, but she was hideous—without going into details.
—FARRAH FAWCETT

There's a lot I don't remember about that movie. It was a major catastrophe in its day. Why focus on the negative? . . . I scarcely remember anything about her.
—RAQUEL WELCH, on *Farrah Fawcett*

Eva [Gabor] was kind of decorative on the [*Green Acres*] set, and she didn't look her age, though she had big ol' massive legs. . . . When it came to any acting ability, Eva was 'bout as useless as teats on a boar hog. **—PAT "MR. HANEY" BUTTRAM**

Darling, I didn't get to spend much time with most of the supporting players.

—EVA GABOR, on *Pat Buttram* and two other cast members

Cecil Beaton was always interfering, Mr. Know-It-All—wanted to tell me how to do *my* job. And then he wins an Academy Award! . . . *And* he was a vicious gossip.

—Hairdresser SYDNEY GUILAROFF (Both men worked on *Gigi*, but Guilaroff wasn't eligible for an award.)

Imagine a hairdresser denying he's [gay]. He passed off his boyfriends as relatives! Typical of the Hollywood mentality. . . . I'm sure Mr. Guilaroff turned green when I received two more Oscars for *My Fair Lady*. **—Photographer SIR CECIL BEATON, who also designed sets and costumes**

The Liberace, the token queen of rock. . . . I consider myself responsible for a whole new school of pretensions—they know who they are. Don't you, Elton?

—DAVID BOWIE, on fellow "bisexual" singer *Elton John* (Bowie later went back in the closet, while Elton came out as gay.)

I didn't retaliate when Bowie said I was a token queen, even though he's had a couple of go's since. . . . I'll always remember going out for dinner with him, and over dinner he admitted to me that he always wanted to be Judy Garland, and that's the God's honest truth. **—SIR ELTON JOHN**

The trouble with Barbra [Streisand] is that she became a star long before she became an actress. Which is a pity, because if she learned her trade properly she might become a competent actress instead of a freak attraction—like a boa constrictor.
—WALTER MATTHAU, on his first-billed *Hello, Dolly!* co-star

What a sour disposition. . . . He sounds like a broken record.
—STREISAND, on *Matthau*'s frequent verbal attacks

. . . Ego to the *n*th degree, and the sensitivity of a starving elephant.
—Director FRANK PIERSON, on *Streisand*

He resented that, as one of the producers, I had a say in how *A Star Is Born* was made.
—STREISAND, on *Pierson*

When we commenced *On a Clear Day You Can See Forever,* I had the mistaken impression that I was the co-star. I was Miss Streisand's first leading man who can sing, even though this was her third musical. I thought she was my leading lady, a partner. I doubt I will choose to work again in Hollywood.
—French star YVES MONTAND, on *Babs* and his final American film

He was a bit standoffish, but also—it's that older men sometimes resent when a female has any real power. **—STREISAND, on *Montand***

She's sort of tough to work for. **—*Streisand*'s son JASON GOULD,**
who played her son in *The Prince of Tides*

Try not to throw the ball like a girl.
—Director STREISAND, to actor *Jason Gould*

I couldn't believe she made it on her own. When she won the Academy Award for Best Actress, I couldn't believe it even more.

—SONNY BONO, on ex-wife *Cher*

Not unless I have to. We have absolutely nothing in common. I think he's a bit of a sad character.

—CHER, on *Sonny Bono*, to whom she seldom spoke

If I hadn't gotten into politics and won, I could never have held my head up after Cher became a movie star with an Oscar and everything.

—SONNY BONO

I have no belief in the system. So Sonny is perfectly at home [in Washington, D.C.]. Politicians are one step below used-car salesmen.

—CHER

I don't think it's a very good area for her to start going into.

—SONNY BONO, on *Cher* directing (*If These Walls Could Talk*)

I told my father that it's legal to discriminate against gay people on the job, that in forty states you can be fired just for being gay. He was amazed and said that's un-American.

—CHASTITY BONO, openly gay daughter of *Sonny* and Cher

I believe in equal rights and opportunity for all Americans.

—CONGRESSMAN SONNY BONO (R-CA), days before voting against ending job discrimination against gay people

Intentional infliction of emotional distress.

—From a $6 million lawsuit brought by JAMES WOODS against co-star and alleged former lover *Sean Young*, who supposedly sent him hate mail, photos of corpses and mutilated animals, and a voodoo doll

There were signs all along that this person was really a liar. He would say things, then change the story. I was really innocent. My detectives had found out some bad stuff about him and [wife] Sarah Owen. I had rights to all their medical records. She had a police record, and he had a whole history of taking medication.

—SEAN YOUNG, on *James Woods*

I was furious with her when I thought she'd done those ugly things. . . . We did *not* have an affair.

—JAMES WOODS, on *Sean Young*

He dropped [the lawsuit] because I came up with such incriminating evidence that he went, "Uh, sorry!" It was all stupid and inane, and very hurtful to my career.

—SEAN YOUNG, who recovered $277,000 in legal costs for defending herself against *Woods*'s suit

I love and admire Sean, and she's actually half right.

—JAMES WOODS, looking back in *Entertainment Weekly* in 1992

I think it's important that [George Michael] got caught with his trousers down. I've been telling him to come out for ten years. . . . It's justice [the arrest in a Beverly Hills john], and while George did nothing wrong, I applaud him for finally coming out. It's long overdue for a man with $50 million in the bank.   **—BOY GEORGE**

Boy George boasts that he's never been in the closet. For starters, what use would it have been for *him* to be in the closet? The gays who can pass are the ones who do. . . . Besides, I remember when Culture Club was the big thing and Boy George went to the States and, just like most people who go there, he was covering up his sexuality in one interview after another.   **—GEORGE MICHAEL**

That old coot. . . . Acting with him was sheer drudgery.
—**VIVIAN VANCE, on *William Frawley*, her *I Love Lucy* co-star**

A loser.   —**LUCILLE BALL, on ex-husband *Desi Arnaz***

Her tongue is a lethal weapon. She can be very cruel when she
wants to be.   —**DESI ARNAZ, on *Lucy***

Viv's career really ended when she left [*The Lucy Show*] and went
back east to live with her artistic young husband.
—**LUCILLE BALL, to friend and actress *Mary Wickes***
(*I Love Lucy* co-star *Vivian Vance*'s last husband
was a younger gay publishing editor.)

Sure, I became famous—as frumpy old Ethel Mertz—and spent the
rest of my working life in the big redhead's shadow.
—**VIVIAN VANCE, to Mary Wickes**

Cindy [Williams] decided to start acting like a diva. She'd been in
the movies. This was her chance. I was strictly from TV. I think I
kept a more level head once we became number one.
—**PENNY MARSHALL, on her *Laverne and Shirley* co-star**

Penny had her brother Garry and other family members working
on the show. They supported her fully, and eventually I felt kind of
ganged-up on.   —**CINDY WILLIAMS**

There's a central dumbness to her.   —**MICK JAGGER, on *Madonna***

He looks like he's on monkey glands or something.
—**MADONNA, on *Mick Jagger***

She's more of a gimmick than a real singer.

—MADONNA, on *Sinéad O'Connor*

Madonna said I looked like I had a run-in with a lawnmower and that I was about as sexy as a Venetian blind. Now there's a woman that America looks up to as being a campaigner for women, slagging off another woman for not being sexy.

—SINÉAD O'CONNOR

Everything was all right until on location in Arizona. I had a four-page monologue, and because of my stage and radio background, I knew all the lines. We shot it in one take, and the crew applauded. Joan was in her trailer and heard the applause—and that started it. It made Joan mad, and *she* was the star of the picture.

—MERCEDES MCCAMBRIDGE, on her *Johnny Guitar* **leading lady,** *Joan Crawford*

On *Johnny Guitar* we had an actress [McCambridge] who hadn't worked in ten years, an excellent actress but a rabble-rouser. Her delight was to create friction. "Did you hear what *he* said about you?" she'd tell me. "And in front of a group of people!" I couldn't believe it. She would finish a scene, walk to the phone on the set, and call one of the columnists to report my "incivilities." I was as civil as I knew how to be. **—JOAN CRAWFORD**

Poor old rotten-egg Joan. I kept my mouth shut about her for nearly a quarter of a century, but she was a mean, tipsy, powerful, rotten-egg lady. I'm still not going to tell what she did to me. Other people have written some of it, but they don't know it all, and they never will because I am a very nice person and I don't like to talk about the dead even if they were rotten eggs.

—MCCAMBRIDGE, in her memoirs

He couldn't cut it, hadn't the maturity to keep the pace of a weekly one-hour series. He preferred to keep escaping into drugs. . . . It's too bad for him, he wasn't a bad guy, but he is no irreparable loss to the series, not at all.   **—CARROLL O'CONNOR, on *Howard Rollins*,
who had to leave *In the Heat of the Night***

I kept hearing "He's nothing like Archie Bunker." You could've fooled me, some of those times. . . . He acted like it was a favor he did everybody by just bringing his big ole self to the set.
—HOWARD ROLLINS, on *Carroll O'Connor*

He could occasionally be overbearing. . . . His pride was considerable, and now and again he liked to take more credit for [*All in the Family*'s] success than was truly warranted.
—JEAN STAPLETON (a.k.a. Edith Bunker), on *Carroll O'Connor*

We'll miss her—some of us more than others.
—CARROLL O'CONNOR, when *Jean Stapleton* voluntarily left the sitcom

Bette Davis started by snapping at me the first day. I said, "Good morning," and she looked right through me. Later, when the [*Murder with Mirrors*] cast gathered for introductions, our eyes met, and I waved. "What's that mean?" she snapped. "I was saying good morning," I answered. "You already *did* that!" she snapped back.
—HELEN HAYES

I was never so scared in my life. And I was in the war!
—SIR JOHN MILLS, on working with *Davis* in *Murder with Mirrors*

[Lillian Gish] ought to know about close-ups. Jesus, she was around when they invented them!

— **BETTE DAVIS, on** *The Whales of August* **co-star** *Gish,*
who became a star in *Birth of a Nation* **in 1915**

That face! Have you ever seen such a tragic face? Poor woman. How she must be suffering! I don't think it's right to judge a person like that. We must bear and forbear.

— **LILLIAN GISH, on co-star** *Bette Davis*

While Bette Davis has indeed always been one of my idols, she did make mincemeat out of poor Lillian when they made *The Whales of August* [1987], a lovely picture. Lillian swears she'll never act again. So first she drove me from the screen, now she's driven Lillian. She's making a clean sweep of everyone our age!　　— **HELEN HAYES**

I don't get his clothes. I just don't get it. I don't get the pushed-up sleeves, the luminescent ties.

— **DAVID LETTERMAN, on** *Jay Leno***'s wardrobe**

Dave's biggest desire was to host *The Tonight Show*, and when he didn't get it. . . .

— ***Tonight Show* host JAY LENO, on** *David Letterman*

I've never seen [*The Tonight Show*] with Leno hosting.

— **DAVID LETTERMAN**

I watch David Letterman every now and again [on TV]. . . . He has, you might say, almost a chronic petulance.

— **LENO, on** *Letterman*

The Marie Antoinette of American politics.

—Author GORE VIDAL on *William F. Buckley*

A celebrity endorsement doesn't change many votes. . . . I don't think that any American much cares to plumb the shallows of Charlton Heston's mind and follow his advice.　　**—GORE VIDAL**

He's always saying he co-wrote *Ben-Hur,* but it's funny, I don't remember him being on the set or seeing him there.

—*Ben-Hur* lead CHARLTON HESTON, on *Gore Vidal*

Most actors go to Hollywood to try and become someone else. Unfortunately, Charlton Heston didn't succeed.

—Talk-show host RICKI LAKE

Her show has too many weirdos on it for me to watch.

—CHARLTON HESTON, on *Ricki Lake*

Martin is like my brother.　　**—TISHA CAMPBELL in 1994, on her
Fox-TV co-star *Martin Lawrence,* against whom
she filed charges of sexual harassment two years later**

She got no sense of humor, man.

—MARTIN LAWRENCE, on *Tisha Campbell*

She even fools some of the males. They believe her. They believe her side of it.　　**—CLINT EASTWOOD, on former
companion *Sondra Locke,* who unlike him told her side in a book**

He has two faces. He completely fooled me. . . . I thought he was in love. I thought he was helping me, not hurting me behind my back. He ended my career in Hollywood, as an actress and a director. I was left shattered and physically diminished.

—SONDRA LOCKE, on *Clint Eastwood*

[Sondra Locke] writes how [Eastwood] forced her to have two abortions, then get surgery that rendered her infertile—after which she found out he had three kids with two other women he was living with while he was living with her. And how he wanted her to call him Daddy. And how *Daddy* turned out to be a control freak.

—Columnist JACK MARTIN, reviewing the 1997 book *The Good, the Bad, and the Very Ugly*

Clint Eastwood and I will never win an Oscar. We're too popular.

—BURT REYNOLDS, who was half right: his co-star later won directing and producing Academy Awards

[I] hated that bastard. **—WILLIAM HOLDEN, on *Sabrina* co-star *Humphrey Bogart*, who was jealous of the younger Holden and of Audrey Hepburn**

He looked lousy with blond hair. Who was he trying to fool?

—HUMPHREY BOGART, on *William Holden* in *Sabrina*

I could have shot Fred [Astaire], but didn't. Fred had no feeling at all. Fred was impatient. Fred yelled at Audrey [Hepburn, first-billed in *Funny Face*]. Fred was irritating, a most disconsolate person. . . . He was just somebody who was frightened.

—Co-star KAY THOMPSON

She was somewhat too powerful, almost mannish, for the screen. Musically, very talented of course. **—FRED ASTAIRE, on actress-musician-arranger-author** *Kay Thompson*

Michael didn't invent the Moonwalk. He learned it from a dancer named Geoffrey who was on *Soultrain,* and he called it the Backslide, but Michael renamed it the Moonwalk. **—A 2004 revelation from sister LATOYA JACKSON**

LaToya always wanted lots of attention. **—MICHAEL JACKSON, whose memoirs were titled** *Moonwalk*

They are trying to show he's a great lover, but they'll never prove it to me. **—ZSA ZSA GABOR, on** *Cary Grant*

Miss Gabor is a prime example of the type of personality that television tries to pass off as a star. **—CARY GRANT, on** *Zsa Zsa Gabor*

I really wanted to sue the pants off her, but she doesn't wear any. **—Beverly Hills jeweler Harry Winston's son, after** *Sharon Stone* **kept a $400,000 diamond necklace she'd been loaned to wear while publicizing a movie (She finally returned it, but Winston had to make a donation to Stone's favorite charity.)**

I rarely wear jewelry, unless I'm asked. If you have natural beauty, jewelry can sometimes detract. **—SHARON STONE**

I was in Hitchcock's *Lifeboat.* So was Tallulah Bankhead, who didn't wear panties, and each morning when we climbed into a lifeboat— up on a mechanical rocker—she gave the cast and crew a hell of a view, hiking up her skirt! Eventually someone complained to Hitch, who didn't want to get involved. He explained it was an interdepartmental matter—involving wardrobe, costume, and possibly hairdressing. **—HUME CRONYN, in his memoirs**

He doesn't really direct you, dahling. He merely presides, along with the camera. He's very attached to the camera—at least until lunchtime. **—TALLULAH BANKHEAD, on portly *Alfred Hitchcock***

Fat is a choice, and it's an unhealthy one, apart from not being very nice to look at. **—CLORIS LEACHMAN (*The Mary Tyler Moore Show*)**

I took [Leachman's remarks] personally, because I've been overweight for a long time, and I don't know I could ever be thin again. I'm fat, all right. Now it's part of me. . . . Some people, including her, don't even have to try and stay thin. They have a lucky metabolism, though I admire the ones who have to struggle with it daily. **—JOHN CANDY, who died prematurely**

Anna Nicole Smith is giving golddigging a bad name.
—Novelist BARBARA CARTLAND

[Anna Nicole Smith] gives sleaze a bad name. **—ROSEANNE**

Roseanne will never see a bikini again, except from the outside.
—ANNA NICOLE SMITH, after her weight loss

The fans are so young! Their parents could hardly have been born when Bette [Davis] started out.
—Co-star OLIVIA DE HAVILLAND, at the New York premiere of *Hush, Hush . . . Sweet Charlotte* in 1964

You were very good in it, Olivia. When you weren't in a scene with me, you managed to keep the audience's attention.

—**BETTE DAVIS, to** *de Havilland*, **after a press screening of their film**

Mick [Jagger] and I have had our differences. We still do. It's like a marriage—the differences get more aggravating over the years. It's gotten to where it's hard to be in the same recording studio together. I don't look forward to touring together, but we'll see. . . .

—**Fellow Rolling Stone KEITH RICHARDS**

It's really stupid how he accepted it, because we were always anti-establishment, we were a symbol of it. It's appallingly hypocritical. . . . I'm appalled.

—**KEITH RICHARDS, after his bandmate was created** *Sir Mick Jagger* **by Queen Elizabeth II**

Keith [Richards] doesn't have many tantrums anymore. He's mellowed out a bit. He just has semi-constant irritations.

—**SIR MICK JAGGER**

He writes songs for dead blondes.

—**KEITH RICHARDS, dissing** *Elton John* **for adapting his** *Marilyn Monroe* **tribute** *Candle in the Wind* **into a record-breaking tribute to** *Princess Diana*

I am glad I have given up drugs and alcohol. It would be awful to look like [Keith] Richards. He's pathetic, poor thing. It's like a monkey with arthritis trying to go on stage and look young.

—**SIR ELTON JOHN**

If I'm old, he's a rock fossil, and I think the drugs have fried or frazzled his brain.

—**ELTON JOHN, on** *Richards*

They arrested Helen Reddy for loitering in front of an orchestra.

—Singer **BETTE MIDLER**

Bette Midler is more interesting when she talks than when she sings.

—**HELEN REDDY** (*I Am Woman*)

Richard Attenborough did what most middling actors dream of doing—he became a director. All of a sudden, he gives the orders, and he looks good because he's behind the camera, not in front of it.

—*A Chorus Line* co-creator and director **MICHAEL BENNETT**

I think in several respects my movie of *A Chorus Line* is superior to Michael Bennett's [stage] version. —**SIR RICHARD ATTENBOROUGH,** whose film was roundly reviled and a big fiscal flop

Looking back, it was a huge blunder to hire somebody who's straight and British to even try and make a movie out of *A Chorus Line*. The guy doesn't have a clue and doesn't have the sensibility.

—**MICHAEL BENNETT,** confidentially, to friends

Don't ask Liz Hurley to be in the same room as actress Ashley Judd. Hurley bailed out of a luncheon in New York recently because Ashley would be attending. The bad blood stems from Hurley being hurled from a Kohl cosmetics campaign because the theme is *American Beauty* and Liz, being a Brit, was disqualified. Liz was a gracious loser until Ashley, at a party a few weeks before, allegedly snarled, "Don't you wish you were an American? Tough luck."

—Columnist **CATHY GRIFFIN**

Sophia Loren plays peasants. I play ladies.

—Fellow Italian **GINA LOLLOBRIGIDA**

It is a shame that Miss Lollobrigida never won the Academy Award. But she likes to play herself instead of other characters.

—Oscar-winner SOPHIA LOREN

Whose [bosom] is bigger, I have no idea and could not care less. I became a star without a husband producing my pictures, and I became a star in respectable pictures! **—GINA LOLLOBRIGIDA,**
on *Sophia Loren* (married to producer *Carlo Ponti*)

Who? I never criticize my elders.

—Seven-years-younger LOREN, on *Lollobrigida*

I know who you are! You don't live here, you *rent*!

—SHANNEN DOHERTY, not welcoming new neighbor *Molly Ringwald*

She has problems—scary. I heard she's taking anger-management therapy. She needs it, or a good lawyer.

—MOLLY RINGWALD, on *Shannen Doherty*

The only thing that dikey b*@&# and I ever had in common was Billie Burke [a.k.a. Glinda the Good Witch], who supported both of us in our first pictures.

—1930s star MARGARET SULLAVAN, on *Katharine Hepburn*

She cared less about her career than climbing in her social life.

—KATHARINE HEPBURN, on *Margaret Sullavan*,
who married their prestigious agent, Leland Hayward
(Henry Fonda was a previous husband.)

She's a good actress, but she's not the director. She has all kinds of ideas. . . . She's subtle, but she is headstrong.

—RUSSELL CROWE, on *Cinderella Man* co-star *Renée Zellweger*

Russell is very old-fashioned. He sees women in just one way.

**—RENÉE ZELLWEGER, who reportedly didn't
want to do joint publicity with *Russell Crowe***

One minute she's so coarse, and the next she turns out to be your mother.

—SIMON COWELL, on colleague *Sharon Osbourne*

I've had my doubts about everything he does.

**—SHARON OSBOURNE, who didn't speak with *Simon Cowell*
for three days because she believed *The X-Factor* was rigged**

I'd hate for Donald Trump to beat us in the ratings. I'd also hate to have to try and converse with him.

—SIMON COWELL

It's hard to tell some of those English guys apart.

—DONALD TRUMP, referring to *Simon Cowell*

He's spent a lot more time in front of a mirror than in front of books. . . . Major gaps in his knowledge, hardly knew there'd been a political blacklist in this country, thought I moved to Europe for the art or the views, not 'cause I was deprived of my work in the United States for being supposedly too liberal. I like him, but he can be a bonehead.

**—LIONEL STANDER, who played
Max on *Hart to Hart*, starring *Robert Wagner***

He brings a lovable, gruff personality to our show, but he is pretty identical in every part.

—The versatile ROBERT WAGNER, on *Lionel Stander*

She is a movie star. I am an actress.

—BETTE DAVIS, on *Joan Crawford*

She may have more Oscars. . . . She's also made herself into something of a joke. **—JOAN CRAWFORD, on *Bette Davis***

Joan Crawford—I wouldn't sit on her toilet! **—BETTE DAVIS**

Bette will play anything, so long as she thinks someone is watching. I'm a little more selective than that. **—JOAN CRAWFORD**

Joan Crawford—Hollywood's first case of syphilis. . . . She was in silent pictures before I even *heard* of Hollywood! **—BETTE DAVIS**

I don't hate Bette Davis, even though the press wants me to. I resent her—I don't see how she built a career out of a set of mannerisms instead of real acting ability. She's phony, but I guess the public likes that.
—JOAN CRAWFORD, on her *What Ever Happened to Baby Jane?* co-star

Hah! Joan must be rolling over in her grave! Long ago, they asked her if she liked any of the current crop of actresses, and she admitted to only one—Faye Dunaway. Now Miss Dunaway is trashing Joan's memory in that horrendous movie [*Mommie Dearest*]! **—BETTE DAVIS**

I think I'm in so many of his pictures because no other actress would work with him. **—JILL IRELAND, on husband *Charles Bronson***

Jill is a fine actress, but her accent makes her sound better than she is. **—CHARLES BRONSON, on *Jill Ireland***

Mick Jagger is too old for that role, and I'd have done it better.
—BOY GEORGE, who lost the drag role in the film *Bent*

Acting's supposed to be a stretch. Boy George in a dress—how unusual.
—**MICK JAGGER**

Mick Jagger's lips—he could French-kiss a moose! —**JOAN RIVERS**

I wonder what Joan [Rivers] puts down where it says "Occupation." She's tried everything but streetwalking, I assume. I guess she could put down "Jill of all trades, and mistress of none."
—**MICK JAGGER**

A sister stops being very grateful the moment she gets into show business. It's show-no-gratitude business. . . . I got her into the music business, I'm happy for her, but anyone likes to hear "thank you."
—**JESSICA SIMPSON, on younger sister *Ashlee*'s recording success**

What I'm proudest of is it's happening all on my own. I'm doing it on my own.
—**ASHLEE SIMPSON**

I don't think Blake Edwards will ever receive as much respect as he feels he's entitled to.
—**WILLIAM HOLDEN, on the director of *The Pink Panther* and *Breakfast at Tiffany's***

Bill [Holden] drinks when he has occasion. Also when there's no occasion.
—**BLAKE EDWARDS**

I think their careers might have gone further if they hadn't married, or at least not kept working together.
—**WILLIAM HOLDEN, on *Edwards* and wife *Julie Andrews***

He's like all these drunks. Impossible when he's drunk and only half there when he's sober. Wooden as a board with his body, relies on doing all his acting with his voice.

—Director JOHN BOORMAN, on *Richard Burton*

Directors like Mr. Boorman are one of the leading factors in actors drinking.

—RICHARD BURTON

He tries to drown his troubles in drink. But they just float.

—W. C. FIELDS, on *John Barrymore*

A friend gave Bill a book about the sin of drinking. Bill took it to heart. He gave up reading.

—JOHN BARRYMORE, on *W. C. Fields*

I feel sorry for Madonna, because she doesn't know who she is. That's why she dyes her hair so much. She tries to steal other people's identities.

—Former girlfriend SANDRA BERNHARD

I can hear Dietrich screaming from her grave, "Kill that trash!"

—SANDRA BERNHARD, when *Madonna* was doing *Marlene*'s look

You can be a celebrity and not get too noticed. Unless you're out with a publicity hog like Madonna.

—SANDRA BERNHARD

Did I tell you about my nightmare? I dreamt I was Madonna, shopping at Tiffany's, where I was trying to buy some class.

—SANDRA BERNHARD

Sandy wants too much from her friends. . . . She's too much.

—MADONNA, on *Sandra Bernhard*

I felt used. There is such a thing as loyalty.

> **—SANDRA BERNHARD, whose romantic friendship with**
> ***Madonna* ended when Madonna appropriated her best friend**

She wanted to be the sole star of the thing. . . . Besides, my age threatened her. I was funny and *young*. She was really too old to play Mame Dennis, by twenty years or so. She had cast approval. I was released . . . replaced by an actress who was funny and *not* young.

> **—MADELINE KAHN, on being fired as Agnes Gooch**
> **in the movie *Mame,* starring *Lucille Ball***

Madeline Kahn didn't want to play the character. . . . She did see to it that her contract ensured she got paid, whether she stayed in the picture or not.

> **—LUCILLE BALL**

Truman Capote is a Republican housewife from Kansas with all the prejudices.

> **—Fellow author GORE VIDAL**

Gore Vidal has never written a novel that's readable, with the exception of *Myra Breckenridge,* which you can sort of thumb your way through. His novels are unbelievably bad.

> **—TRUMAN CAPOTE**

Truman Capote has made an art of lying. A minor art.

> **—GORE VIDAL**

I was visiting Italy some time after Gore moved there, and eventually we connected on the telephone. He called me to say, "I passed by your hotel yesterday." I was perfectly candid and said, "Thank you so much."

> **—TRUMAN CAPOTE (*Breakfast at Tiffany's*)**

You keep reading about these Hiltons. I thought they were motels or something, and they're not even actresses, they just had rich grandparents or something. What'd they ever do to get on TV, get your own show? What'd they do—or *who* did they do? . . . One of them's even on a sex tape, one of those like "accidentally" taped things.

—SHANNEN DOHERTY

I wouldn't want to go the Shannen Doherty route. She does one series, then she has to host third-rate reality stuff or wait to be asked by Aaron Spelling or whoever to come be on somebody else's new show when it's in the ratings cellar and they need two paragraphs in *TV Guide* about her latest attempted stab at a job.

—PARIS HILTON

That dreadful picture [*The Producers*]. I can't bear to watch it, even on a small television. I'm rather sorry I did it. I must have needed the money—living in Hollywood weakens one's motives. [Mel Brooks] reminds me of the saying that nobody ever went broke underestimating the American public's taste.

—ESTELLE WINWOOD (1883–1984)

Estelle [Winwood] was wonderful in the role, as a rather pickled old lady. She was rather pickled-looking—in fact, mummified.

—MEL BROOKS

That was a negative experience. Erik Estrada didn't care for competition, and the producers made me look less than beautiful so I wouldn't detract from him.

—MORGAN FAIRCHILD, on the TV movie *Honey Boy*

All her career, so far as I know, comes from being a blonde who's beautiful but has a bitchy image.

—ERIK ESTRADA, on *Morgan Fairchild*

I watched Barbara Stanwyck in *The Thorn Birds*. Augh! It was painful! *I* should have played that part! She was supposed to be a passionate older woman in love with this beautiful young priest. She and Richard Chamberlain were completely miscast. . . . She had no fire or passion, not for a man in or out of the cloth!

—BETTE DAVIS

Miss Davis wonders why she doesn't get the choice roles in her age bracket. Perhaps she might ask some of the directors who have had the *alloyed* joy of working with her. **—BARBARA STANWYCK**

My favorite American lesbian!

—CLIFTON WEBB, on *Barbara Stanwyck*

He more or less played my husband [in the 1953 *Titanic*].

—BARBARA STANWYCK, on the also-gay *Clifton Webb*

I always heard that Noel Coward wrote that song [*Mad About the Boy*] because of his friend Cary Grant. **—DOUGLAS FAIRBANKS JR.,**
refuting a rumor that *he* inspired the song

He's not a star on the order of his late father, of course, but he's already moving into producing, [and] he aspires to the English aristocracy. **—SIR NOEL COWARD, on *Douglas Fairbanks Jr.***

You don't expect a friend to sleep with your boyfriend, but she did, and that's that, and it's over. **—Mick's daughter JADE JAGGER,**
on her two-year estrangement from *Kate Moss*

It just happened. She sent me a diamond necklace that said "slut" on it! I didn't know whether to thank her or be insulted.

—Supermodel KATE MOSS, on jewelry designer *Jade Jagger*

Kate Moss and Jade Jagger are burying the hatchet and went back to being friends again. . . . [They] must have decided that it works to their advantage to keep the friendship going.

—Columnist ARLENE WALSH

I could see that the friendship we'd developed was starting to come apart when the Fonz was more popular than Richie. . . . To his credit, Ron did try to hide the fact. He wasn't confrontational.

—HENRY WINKLER, on his and *Ron Howard*'s
characters in the sitcom *Happy Days*

I didn't know how I was going to take it if they made the Fonz or Fonzie the main character. I was supposed to be the star of the show, and it was all kinda embarrassing. **—RON HOWARD**

She came in thinking she was the *star* of the show. Though how she thought that, without first billing. . . . And it was *Gilligan's Island*, not *Ginger's Island*. **—BOB DENVER, on *Tina Louise***

My character was meant to be a cross between Marilyn Monroe and Lucille Ball. . . . I was never snobbish about the program, as several writers and even a few cast members have suggested. But it did hurt my film career, and I didn't keep returning [for TV reunions] because I did not want a career that revolved around something I did for a few years. I also didn't jump at the chance to make a big, fast buck—and the money was tempting, but I never get credit for resisting that. **—TINA LOUISE**

It was the same old story: I'm too good for TV, I think I'll become a movie star . . . and that almost never works for a woman. But she left, and made a movie with Donald Sutherland—about a seal, I think—and it was no hit, so she went back to the *small* screen and TV and infomercials, books, what-have-you. But it came from *greed*, and at first it jeopardized our whole show and all our jobs.

—JOYCE DEWITT, on former *Three's Company* castmate *Suzanne Somers*

John [Ritter] came around . . . we made up. Joyce [DeWitt] is sometimes too hard on people, and when you're hard on others, you're also being hard on yourself. **—SUZANNE SOMERS**

I'll play at being a tough character sometimes. *She's* the real thing, and I don't think she enjoys it.

—BRITNEY SPEARS, on *Christina Aguilera*

When someone goes from A to Z, like she has, from virginal to whorish, you know it's a calculated, money-oriented act. I don't think she has a strong sense of personal identity, just a sense of what she thinks will sell, or shock. . . . She's covering a lot of Madonna's ground. **—CHRISTINA AGUILERA, on *Britney Spears***

I'm being touted as the new Martha Stewart, for a younger and hipper crowd. . . . Our show is retro, which is fashionable now. We do decorating, personal style, grooming, cuisine, etc. Unlike Martha, though, I don't cook the books! **—BRINI MAXWELL**

The Brini Maxwell Show is a clever idea, certainly a specialized one—with a young man in drag. I don't see it having any real connection to what *I* do. **—MARTHA STEWART in 2004**

I'm not going to bad-mouth her. She's a lovable character, everyone's favorite aunt and homemaker. But Frances [Bavier] had very set ideas about things and about her status. And she was an older actress with a lot of experience, so we tried to accommodate her.
—ANDY GRIFFITH, on "Aunt Bea"

He's a good man, but bossy. Oh, very bossy. . . . And certainly the center of things, of attention.
—FRANCES BAVIER, on the star and co-owner of *The Andy Griffith Show*

Like, she always wants to be noticed. I think she's in physical pain when she's not noticed.
—AMANDA BYNES, on *Lindsay Lohan*

Can teen queen Lindsay Lohan get along with any girls her own age? She's had feuds with Hilary Duff and Amanda Bynes, and now comes word she began fighting with Mila Kunis, who stars on *That '70s Show* with Lindsay's boyfriend Wilmer Valderrama.
—Columnist CATHY GRIFFIN

You shouldn't hang around our set so much, acting like some movie queen!
—MILA KUNIS to *Lindsay Lohan*, who reportedly responded with several unprintable words

If a young guy thinks he's handsome and funny, he sometimes thinks he can take over your [TV series]. Or worse, he thinks he can charm you out of it. . . . These kids don't respect age and experience or persistence, and they don't know about climbing the ladder. They want to fly up the ladder.
—TED KNIGHT, on his *Too Close for Comfort* co-star JM J. Bullock

Ted [Knight] had the impression that having been part of *The Mary Tyler Moore Show* had placed him on Mount Rushmore. . . . He was sometimes too suspicious to believe the fact that I liked him!

—**JM J. BULLOCK (*Hollywood Squares*)**

Sean Penn likes to get in touch with his inner pit-bull now and again.

—**SANDRA BERNHARD**

She didn't make it in movies. She's trying to make it in and with everything, anything else. —**SEAN PENN, on *Sandra Bernhard***

She has a career. She should get a life.

—**MICHELLE BRANCH, on *Hilary Duff***

She could "branch" out and try being more of a human being.

—**HILARY DUFF, on *Michelle Branch***

I hear she's doing a wonderful infomercial now. . . .

—**JOAN COLLINS, on former *Dynasty* co-star *Linda Evans***

It takes her longer to make up than it does me. I only have one face.

—**LINDA EVANS, on *Joan Collins***

My sister and I have never feuded. Never. At worst, an active estrangement. —**JOAN COLLINS, on her and *Jackie Collins***

Once in a while he'll pontificate, go on about "film" in contrast to just plain movies. —**ROGER EBERT, on fellow film critic *Gene Siskel***

Roger [Ebert] would be more inclined to a feud than I am, and the public would love it. But I just grin and bear some of his more juvenile tastes.

—GENE SISKEL

I told him he's perfect for horror movies, and he took it as offense. He did a few for Andy Warhol, is all I meant. . . . He's touchy and kind of weird.

—RIVER PHOENIX, on *My Own Private Idaho* castmate *Udo Kier*

Hypocrites don't like being reminded. One day I said, "Why bother with being a vegetarian if you don't give up the drugs?"

—UDO KIER, on *River Phoenix*, who eventually died of a drug overdose

When humor didn't work for her, she tried vitriol.

—VICTORIA PRINCIPAL (*Dallas*), on *Joan Rivers*

I've relished a feud or two in my time, and heaven knows Victoria Principal—Little Miss Moisturizing—is a worthy target. But after a point, one chooses to get on with real life and move forward.

—JOAN RIVERS

The prejudice from fans and peers alike is toward handsomer, more svelte actors, and if you aren't encased in that, it's easy to be overlooked.

—ROD STEIGER, a year younger than *Marlon Brando*, whose older brother he played in *On the Waterfront* (1954), for which Brando won his first Oscar

It took Rod [Steiger] longer to make it, and he's pissed.
—MARLON BRANDO, theorizing about their estrangement

I can't remember why we're not speaking.
—ROD STEIGER, after forty-four years, on bumping into
***Marlon Brando* at a Montreal restaurant (The actors then**
embraced and settled their differences.)